D0784033

AVCE
Information and Communication Technology
Technology
Units 1 - 3

R. P. Richards, B.Sc.(Hons), M.A.
&
P. M. Heathcote, B.Sc.(Hons), M.Sc.

Published by
Payne-Gallway Publishers Limited
26-28 Northgate Street
Ipswich IP1 3DB
Tel: 01473 251097   Fax: 01473 232758
E-mail: info@payne-gallway.co.uk
Web site: www.payne-gallway.co.uk

2001

Acknowledgements

We would like to thank Nick Burridge, Managing Director of Merrell, for answering innumerable questions to explain how a footwear distributor operates. The case study ShoeShock is based on the concepts he explained while being changed in most essential details.

Cover picture © 'Island Sunset' reproduced with the kind permission of James Judge

Cover photography © Mike Kwasniak, 160 Sidegate Lane, Ipswich

Cover design by Tony Burton

First edition 2001. Reprinted 2002, 2003.

10 9 8 7 6 5 4

A catalogue entry for this book is available from the British Library.

ISBN 1 903112 29 X

Copyright © R.P. Richards and P.M. Heathcote 2001

All rights reserved

No part of this publication may be reproduced, stored in a retrieval system, or transmitted in any form or by any means, electronic, mechanical, photocopying, recording, or otherwise, without the prior permission of the copyright owner.

Printed in Great Britain by

W.M.Print, Walsall, West Midlands

Preface

Vocational A Level qualification

The AVCE (Advanced Vocational Certificate of Education) in Information and Communication Technology is one of several vocational A Level qualifications offered by the Examining Boards. The mandatory units and specification for each one is the same for all Boards but the assessment may be different for different Boards.

This book covers three mandatory units for the 6-unit and 12-unit award. All the theory given in the specifications is covered, as well as guidance for both internal and external assessments. Unit 1 is a very practical unit and students are given guidance on creating documents and presentations to put in their portfolios. In Unit 2, practice is given in answering examination-style questions similar to those that are set by Edexcel. In Unit 3, a sample spreadsheet project in Excel is worked through to show students the features they will need to create their own projects for their assessment.

How to use this book

The book is designed to be used in the classroom, and for practice and revision sessions. Suggestions for activities and discussions are found throughout, and questions and exercises to test students' understanding and recall can be used either as homework or as class work. In Unit 3, students can work through the sample application at their own pace, learning the capabilities of MS Excel as they work through, so that they can then design and implement their own projects.

Extra resources

Extra resources for teachers can be found on our web site www.payne-gallway.co.uk.

Documents used in the exercises in the text may be downloaded by students from the web page www.payne-gallway.co.uk/avce. These are:

    Draftcopy.doc (Chapter 1)

    Paraformatting.doc (Chapter 2)

    Reporttext.doc (Chapter 3)

Contents

Table of Contents

Unit 2
ICT Serving Organisations 79

Unit 3

Spreadsheet Design   **127**

Appendices

Unit 1

Presenting Information

This unit is all about communicating. We communicate with each other in many different ways – speech, body language, text messaging, writing letters, books, newsletters or reports, filling in forms, making presentations and so on.

You will mainly be using Microsoft Word and PowerPoint to create different styles of documents and presentations. You have probably used both these pieces of software before so you're off to a flying start! But the new tips and techniques you'll learn will be useful to you not only to help you pass the unit, but also in the career you eventually choose.

You can look at other people's (and organisations') efforts at communication and judge how well you think they get the message across to the intended audience.

The unit is assessed through portfolio work, and you will be putting together six different types of original document or presentation together with a report comparing and evaluating documents from other organisations. As this is largely a practical unit, you will do most of the work at the computer and there are lots of short exercises for you to try out as you work through each chapter. At the end of each chapter longer assignments are included as examples of the type of work you will need to put into your portfolio.

Chapter 1 – Accuracy and style of writing

Objectives

✓ Use tools to check the spelling accuracy of documents
✓ Use tools to check the grammar in documents
✓ Use different writing styles for different purposes
✓ Produce draft copies of documents
✓ Use manual or electronic techniques for proofreading

*Note: You will need to download **Draftcopy.doc** from www.payne-gallway.co.uk/avce to complete the exercises in this chapter.*

1.1. Spelling and Grammar – get it right!

Getting the content of a document correct is obviously pretty important. People rightly get rather annoyed if they are sent a bill for the wrong amount (though they may not complain if the amount is too little) or if the directions they are given for attending an important meeting are wrong.

"He said right, but did he mean left?"

Once you're sure the content is right, you can check the spelling and grammar – and luckily, the days of thumbing through a dictionary are long gone for most of us. Microsoft Word has several ways to check spelling and grammar, and you can choose the options you find most convenient. The main thing is to realise just how important correct spelling and grammar are in any sort of business communication – for example, you'll have great difficulty in getting a job if your CV has these sorts of mistakes in it!

You need to be logged on at a computer running Word (version 97 or 2000) for the rest of this chapter. Then you can try things out instead of just reading about them.

Automatically correct spelling and grammar

To fix spelling and grammatical errors without having to confirm each correction, use the **Autocorrect** feature. For example, if you type **adn** plus a space, AutoCorrect replaces what you have typed with **and**.

- Open a new Word document.
- From the **Tools** menu, select **Autocorrect**.
- Select the **Autocorrect** tab.
- A list of autocorrections are displayed (it is also possible to add your own autocorrections).
- Make sure that the **Replace text as you type** option is selected.
- Type in the following text, including the mistakes.

the day came when caesar had to return to his home adn his poeple.

The **Autocorrect** feature should have corrected your mistakes automatically.

Automatically check spelling and grammar as you type

To check for spelling and grammatical errors "behind the scenes," use **automatic spelling and grammar checking**. As you type, the spelling and grammar checkers check the text and then mark possible errors with wavy underlines (red for spelling, green for grammar). To correct an error, display a shortcut menu and select the correction you want.

- From the **Tools** menu, select **Autocorrect**.
- Click the **Autocorrect** tab.
- Ensure that the **Replace text as you type** option is not selected, and click **OK**.
- From the **Tools** menu, select **Options**.
- Click the **Spelling and Grammar** tab.
- Ensure that the **Check spelling as you type** and **Check grammar as you type** options are selected and click **OK**.

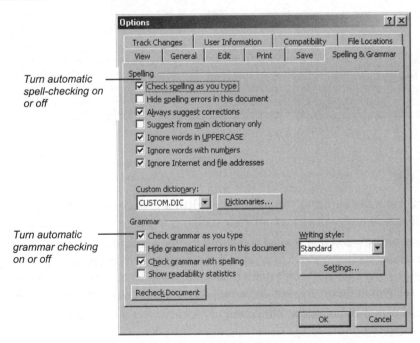

Figure 1.1: Controlling automatic spelling and grammar check

- Type in the same text as before, including the mistakes.

  the day came when caesar had to return to his home adn his poeple.

This time you should see green and red wavy lines indicating the mistakes.

- Right-click on each mistake and select the correction you want from the shortcut menu.

Check spelling and grammar all at once

You need to put the spelling mistakes back again now! Either press the **Undo** button until the mistakes are back, or type the line in again with all the mistakes.

- Click the **Spelling and Grammar** button on the Standard toolbar.

- When Word finds a possible spelling or grammatical error, make your changes in the **Spelling and Grammar** dialogue box as shown in Figure 1.2 below.

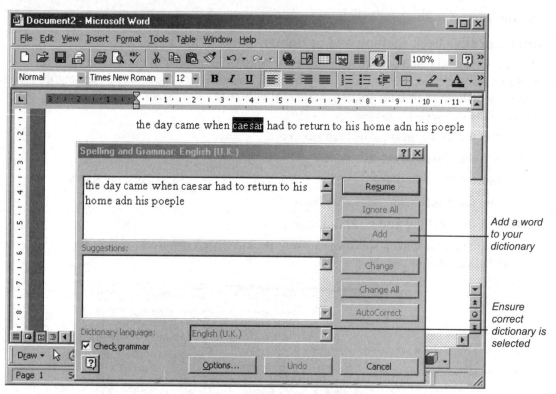

Figure 1.2: Checking spelling and grammar

1.2. Dictionaries

When you run the spell checker make sure that you have the English dictionary set as the default rather than the U.S. English dictionary, which will change all your spellings to the American version.

Sometimes the spell-checker will suggest that a word is incorrect when you know that it is correct. This often happens with proper names such as 'AVCE' (though if you have turned on the option to ignore words in UPPERCASE – see Figure 1.1 – it won't mark that one). You can add words to the dictionary by clicking the **Add** button shown in figure 1.2, but do be careful not to add wrongly-spelt words!

You can also create a special personal dictionary, additional to the main dictionary, which contains any unusual words you may wish to use.

Task 1.1: Create a custom dictionary to hold words that you are going to use in an article about text-messaging.

- On the **Tools** menu, click **Options**, and then click the **Spelling & Grammar** tab.

- Click **Dictionaries** and **New**.

- In the **File name** box, type the name **Texting** for the custom dictionary and click **Save**.

- Before you can use the custom dictionary to check spelling, you must activate it: In the **Custom Dictionaries** dialog box, make sure the check box beside the dictionary's name is selected.

- Ensure that your dictionary is displayed on the options dialogue box (see figure 1.3 below).

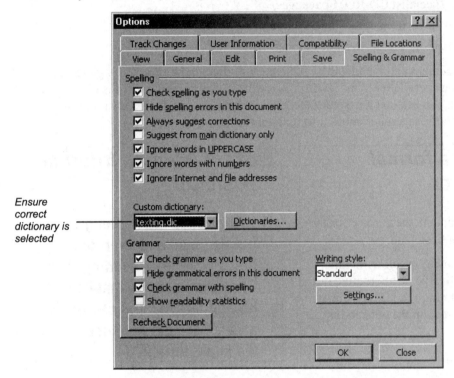

Ensure correct dictionary is selected

Figure 1.3: Creating a new dictionary

- Enter the text below into a new Word document.

Compose your message by using the letter and number keys on your phone. For example:

HaPEBday	*Happy Birthday*
MkeMyDaSa+!	*Make my day, say yes*
ItsOnlEAGAmShO	*It's only a game show*

(add your own text!)

- You can now add words to your custom dictionary while you check spelling.

- Try spell-checking your document with your new dictionary activated and deactivated from the custom dictionaries dialogue box. Note each time you rerun the spell-check on the same piece of text you must click on the **Recheck Document** button shown in figure 1.3.

1.3. Writing Style

The test of good writing is whether you can convey to your readers exactly what you intend. You have to be aware of who your audience is likely to be and what type of language they are likely to understand and expect. You don't want to send your audience to sleep, be patronising, mislead them or even unwittingly cause offence by using the wrong language.

Also, consider the purpose of the document. All written products are created for a reason, which can include:

- ❑   to inform (e.g. business letters, memos, instruction manuals)
- ❑   to entertain (e.g. internal newsletters, web pages)
- ❑   to educate (e.g. specialist CD-ROM packages)
- ❑   to persuade (e.g. advertisements, publicity flyers)
- ❑   to collect information (e.g. forms, questionnaires)

The purpose of the document and the intended audience will dictate the style of language that should be used. For example a business letter to a client informing them that their payment is overdue would demand a formal style. An internal newsletter, perhaps including a report on the organisation's Christmas party to entertain the staff use a much more informal approach:

Extract from a formal business letter	*Extract from an internal newsletter*
In spite of several reminders the invoice for the goods supplied has not been paid. Unless we receive payment in full within the next seven days, I shall have no alternative but to pursue this matter through the Courts and a claim will include interest on the outstanding amount and full costs.	**The Christmas Party was great fun as usual and everyone had a wonderful evening. The Chairman showed that he was human after all and obviously a very keen disco dancer in his spare time!!!!**

Figure 1.4: Different styles of writing

1.4. Using different writing styles to meet different needs

Organisations produce many types of document, each of which requires a different writing style to meet different needs together with an appropriate document structure. To illustrate the different documents that an organisation might produce, a fictitious company called Victory Publishing, described in Appendix B, is used. Basically Victory Publishing produces a range of educational textbooks for schools and colleges.

Examples of some of the documents that Victory Publishing produces together with a description of their styles are listed below.

- ❑   **Advertisements**
    Short, bold headlines to attract attention e.g. **Half-price Books!**
- ❑   **Software instruction manuals**
    Facts set out clearly using short sentences and simple words. Use of bullet points, figures and diagrams.
- ❑   **Questionnaires** for market research

Simple, unambiguous, easy to answer questions which are often multiple choice with tick boxes.

❏ **Reminders**

Short sentences in informal note form using appropriate abbreviations.

❏ **Invoices**

Clear table structure with appropriate column headings.

❏ **Contracts**

Longer sentences using more complex wording.

❏ **Letters to customers and suppliers**

Formal language.

❏ **Reports**

Longer sentences in paragraphs which are organised into a consistent format of sections and subsections.

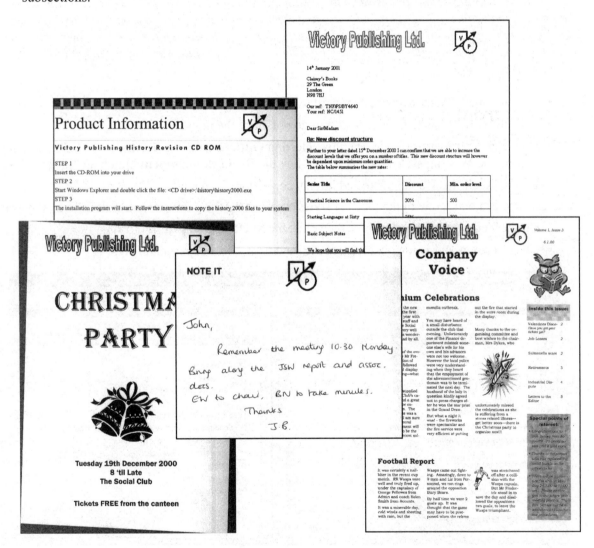

Figure 1.5: Sample documents from Victory Publishing

1.5. Using tools to help with style

Software tools exist to help with writing style. For example in MS Word you can select, customise or create different grammar and writing styles. Figure 1.6 below shows the type of checks you can choose to apply to your document. You can choose between Casual, Standard, Formal, Technical and Custom styles.

- Open a new Word document.

- On the **Tools** menu click **Options**, click the **Spelling and grammar** tab and then select **Casual style** from the **Writing style** box. Click **OK**.

- Type in the following extract[1]:

"Now it is autumn again; the people are all coming back. The recess of summer is over, when holidays are taken, newspapers shrink, history itself seems momentarily to falter and stop. But the papers are thickening and filling again; things seem to be happening; back from Corfu and Sete, Positano and Leningrad, the people are parking their cars and campers in their drives, and opening their diaries, and calling up other people on the telephone. The deckchairs on the beach have been put away, and a weak sun shines on the promenade; there is fresh fighting in Vietnam, while McGovern campaigns ineffectually against Nixon."

- Run the **Spell Check** from the Standard toolbar.

- Note the corrections that it suggests, but do not make them.

- Now change the writing style again by selecting **Options** from the **Tools** menu. Select **Formal** from the **Writing style** box this time. Click the **Recheck document** button and then click **OK**.

- Run the spell check and note the additional corrections it suggests.

You can also customise one of the existing styles by selecting the grammar and style options you want.

- On the **Tools** menu click **Options** then click the **Spelling and grammar** tab.

- Click **Settings** and you will see the options available for that particular style.

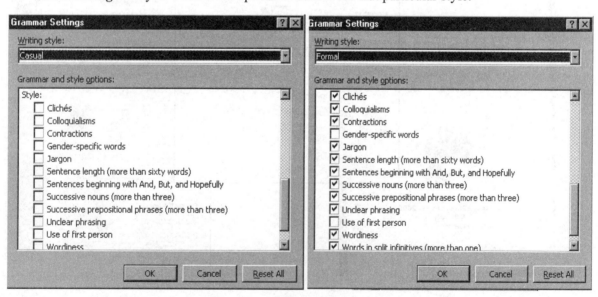

Figure 1.6: Casual and formal writing style default options

---

[1] Bradbury, Malcolm. *The History Man*, Martin Secker and Warburg 1975

> **Note:** You can also create a new style by selecting the custom style of writing and then selecting the
> grammar and style options you require.

1.6. Using a thesaurus

A thesaurus helps you to replace particular words with either more appropriate ones or different ones to prevent repetition.

Try this out on the text you typed in section 1.5:

- Highlight the word *shrink*.

- On the **Tools** menu, select **Language**, **Thesaurus**.

- You will see a list of meanings of the word and a list of synonyms (i.e. words that could be used instead). Click on a synonym e.g. *reduce in size* and click **Replace**.

You can also find a common synonym for a word by right-clicking the word, pointing to **Synonyms** on the shortcut menu and then clicking the synonym you want.

1.7. Producing draft copies

After you have used the tools discussed above and read through your work on the screen, you may want to print a quick **draft copy** to check it through.

When printing a document in draft quality, Word omits formatting and most of the graphics, which usually makes the document print faster. However, some printers do not support this option, so check first.

You can download a document **Draftcopy.doc** from the web site www.payne-gallway.co.uk/avce to try this out.

- Open the file **Draftcopy.doc** that you have downloaded from the Payne-Gallway web site.

- On the **Tools** menu, click **Options**, and then click the **Print** tab.

- Under **Printing options**, select the **Draft output** check box.

- From the **File** menu, select **Print** and click **OK**.

The document displayed on your screen will be printed in draft mode with no figures printed.

Many printers have economy or draft quality print settings which save time and ink, so look out for these, usually accessed from the **Properties** button in the **Print** dialogue box.

1.8. Displaying readability statistics

The Flesch Reading Ease index calculates readability based on the average number of syllables per word and the average number of words per sentence. Scores range from 0 to 100. The average writing score is approximately 60 to 70. The higher the score a piece of writing is awarded, the greater the number of people who can readily understand the document. Standard writing approximately equates to the seventh to eighth grade level on the Flesch-Kincaid scale as shown in Figure 1.7. (equivalent to Year 8 in our schools).

- Open a new Word document.

- On the **Tools** menu, click **Options**, and then click the **Spelling & grammar** tab. Select the **Check grammar with spelling** check box. Select the **Show readability statistics** check box, and then click **OK**.

- Type in the following text which is an extract from a contract between Victory Publishing and one of their authors.

The Author shall not during the continuance of this Agreement without the consent of the Publishers publish any abridgement of the work nor shall the Author prepare otherwise than for the Publishers any work which reproduces in identical or similar form any considerable part of the work.

- Click the **Spelling and Grammar** button on the Standard toolbar.

When Word finishes checking spelling and grammar it displays information about the reading level of the document (see Figure 1.7 below).

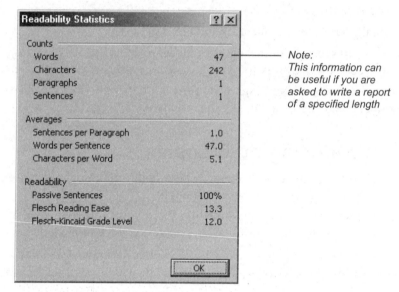

Figure 1.7: Readability statistics

The Reading Ease Score for the passage was only 13.3, which is hardly surprising. The passage could have been written as follows to convey almost the same information.

The author must not publish any of this work elsewhere unless the Publisher agrees.

- In a new Word document type in the new version and check its Flesch Reading Ease score

In this case there is a Flesch Reading Ease score in excess of 50, which means it is much easier to understand. However, legal documents which have to make sure that every detail is spelled out are often very hard to understand.

Task 1.2: Select a piece of your own written work. Type it into Word and produce readability statistics.

Before you submit assignments try using these tools to test the readability of your work. If a piece of writing intended for the general public scores less than 60, look at it again and simplify it!

1.9. Proofreading

The software tools that you have been using to check your documents will not guarantee that there are no errors. To check that your document makes sense, that it is correctly laid out and that the spelling and grammar are correct and consistent you must also proofread it carefully. When a document is proofread it is marked by hand to indicate the changes that are needed. There is a British standard for proofreaders' symbols. The most commonly used ones are reproduced in figure 1.8.

Discussion: Check the last 6 lines. There are two errors (inconsistencies) in them. Can you find them?

Correction	Textual Mark	Margin Mark
Deletion	 / through character or  — through words to be deleted	
Start new paragraph		
Insertion		
Run on (no new paragraph)		
Change to capital letters		
Change to lower case	encircle characters to be changed	
Indent		
Use italic letters	under characters	
Use bold letters	 under characters	
Centre text	Enclosing matter to be centred	[ ]

Figure 1.8: Proof correction marks

You should get into the habit of using these as they are a clear, quick way of showing corrections that need to be made. You need a pencil with a very fine point to make the marks in exactly the right place.

It is often a good idea to ask someone else to check your work for you – we often see what we want to see, not what is really there!

A good proofreader should check for obvious mistakes such as spelling, grammar and typographical errors and also for clarity, sense and consistency. For example, a section of a report may refer to a diagram or a chart that has actually been taken out at some stage. It is easy to lose track and not remove the reference. Another potential area for mistakes is the use of the wrong word. In Microsoft Word Help you can view their list of commonly-confused words, for example 'advice' and 'advise' are often confused, as are 'affect' and 'effect'.

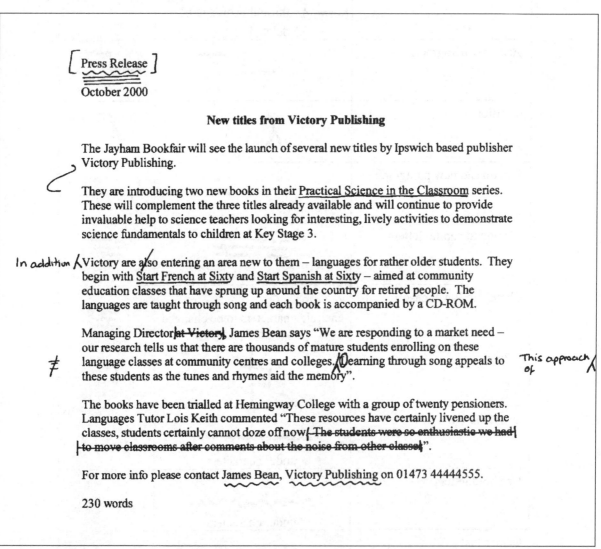

Figure 1.9: A piece of corrected text

Task 1.3: Open a new Word document. Enter the text shown in Figure 1.9 but incorporating the amendments marked.

1.10. Software tools to help with proofreading

When several people review and edit a document in Word, the changes can be tracked using a feature called **Revision Marks**. These marks are similar to editing marks you might use if you were editing on paper as described above, but with some major advantages. First you can change your mind and reverse an edit without making the document messy. Word can capture the edits of numerous reviewers and keep track of each one's comments individually. Revisions by different people are shown in different colours. By default any proposed additions are shown as underlined text and deletions as strikethrough text.

Inserting proposed changes and comments

- Open a Word document that contains some text.
- On the **Tools** menu, select **Track Changes**, **Highlight Changes**.
- In the **Highlight Changes** dialogue box, select **Track Changes While Editing** and **Highlight Changes on Screen** check boxes and click **OK**.
- Try adding some text – it should appear as underlined text. You should see a vertical change line appear in the margin, identifying lines containing changes.
- Try deleting some text. The text should appear with a line drawn through it (a strikethrough).
- To insert a comment, click after the word you want to comment on.
- On the **Insert** menu, click **Comment**.

A comment reference mark with a sequential number is inserted in the document. The comment pane is opened at the bottom of the Word window and the insertion point is automatically positioned in it next to the new comment reference number.

- Type your comment in the comment pane.
- Click the **Close** button in the comment pane and **Save** the document.

When you move your mouse over the position of the comment, the comment will be displayed.

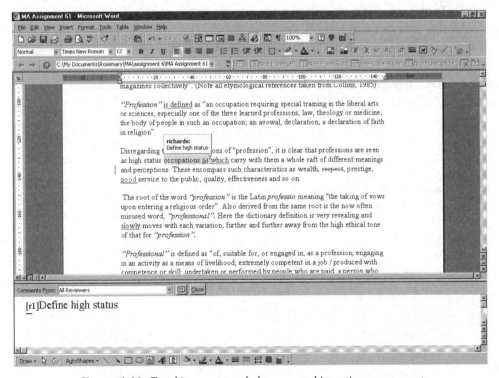

Figure 1.10: Tracking proposed changes and inserting a comment

Reviewing the proposed changes and comments

- On the **View** menu select **Toolbars**, **Reviewing**. The Reviewing toolbar appears.

- Press **Ctrl-Home** to move to the beginning of the document.

- On the Reviewing toolbar click the **Next Change** button to move through the proposed changes you made to the document.

- Click the **Accept Change** button or the **Reject Change** button to either accept or reject the proposed changes.

- After you have read a comment you can delete it by clicking the **Delete Comment** button.

Figure 1.11: The Reviewing toolbar.

1.11. Building your portfolio

Produce one of the six original documents required for your portfolio using the techniques discussed in this chapter to check your accuracy and style of writing.

For example write *either* an instruction leaflet for a machine your parents have difficulty with, such as a video recorder, mobile phone etc. *or* an instruction leaflet for a new board game:

- Before you begin identify who your readers will be – this will help you to use a suitable style and to make sure it is at a level that suits them.

- Experiment with different layouts and keep copies of your different attempts as evidence.

- Print out draft copies showing hand-written annotation marks and/or revision marks inserted with Microsoft Word.

- Run readability statistics and identify any changes you have made to improve the readability of the document. Use **Print Screen** or a screen capture utility as described in Unit 3, Chapter 21 to provide screenshots as evidence.

- Provide evidence that you have run the spell checker, grammar checker and used the thesaurus (use screenshots as above).

Chapter 2 – Styles of Presentation

Objectives

- ✓ Produce different page layouts
- ✓ Use different textual styles
- ✓ Use special presentation styles appropriately
- ✓ Incorporate lists, columns and tables into documents

*Note: You will need to download **Paraformatting.doc** from www.payne-gallway.co.uk/avce to complete the exercises in this chapter.*

Information has to be presented clearly if you are not going to annoy or confuse your readers. Also, you have to think about what you want to achieve with your document and what will appeal to your readers.

Different styles of presentation are used to suit different purposes. If you are trying to sell a new brand of Cola, invite people to send for a pizza or try travelling by rail, you will need a different presentation style from one used in a document informing them that their house is about to be demolished or a new motorway is to be built through an area of outstanding natural beauty.

2.1. Page Layout

Different documents use different page layouts to make them easier to read, attract the reader's attention and make them generally pleasant to look at. You can normally recognise at a glance the type of document from its layout.

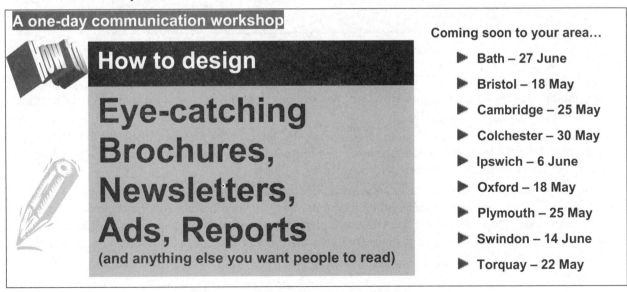

Figure 2.1: An advertising leaflet

Page Setup

In Microsoft Word page specifications can be viewed and modified from the **File** menu, **Page Setup** command. Settings that are most often modified are paper size and margin sizes.

In countries that use the metric system (such as the UK), the standard paper size is **A4** (210 by 297 millimetres), which is narrower and longer than the standard paper size for some other countries, such as the United Sates, which uses **Letter** (8.5 by 11 inches). You will often find that the Page Setup in Word, for example, has a default of **Letter** paper size. You don't need to worry about this because Word can automatically adjust documents so that they print correctly on a different standard paper size (for example, **A4**).

- On the **Tools** menu, select **Options**. Click the **Print** tab.
- Under **Printing options**, select the **Allow A4/letter paper resizing** check box.

Most business documents are produced in Portrait orientation ('tall') but some advertising documentation, large spreadsheets or charts for example, may be better presented in Landscape orientation ('wide'). This can be set from the **File** menu, **Page Setup** command.

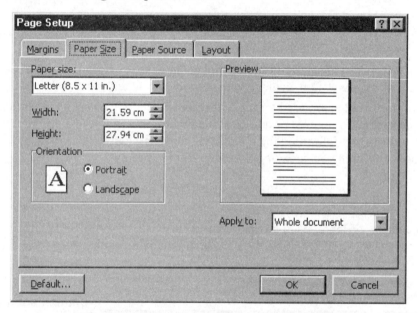

Figure 2.2: Selecting paper size and orientation

Page margins are the blank space around the edges of the page. In general, you insert text and graphics in the printable area inside the margins. However, you can position some items in the margins – for example headers, footers, and page numbers.

Word offers several page margin options. You can use the default page margins or specify your own, either from the **Page setup** dialogue box (see Figure 2.3) or switch to print layout view and drag the margin boundary on the horizontal or vertical ruler bar.

If you are producing a lengthy document such as a report, you may want to bind the document. To prevent any text becoming obscured by the binding process you should use a gutter margin to add extra space to the side or top margin of a document you plan to bind. If you plan to print back-to back you should also turn on mirror margins to place the gutter margin on facing pages rather than on the left side of every page, as shown in Figure 2.3.

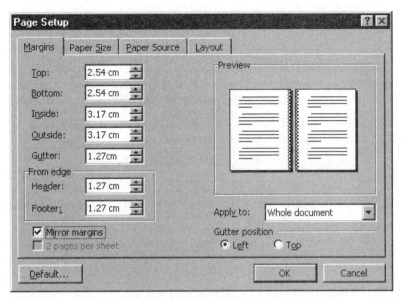

Figure 2.3: Setting margins

Pagination

When you fill a page with text or graphics, Microsoft Word inserts an automatic page break and starts a new page. To force a page break at a specific location, you can insert a manual page break from the **Insert** menu. However, if you insert manual page breaks, you might have to frequently adjust the page breaks as you edit the document.

Instead, you might want to set pagination options to control where Word positions automatic page breaks. Most of these options are set from the **Format** menu, **Paragraph** option, **Line and Page Breaks** tab as shown below.

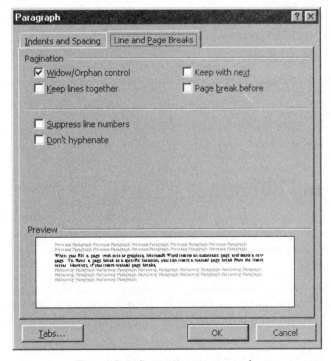

Figure 2.4: Setting pagination rules

These pagination rules are summarised in the table below.

Option	Description
Widow/Orphan control	Prevents the last line of a paragraph being printed at the top of a new page (widow) or the first line of a paragraph being printed at the bottom of a page (orphan).
Keep lines together	Keep all lines of a paragraph on the same page.
Keep with next	Keeps two paragraphs on same page.
Page break before	Forces a page break before a specified paragraph.
Suppress line numbers	Line numbers are suppressed if the line numbering feature has been selected.
Don't hyphenate	Ensures words are not hyphenated at the end of a line.

Task 2.1: Experiment with formatting options as described below.

- Download the file **Paraformatting.doc** from www.payne-gallway.co.uk/avce
- Select **Format**, **Paragraph** and click the **Line and Page Breaks** tab.
- Ensure that the **Widow/Orphan control** option is not selected.
- Scroll through the document and note the widow at the top of page two and the orphan at the bottom of page two.
- Go back and select the **Widow/Orphan control** option.
- Scroll through the document to see the effect.
- Click before the last paragraph on the first page.
- From the **Insert** menu, select **Break**, **Page Break**.
- Click on the **Print Preview** button on the Standard toolbar.
- Click the **Multiple Pages** button.
- You should now see four pages of text.
- **Close** Print Preview.
- Experiment using the other pagination rules shown in the table above.
- Close the file without saving the changes.

2.2. Headers and Footers

A header consists of text and/or graphics appearing at the top of every page; text or graphics placed in a footer will appear at the bottom of every page. A header is typically used to identify the section or chapter in a book, and the footer may contain the page number, a document identification of some kind, the author's name and so on.

Headers and footers are also useful when you are designing a letterhead. The header can incorporate a logo and the organisation's name. The footer can include the company address (which could alternatively be placed in the header) and information such as the directors' names, VAT registration number and so on.

- In a new Word document, select **View**, **Header and Footer**.

- By default you're placed in the Header area at the top of your current page. If you already have text in your document it will appear dimmed, in light-grey text.

- The Header and Footer toolbar is displayed, with buttons to insert various items such as page number, date, time and so on. The only button you'll need at the moment is **Switch between Header and Footer**.

Figure 2.5: The Header and Footer toolbar

- Insert a text box using the **Text Box** tool from the Drawing toolbar. A cross-hair appears allowing you to make the text box the required size, and you can then type text into it.

- Type in a fictitious Company and address – See Figure 2.6.

- Select the text and change the font size or typeface if you like. You can use the **Line Color** tool to remove the border, and the **Fill Color** tool to shade the box.

- Insert some clip art into the header too. Select **Insert**, **Picture**, **Clip Art**.

- Select a suitable image and click **Insert clip**.

- Size the image as required and position it in your header.

- Use the **Line** tool to draw a line under the text.

- Use the **Switch between Header and Footer** button in the Header and Footer toolbar to move to the Footer.

- Type additional company information in the footer.

- Press the **Close** button to return to the main document.

- Save this document as *Headandfoot.doc*.

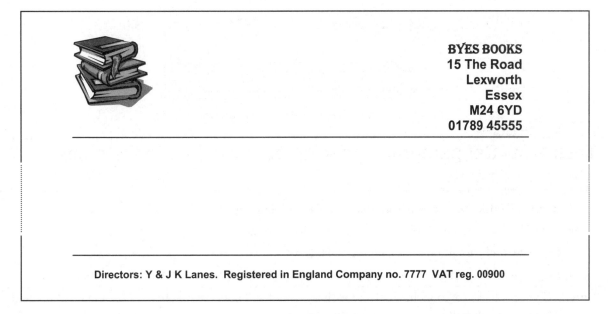

Figure 2.6: Header and footer

Task 2.2: Reopen the file **Paraformatting.doc** and create a footer to display page numbers.

2.3. Paragraph formats

Indents

Several types of indents are available in MS Word to format text. If you select **Paragraph** from the **Format** menu and then click on the **Indents and spacing** tab you will see the various options available. You can specify indentations from the left or the right of selected text and also some special indents. These include a **first line** indent which, as you may have guessed, indents the first line only and a **hanging** indent, which indents all of the paragraph text *except* for the first line.

Hanging indents are most useful in numbered and bulleted lists, where the numbers or bullets line up at the left margin and the rest of the text is indented. Look at the bulleted list in paragraph 2.2.

In that same dialogue box you can also specify line spacing – normally **Single** or **Double**. **Spacing Before** and **Spacing After** allows you to leave space between paragraphs. The text in this book is set with **Spacing Before** equal to 6 points. The paragraph headings, like **2.3. Paragraph formats** above, are set with **Spacing Before** equal to 18 points.

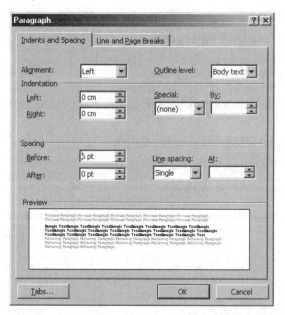

Figure 2.7: Specifying indents, spacing and line spacing

Task 2.3: Set paragraph spacing as described in the steps below.

- Reopen the file **Paraformatting.doc** if it is not already open.
- In the first paragraph of this document set a first line indent.
- In the second paragraph set a hanging indent.
- Indent the third paragraph by an additional two centimetres from the left and the right.

Note: If your ruler is set to inches, select **Options** from the **Tools** menu, click on the **General** tab and change the measurement units to centimetres.

- Set the fourth paragraph to double line spacing.
- Save and close the document.

Hyphenation

You can use the hyphenation feature to give your documents a polished and professional look. Hyphenation helps eliminate gaps or "rivers of white" in justified text and also helps maintain even line lengths in narrow columns. On the other hand, hyphenated words are sometimes awkward to read and many people prefer not to allow hyphenation.

Microsoft Word provides several ways to hyphenate all or part of your document. You can:

Automatically hyphenate text as you type

When you turn on automatic hyphenation, Word automatically inserts hyphens where needed in the document. If you later edit the document and change line breaks, then Word rehyphenates the document.

- On the **Tools** menu, select **Language**, and then click **Hyphenation**.
- Select the **Automatically hyphenate document** check box.

Hyphenate text all at once

When you choose manual hyphenation, Word searches for text to hyphenate, asks you to confirm each proposed optional hyphen, and then inserts it. If you later edit the document and change line breaks, Word displays and prints only the optional hyphens that still fall at the ends of lines. Word does not rehyphenate the document.

- To hyphenate part of the document, select the text you want. To hyphenate the entire document, make sure no text is selected.
- On the **Tools** menu, select **Language**, and then click **Hyphenation**.
- Click **Manual**.
- If Word identifies a word or phrase to hyphenate, either insert an optional hyphen in the location Word proposes, click **Yes**, or insert an optional hyphen in another part of the word, use the arrow keys or mouse to move the insertion point to that location, and then click **Yes**.

Task 2.4:   Hyphenate a piece of text

- Reopen the file **Paraformatting.doc**.
- Practise hyphenating the text as described above.
- Close the document without saving the changes.

2.4.   Textual styles

The art of designing, selecting and producing typefaces is called typography. There are thousands of different typefaces and each can have its own variation within that style. A single size and style of a particular typeface is called a font. There are two main groups of typeface, **serif**, which are more decorative, and **sans serif** which are plainer.

```
                    Serif
     (serifs are the little lines at the top and bottom of the letters)
                  Sans serif
```

Figure 2.8: Examples of serif (e.g. Times New Roman) and sans serif (e.g. Arial) typefaces

Type may be *italic*, **bold** or <u>underlined</u>, or in any ***<u>combination</u>***. Other, seldom-used, styles are ~~strikethrough~~ and SMALL CAPS. Sizes of typefaces are measured in different ways, and the *point* system is used in MS Word. There are 12 points in a *pica*, and 6 picas in one inch. Another way to emphasise text is to adjust the justification or the alignment. The easiest way to do this is to select the text and use the toolbar buttons to align the text – **Left**, **Right** or **Centre**. The **Justify** option means that the text is aligned down both margins.

Typefaces can also be divided into **text** or **book** faces which are used for blocks of text as they are easy to read even when printed quite small, and **display** faces which are used to attract attention and so are used for headings and titles. In a long document it is vital to be consistent with the typefaces you use for body text (**Times New Roman 11pt** in this book), chapter headings (**Antique Olive 28pt** in this book) and so on.

Ways to raise or lower text

Text in a document is positioned along an invisible horizontal line called the baseline. You can raise or lower text along the baseline by making it subscript or superscript (this text will be smaller than the text around it).

- Type the following sentence into a new Word document

  The formula for water is H2O

- Highlight the number **2**.
- Select **Font** from the **Format** menu and click on the **Font** tab.
- Click on the **Subscript** check box.

Now the formula reads *The formula for water is H_2O*

- On a new line, type the following equation

  22 = 4

- Highlight the second number **2**.
- Select **Font** from the **Format** menu and click on the **Font** tab.
- Click on the **Superscript** check box and click **OK**.

The equation now looks a bit more sensible! It should say $2^2 = 4$.

You can also shift text vertically without changing its size. You specify the number of points by which the text is raised or lowered along the baseline.

- Type in the first sentence again.
- Select the text to be raised or lowered.
- On the **Format** menu, click **Font** and then click the **Character spacing** tab.
- In the **Position** box, click **Raised or Lowered**.
- Experiment with raising and lowering the text by different numbers of points.

On-screen text animation

Word has a number of built-in text animations which can add visual interest or emphasis to a document. However it is clearly only effective in documents that will be displayed on screen because in a printed document, the animations appear as regular text. For example, animating the title of an e-mail memo would be effective, but animating the headings for a printed report would be completely pointless.

- Prepare the following memo in a new Word document that will later be attached to an e-mail.

MEMORANDUM

From: Mr Smith

To: All staff

Date: 2.2.01

Subject: Annual holidays

Please note that all holidays for the current year must be booked with my secretary, Miss Peel, by February 15th.

- Select the heading MEMORANDUM.
- Select **Format**, **Font** and click the **Text Effects** tab.
- In the Animations box, click the effect you want.

2.5.   The Drawing toolbar

In Paragraph 2.2 the Drawing toolbar was used to create text boxes and insert clip art. It can also be used to create lines, arrows, stars, banners and callouts (text used to call attention to pictures and graphics). Existing graphics can be modified by filling with colour, changing the line size, style or colour or by adding a shadow or 3-D effect. The **WordArt** button on the toolbar adds special effects to text which can then be rotated, sized and fitted to a predefined shape.

These effects can be useful for drawing simple diagrams or to add interest to newsletters, posters, letterheads and so on.

Task 2.5:   Follow the instructions below to create a header and footer incorporating a company logo for Victory Publishing.

- Open a new Word document.
- Select **View**, **Header and Footer**.
- Insert some blank lines into the header.
- Click the **WordArt** symbol in the Drawing toolbar.

The WordArt gallery opens.

- Select your desired effect and press **OK**. (The top left-hand one was chosen in Figure 2.12.)
- A new window opens. Type the name of the company e.g. *Victory Publishing Ltd* and click **OK**.

You can edit the text using the WordArt toolbar.

Format
WordArt

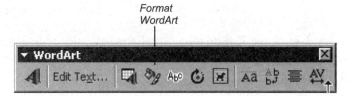

Figure 2.9: The WordArt toolbar

For example, you could change the colour of the text to black by clicking the **Format WordArt** button. Then select the **Fill** and **Line Color** from the dialogue box, or click **Cancel** if you change your mind.

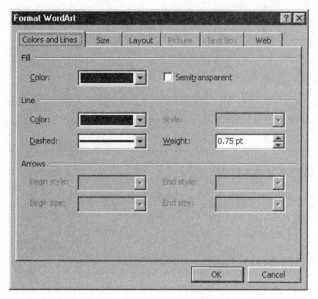

Figure 2.10: Formatting WordArt

- Move and size the WordArt to fit in the header. You can size the WordArt object by clicking it and dragging one of the corner handles, and move it by dragging.

You can now use the tools on the Drawing toolbar to create the logo shown in Figure 2.12.

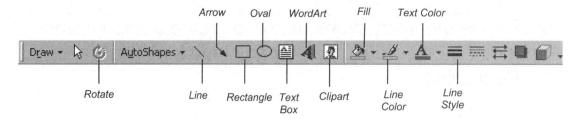

Figure 2.11: The Drawing toolbar

- On the right-hand side of the header draw a square using the **Rectangle** tool (keep your finger on the **Shift** key to draw a perfect square).
- Draw an overlapping circle using the **Oval** tool.
- Right-click in the square and select **Add Text**. Insert the letter *V*, adjusting the size and style from the Formatting toolbar.
- Repeat for the circle.
- Use the **Arrow** tool to draw an arrow across the shapes.
- With the arrow selected, click the **Rotate** tool. Small green circles will appear at each end of the arrow. Drag these to rotate the arrow to the correct angle.
- Drag the arrow into position.

- Click on each shape and increase the line width by clicking the **Line Style** button.

- Select the three shapes in the graphic by clicking the **Select Objects** tool and dragging around them.

- Click on **Draw**, **Group** from the Drawing toolbar. All the items will be grouped together as one object.

- Drag to the correct position.

- The logo consists of the text and the graphic, so group both these objects together. The logo should look something like Figure 2.12 but it may be a different size, colour or shape – just be creative!

Figure 2.12: The completed header

- Switch to the footer (use the **Switch between Header and Footer** button on the Header and Footer toolbar) and insert a text box with the company address details.

Figure 2.13: The completed footer

- Save this document as *Victoryheader.doc*.

2.6. Special Presentation styles

Borders and shading

You can add a border to any or all sides of each page in a document, to pages in a section, to the first page only, or to all pages except the first. You can add page borders in many line styles and colours, as well as a variety of graphical borders.

- Reopen the file **Paraformatting.doc**.

- From the **Format** menu, select **Borders and Shading**.

- Select the **Page Border** tab.

- Select one of the line styles or artwork from the **Art** selection.

- Specify that you want to apply it to the first page only and click **OK**.

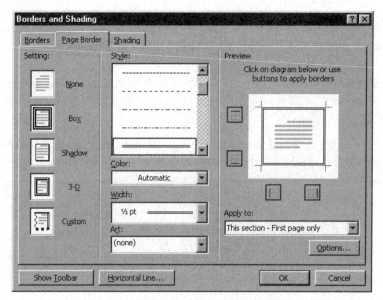

Figure 2.14: Creating a page border

You can draw attention to paragraphs or selected text by adding borders or applying shading.

- Scroll to the second page of the document **Paraformatting.doc** and highlight the first paragraph.
- From the **Format** menu, select **Borders and Shading** and click the **Borders** tab.
- Select a **Setting** and a **Style**, choose a colour and width and click **OK**.
- Click the **Shading** tab and select a fill colour. Click **OK**.

Use of sounds

To insert an existing sound file into a Word document, you must have a sound program such as Sound Recorder – a Microsoft Windows accessory that lets you record, edit, and play sound files. You will also need a sound card and speakers installed in your computer.

- Scroll through to the third page of the document **Paraformatting.doc**.
- Click after the first paragraph on this page.
- On the **Insert** menu, select **Object**, and then click the **Create from File** tab.
- Click **Browse**, and then locate the sound file you want to insert.

> **Note:** In Windows 98 and 2000 you will find some sounds in the folder **C:\windows\media**.

- To display a sound file icon select the **Display as icon** check box. Click **OK**.
- To play the sound file, double-click its icon.

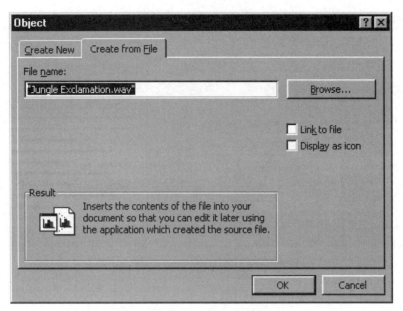

Figure 2.15: Inserting a sound into a Word document

2.7. Bullets and numbers

To create a bulleted list, like the ones we have used for the exercises in this book, click the **Bullets** tool on the Formatting toolbar.

To stop the bullets appearing, press **Backspace** or deselect the **Bullets** tool before typing. You can customise the bullets by selecting your bulleted list and then select **Format**, **Bullets and Numbering**. You can then click on the option you prefer.

Task 2.5: Create a bulleted and a numbered list.

- Open a new Word document.
- Enter the following items as a bulleted list:

  > Art
  > Biology
  > Chemistry
  > English
  > French
  > History

- Highlight the list and select **Format**, **Bullets and Numbering**. Click on the **Bulleted** tab and then on **Picture**.
- Select a symbol to replace the current bullets.

Numbered list

- Now turn the bulleted list into a numbered list by selecting the list and clicking the **Numbering** tool.

You can customise the numbers by selecting **Format**, **Bullets and Numbering** and selecting an option. Sometimes for example you may want your list to start from a number other than 1, or you may want the list to be numbered **Subject 1**, **Subject 2**, **Subject 3** or **a**, **b**, **c** instead of **1, 2, 3**. You may also want to change the alignment and/or indentation of the list.

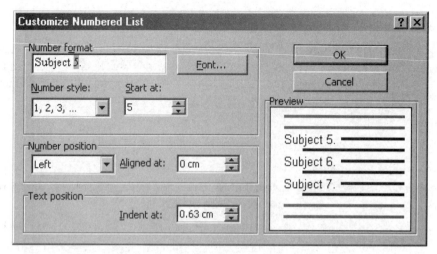

Figure 2.16: Customising a numbered list

- **Save** this file as *Subjectlist.doc*.

Turning off autonumbering

If you start a list by typing a number, Word will automatically number the next line when you press **Enter**. If you want to turn this feature off, choose **Tools**, **Autocorrect** from the menu. Click the **Autoformat as you type** tab and deselect **Automatic numbered lists**.

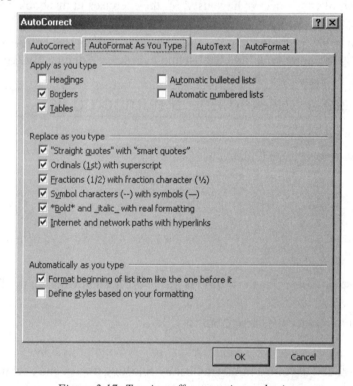

Figure 2.17: Turning off automatic numbering

2.8. Tables

A table is made up of rows and columns of cells that you can fill with text and graphics. Tables are often used to organise and present information, but they have many other uses as well. You can use tables to align numbers in columns, and then sort and perform calculations on them. You can also use tables to create interesting page layouts and arrange text and graphics.

- Open a new Word document.
- From the **File** menu, select **Page Setup** and click on the **Page Layout** tab.
- Select **Landscape** orientation.
- From the menu bar select **Table, Insert Table**. Specify a table of 7 columns and 5 rows and click **OK**.
- Select the cells in the top row by dragging across them, and select **Table, Merge cells**.
- Enter the text as shown below, adjusting column widths where necessary by dragging the column dividers.
- Centre the headings as shown.

Victory Publishing Current Titles

ISBN	Title	Author	No. of pages	Publication date	Price	Stock level
1 904113110	Basic Geography	R. O'Brien	80	1.9.99	6.95	1375
1 904113111	Science for School Years	J. Myers	64	1.8.99	4.95	2195
1 904113112	Basic History notes	K Lightfoot	80	1.2.00	6.95	1775

Figure 2.17: Extract from a table

You can also add borders to a table or an individual table cell, and you can use shading to fill in the background of a table.

- Highlight the top row of the table.
- From the **Format** menu, select **Borders and Shading**.
- Click on the **Borders** tab.
- Click on **Box,** select a line style and click **OK**.
- With the row still highlighted select **Borders and Shading** from the **Format** menu again**.**
- Click on the **Shading** tab.
- Select options for colour or patterns.
- Save the document as *Table.doc*.

Changing the text orientation

Sometimes you may need to enter text into a table cell in a different direction.

- In the table you have just created highlight the second row.
- From the **Format** menu select **Text Direction**.
- Click on an orientation option.

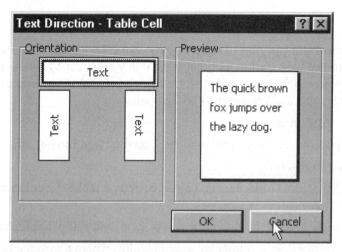

Figure 2.18: Changing the text direction

The table should now look something like this:

Victory Publishing Current Titles						
ISBN	Title	Author	No. of pages	Publication date	Price	Stock level
1 904113110	Basic Geography	R. O'Brien	80	1.9.99	6.95	1375
1 904113111	Science for School Years	J. Myers	64	1.8.99	4.95	2195
1 904113112	Basic History notes	K Lightfoot	80	1.2.00	6.95	1775

Figure 2.19

Task 2.6: Create a time sheet for Victory Publishers Ltd.

Each week employees at Victory Publishing Ltd complete a Time Sheet to show any overtime they have worked. Some employees are paid for overtime and others are not, but it is recorded in any event.

The time sheet you are to create will look like the one below in Figure 2.19. You can copy the logo from the document **VictoryHeader.doc** created earlier in this chapter. Then insert a table of 15 rows and 3 columns, and merge some of the cells as in the figure. You can alter row heights by selecting them and then choosing **Table Properties** from the **Table** menu. To make the word **Overtime** align with the bottom of the cell, right-click it and choose **Cell Alignment** from the pop-up menu.

Discussion: What other software package could you use to produce the time sheet? What are the advantages of each method? Which do you favour?

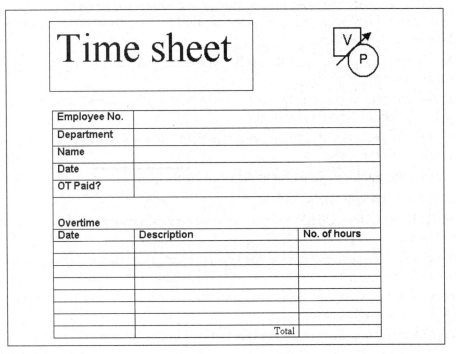

Figure 2.20: A time sheet

- Save the time sheet as **TimeSheetForm.doc**.

2.9. Working with columns

With Microsoft Word you can also create a document with newspaper-style or snaking columns in which text flows from the bottom of one column to the top of the next. You can start a new document with defined columns or reformat an existing document into up to twelve columns. Use the **Column** command from the **Format** menu to make the settings. Remember that you must be in Print Layout view (select this from the **View** menu) to see the column settings.

This type of layout is often used in newsletters produced by companies, clubs, schools etc. However it is often simpler to use a Desk Top Publishing package such as Microsoft Publisher which provides a good selection of standard templates for this type of document.

2.10. Building your portfolio

Use some of the different styles of presentation discussed in this chapter to produce at least two of the six original documents required for your portfolio. Here are three ideas:

1. Write a formal letter from an imaginary company offering employment to an applicant who has recently attended an interview. It should also include joining instructions.

   - Incorporate a header and footer that give the company name and address and a logo (created using the Microsoft Word Drawing toolbar).
   - Lay out the letter in a standard business format.
   - Before you begin identify who your reader will be – this will help you to use a suitable style and to make sure it is at a level that suits them (consider the type of job they have applied for).
   - Print out draft copies showing hand-written annotation marks and/or revision marks inserted with Microsoft Word.

- Run readability statistics and identify any changes you have made to improve the readability of the document. Use **Print Screen** or a screen capture utility as described in Unit 3, Chapter 7 to provide screenshots as evidence.

- Provide evidence that you have run the spell checker, grammar checker and used the thesaurus (use screenshots as above).

2. Produce an A4 landscape advertising leaflet for an event, say, a Murder Mystery weekend to be held at a local hotel, an exhibition or a Pop Festival.

   - Use bullet points, borders and shading, paragraph formatting and different textual styles to enhance the presentation of the leaflet.

   - Incorporate some graphics created using the Drawing toolbar.

   - Include a table of charges on the leaflet.

   - Print out draft copies showing hand-written annotation marks and/or revision marks inserted with Microsoft Word.

   - Provide evidence that you have run the spell checker and grammar checker (use screenshots as above).

3. Create a blank form to collect information of some kind – for example an expenses form, an application form or a questionnaire.

   - Use tables incorporating some of the features covered in this chapter.

   - Make sure the form is easy to understand and to complete.

   - Print out draft copies showing hand-written annotation marks.

   - Provide evidence that you have tested the form out on some sample users.

Chapter 3 – Working with longer documents

Objectives

- ✓ Create a multi-page report
- ✓ Incorporate headers, footers and page numbers
- ✓ Create a contents page, an index and a bibliography
- ✓ Insert figures and captions
- ✓ Set up cross-references

*Note: You will need to download **Reporttext.doc** from www.payne-gallway.co.uk/avce to complete the exercises in this chapter.*

3.1. Layout features for longer documents

There are a number of advanced features in MS Word that you are likely to need in documents containing multiple pages, such as a report. These include the following:

- ❑ **A Contents page** – this normally lists chapter headings, sections and subsections together with the pages on which they appear. It normally appears at the beginning of the document.
- ❑ **An Index** – this lists the terms and topics discussed in a printed document, along with the pages they appear on. It is normally at the end of the document.
- ❑ **A Bibliography** – this lists references to other books, magazines or other sources that have been made in the document. This is normally placed at the end of the document before the index.
- ❑ **Cross-reference** – this is a reference to an item that appears in another location in a document; for example, "See Figure 1 on page 3."
- ❑ **Figures and captions** – automatically numbered captions can be created for diagrams, tables etc.

To include these features in a document you really need to have planned for them before you start. You must use consistent headings for sections, consistent captions for figures or tables and have a consistent method of marking footnotes or endnotes so that you can create a bibliography.

Task 3.1: Create a multi-page report.

In this exercise you will use Word's **Outline** feature to create an outline for a Victory Publishing marketing report. The Marketing Manager has been asked to supply the Managing Director with a report describing the marketing strategy for the following year. You will be able to practise creating a Table of Contents, an index, a bibliography, cross-references and captions.

3.2. Setting up the document outline

Word has a useful feature called Outlining. This enables you to create an outline for your document, breaking it up into sections and subsections, which you can then fill in with text and figures. You can easily add, delete or rearrange headings at any stage, and at the end of it all you will be able to create an automatic Table of Contents and an index.

- Create a new document and save it as *Report.doc*.
- Click the **Outline View** button at the lower left corner of the Word window.

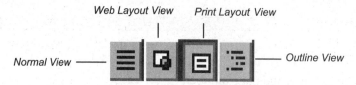

Figure 3.1: The View buttons

The Outline toolbar appears, the Style box displays Heading 1 style and a minus sign appears in the left margin.

Figure 3.2: The Outline toolbar

- Type in headings as shown in Figure 3.3 below using the **Demote** and **Promote** buttons on the Outlining toolbar to enter them at the appropriate level.

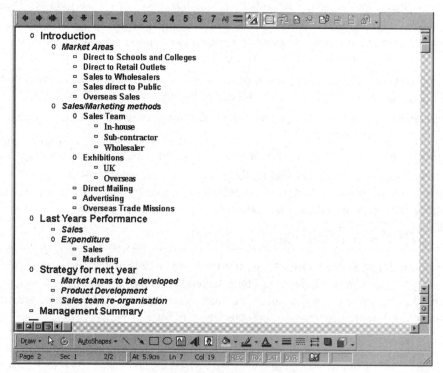

Figure 3.3: Outline for the Report

- Add numbers to these headings by highlighting the outline and then selecting **Format**, **Bullets and Numbering**.

- Click the **Outline Numbered** tab and select a numbering format. Your outline will appear something like Figure 3.4.

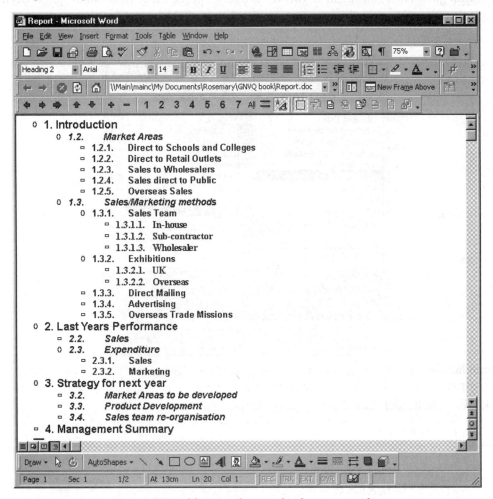

Figure 3.4: Adding numbers to the document outline

- Click the **Normal View** button (see Figure 3.1). All the document needs now is some text.

- Download the file **Reporttext.doc** from www.payne-gallway.co.uk/avce and copy and paste the sample text into the appropriate sections of the report.

3.3.   Adding headers and footers

For a report of this type the header could contain the report title and the section title and the footer could contain your name and the page number.

- Insert page breaks between each of your major sections by pressing **Ctrl-Enter** wherever you want a page break.

- With the cursor at the beginning of the document, select **View**, **Header and Footer**.

- In the header enter the report title on the left-hand side.

- Tab twice to get to the right-hand side of the header so that a field can be inserted to display the name of the section.
- Select **Insert Field** from the **Insert** menu.
- In the **Categories** box select **Links and References**. In the F**ield Names** box select **StyleRef**.
- After the word **STYLEREF** enter the style name *"Heading 1"* in quotes as shown in Figure 3.5.

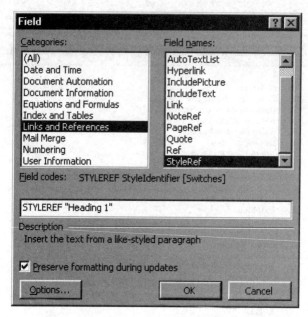

Figure 3.5: Inserting a field into the header

- Click **OK**. The header should appear as in Figure 3.6.

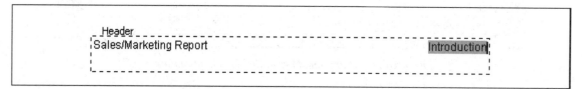

Figure 3.6: The header containing the section name

- Click the **Switch Between Header and Footer** button on the Header and Footer toolbar and insert your name.
- Tab once to the centre of the footer and click the **Insert Page Number** button to insert page numbers.

3.4. Inserting a Table of Contents

The Table of Contents will be inserted at the beginning of the report. This can automatically be updated at any time by clicking in it and pressing **F9**.

- Insert a page break at the front of the heading **Introduction**.
- Click on the **Normal View** button in the bottom left of the Word window.
- With the cursor at the beginning of the document, click **Insert, Index and Tables**.
- Click the **Table of Contents** tab. Leave the other defaults as shown in Figure 3.7.

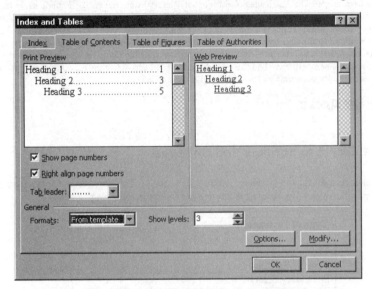

Figure 3.7: Inserting a Table of Contents

The Table of Contents will appear as shown below.

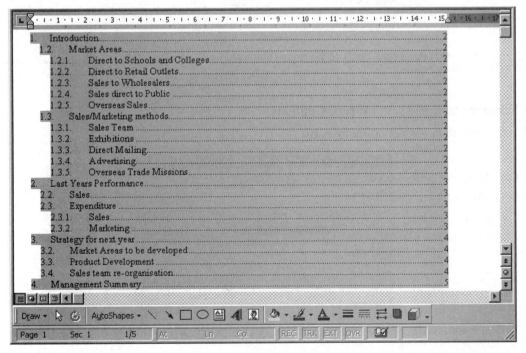

Figure 3.8: The Table of Contents

3.5. Creating captions and cross-references

Insert a table into section 1.2.1 as shown in Figure 3.9.

Sales/Marketing Report   Introduction

•

1. Introduction

This report has been prepared for the management team of Victory Publishing Ltd. It summarises the current sales and marketing situation within the company, outlines the major areas of sales and marketing activity over the past year and proposes some areas for development over the next twelve months. This report will be circulated to the management team during January 2001. It will then be presented by the Marketing Director at the next Sales and Marketing conference to held early in February. It is hoped that all members of management will have had the opportunity to read and digest the report by this time. All queries or issues raised by the report will be addressed at the conference.

1.2. Market Areas

1.2.1. Direct to Schools and Colleges

The main market for the company is direct to schools. This represents approximately 60% of total sales. This market is divided between the following:

Type of Institution	Market %ge
Primary Schools	30
Secondary Schools	40
6th Form Colleges	10
FE Colleges	10
HE Colleges and Universities	5
Special Schools	3
Prisons	2

Figure 1

There is also a small sector of this market that comprises LEA advisors, External

---

Figure 3.9: The table inserted into the report

- Click in the table and select **Insert, Captions**.
- Set the options as shown in Figure 3.10.

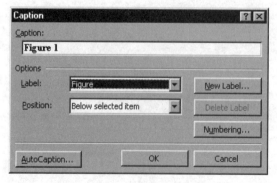

Figure 3.10: Creating a caption

- Under section 2.2 of the report type *The market split for sales direct to schools is shown in.*
- Insert a cross-reference back to the table by selecting **Cross-reference** from the **Insert** menu. Set the options as shown in Figure 3.11.

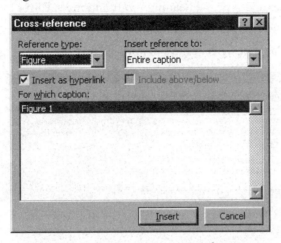

Figure 3.11: Inserting a cross-reference

The figure number will be inserted into section 2.2. When users view this document electronically they can click on this figure number and a hyperlink will automatically take them back to the figure in Section 1.2.1 of the report.

3.6. Creating an index of entries

Firstly you must mark the index entries by selecting the words in the document.

- Highlight the first occurrence of the word **sales** in the Introduction of the report.
- Press **Alt-Shift-X**.

Figure 3.12: Marking an Index entry

- To mark all occurrences of the word click **Mark All**.
- Repeat for the word **market**.
- Press **Ctrl-End** to go to the end of the document.

When you mark index entries, Word displays all the paragraph markers and the index entries which are normally hidden. You should hide these before generating the index because they affect the page numbers on which the text appears. To do this, click the **Show/Hide** button on the Standard toolbar. ¶

- Leave a few blank lines and type the heading *Index* and press **Enter**.
- Select **Index and tables** from the **Insert** menu and click the **Index** tab.
- Select one of the available designs in the **Formats** box as shown in Figure 3.13 below.

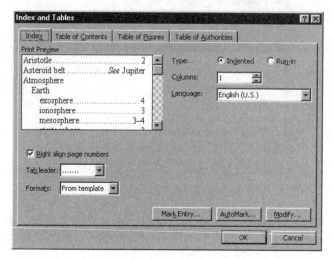

Figure 3.13: Creating an Index

- Click **OK**.

Word then collects the index entries, sorts them alphabetically, references their page numbers, finds and removes duplicate entries from the same page, and displays the index in the document. The Index with just these two entries will look something like this:

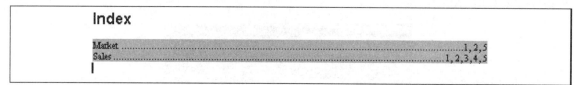

Figure 3.14: The Index so far

Indexing is a skilled task and you will generally find that it is not satisfactory simply to mark every reference to a particular word. People want to be directed to the page where there is a major discussion of a topic, not to every passing reference. In a recipe book, you might have an entry for 'eggs' but you would not expect to be directed to every recipe that used an egg.

You will also need to edit index entries. You do not want separate entries for 'egg' and 'eggs', for example. When you mark a word as an index entry, you can accept the default entry in the **Main entry** box (see Figure 3.12) or you can edit it.

Task 3.1: Complete the index for the whole document.

3.7. Creating a bibliography

A bibliography is used to list references to any other sources that you have referred to in your document. The easiest way to create a bibliography at the end of a Word document is to use the **endnote** feature. An endnote consists of two linked parts – the note reference mark and the corresponding note text. You can automatically number marks or create your own custom marks. When you add, delete, or move notes that are automatically numbered, Word renumbers the note reference marks. You can add note text of any length and format note text just as you would any other text. You can customise note separators, the lines that separate the document text from the note text.

- In Print Layout view, click in front of the text **Interim Report – Sales and Marketing June 1999** in section 1.2.1.

- On the **Insert** menu, click **Footnote**.

- Click **Endnote**. Leave the other options as shown in Figure 3.15 below.

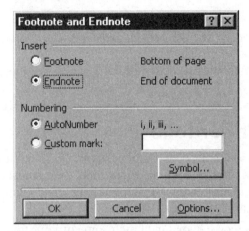

Figure 3.15: Creating an endnote to include in a bibliography

- Word inserts the note number and places the insertion point next to the note number.

- Type the bibliography entry as shown in Figure 3.16.

- Repeat for the reference to **Sales and Marketing Report January 1998**.

- Enter the heading *Bibliography* above the entries.

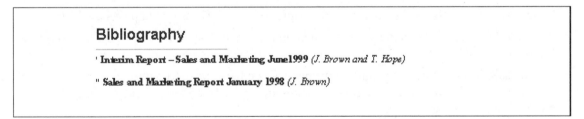

Figure 3.16: The bibliography so far

Note the endnote mark in the text of the document. If you hold the mouse pointer over the text you can view the end note as shown below.

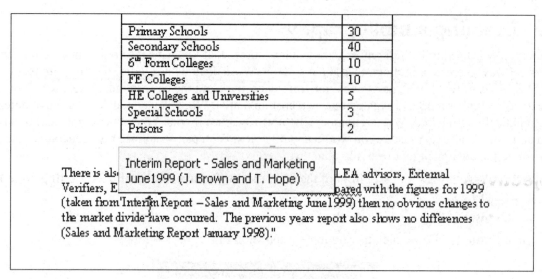

Primary Schools	30
Secondary Schools	40
6th Form Colleges	10
FE Colleges	10
HE Colleges and Universities	5
Special Schools	3
Prisons	2

There is als... Interim Report - Sales and Marketing June1999 (J. Brown and T. Hope) ...LEA advisors, External Verifiers, E... ...ared with the figures for 1999 (taken from 'Interim Report – Sales and Marketing June 1999) then no obvious changes to the market divide have occurred. The previous years report also shows no differences (Sales and Marketing Report January 1998)."

Figure 3.17: Viewing the endnote in the document

You can also put footnotes or references at the bottom of a page – see the footnote in Chapter 1, paragraph 1.5.

3.8. Building your portfolio

Use some of the layout features that have been introduced in this chapter to produce the major document for your portfolio (one of the six original documents required – see Appendix D for unit assessment evidence details). This must be at least three A4 pages in length and incorporate a range of text styles, page layout and paragraph formatting features.

For example, you could create a recipe book containing some of your favourite dishes, a visitors' guide to your local town highlighting places of interest and forthcoming events or a brochure for your school or college.

- The document should be at least three pages long.
- It should also incorporate a Table of Contents, an index and a list of information sources either in a bibliography or as footnotes.
- Use a suitable style and level of writing for your readers.
- Experiment with different layouts and keep copies of your different attempts as evidence.
- Print out draft copies showing hand-written annotation marks and/or revision marks inserted with Microsoft Word.
- Run readability statistics and identify any changes you have made to improve the readability of the document. Use **Print Screen** or a screen capture utility as described in Unit 3, Chapter 7 to provide screenshots as evidence.
- Provide evidence that you have run the spell checker, grammar checker and used the thesaurus (use screenshots as above).
- Show that you have thoroughly proofread the document.
- Include scanned images, clip art or digital photographs to add interest to the document.

Chapter 4 – Maintaining a Consistent Style

Objectives

- ✓ Use, define and modify textual styles
- ✓ Create and use templates
- ✓ Develop a house style

All organisations should attempt to create a consistent style for the documents they produce. As well as creating a professional image, this will also make them immediately recognisable to the recipient, whether it is an internal memo to employees or an external communication to a customer or supplier. A standard layout or *template* may be created for each regularly-used document incorporating a company logo and consistent formats for different types of text, e.g. headings and 'body text', i.e. text used in the main body of a letter or report.

Task 4.1: **Create a letter template for Victory Publishing using instructions given below.**

In this exercise you will create a standard letter template for Victory Publishing Ltd. It will include a header incorporating the company logo and a footer with the company address and details. Styles of text will be created for different parts of the letter. Fields will be inserted to indicate to the user where specific parts of the letter should be located.

4.1.   The letter layout

A standard business letter layout is shown in Figure 4.1 below. The return address is right-aligned with all the other text left-aligned. This is the layout that Victory Publishing wants all external letters to follow. However the company would also like a header and footer to incorporate its logo, address and company details.

Victory Publishing
Teelmark Business Park
Ipswich
IT64 8PW
Tel: 01473 **888999**
Fax: 01473 **444555**
E-mail: vp@rui.com

14th September 2001

Mr G. Holden
Clairey's Books
29 The Green
London
N98 7HJ

Our ref: TNF/PS/BY4640
Your ref: NC/1451

Dear Mr Holden

Re: New discount structure

Further to your letter dated 8th September 2001 I can confirm that we are able to increase the discount levels that we offer you on a number of our titles. This new discount structure will however be dependent upon minimum order quantities.

The table below summarises the new rates:

Series Title	Discount	Minimum order quantity
Practical Science in the Classroom	30%	500
Starting Languages at Sixty	25%	300
Basic Subject notes	25%	300

We hope that you will find this new arrangement satisfactory and we look forward to working with you in the future. I enclose a copy of our latest catalogue.

Yours sincerely

James Bean
Managing Director

Enc

Figure 4.1: A standard business letter layout

4.2. Creating and using a document template

A template is a special type of document used as a basis for new documents. Any document can be saved as a template. When you create a new document you can specify which template to base it on.

For example, headers and footers can be useful when designing a letterhead for a club or company.

- Open the file **Victoryheader.doc** that you created in paragraph 2.5.
- Save the document as *Lettertemplate.dot* as shown below.

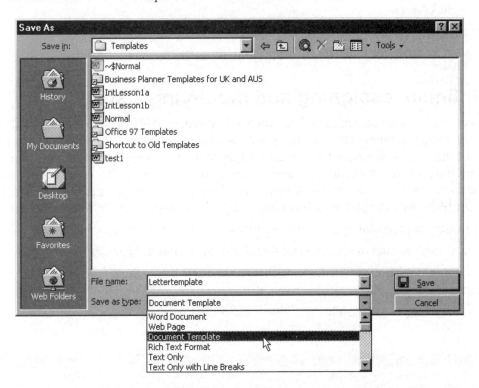

Figure 4.2 Saving a document as a template.

As you will see in Figure 4.2 Word attempts to save the template in the default location for templates. This is fine if you are working at home on a stand-alone PC. However if you are at school or college working on a network with restricted rights you may have to change the default destination drive. The easiest way is probably to save the template onto a floppy disk.

Using a template saved in the Document Template folder

If you were able to save the template saved in the standard Templates folder:

- Select **File**, **New**.

In the dialogue box you should see the name of your new template (lettertemplate).

- Click on the new template, ensure that **Create New Document** is selected and click **OK**.

A new document will open with the Victory header and footer.

- Enter some information into the document.
- Select **File**, **Save As**.
- This time save the document as you normally would, with an appropriate name.

Using a template saved anywhere else (e.g. Drive A:)

If you were not able to save the template in the standard Templates folder you will encounter a problem – you are not given the option to use a template stored in any other folder. So if, for example, you have saved the template on a floppy disk, try the following method:

- Minimise any documents and applications that you have running and return to the desktop.
- From the desktop double-click on **My Computer**.
- Double-click on **A:**
- Right-click on **Lettertemplate.dot** and select **New**.

A new document based on the template will appear on your screen.

4.3. Defining, assigning and modifying a style

In word processing software packages such as Microsoft Word, a **style** is a collection of character or paragraph formatting information that can be applied all at once to any selection of text. If a style is changed, all of the text that has been formatted with that style will change automatically. This feature can be used to enforce consistency within the documents you create so that similar elements (for example, paragraph headings) within documents look alike. The Victory Publishing letter template needs some styles to be defined – for example, the subject line is to be bold, underlined, left-aligned, 12pt Arial.

- Open **Lettertemplate.dot** as a template so that you can modify the actual template.
- Type in a small amount of text in **Arial** font, **bold**, **underlined**, **12pt** size.
- With the insertion point still in the text, click in the **Style** box at the left end of the Formatting toolbar.
- Type a name for your new style e.g. *Subject* and press **Enter**.

The style box

Figure 4.3: Defining a style

Remember that when you create a style in this way, it is associated only with your *current* document. Because in this case the current document is a template, this style will be available to all documents based on the template.

Now try to create two more styles. One style for the recipient's address should be left-aligned, Times New Roman, 11pt, not bold. Name this style *Address*. The other style is for the main body of the letter and should be the same as Address style but with 6pt spacing before paragraphs (see Figure 2.6). Name this style *Letterbody*.

- Save and close the template document.

Now create a letter based on this template.

- Select **File**, **New** and click on your template name. (Or, if you saved the template in a different directory, open a new document as explained in paragraph 4.2.)

- Type in the letter to Clairey's Books shown in Figure 4.1.

- Assign the new **Subject** style to the subject line by highlighting the text and clicking the arrow to the right of the style box.

- Select the style by name and press **Enter**.

- Assign **Address** style to Clairey's name and address.

- Assign **Letterbody** style to the main part of the letter.

- Save the letter as *Claireysletter.doc*.

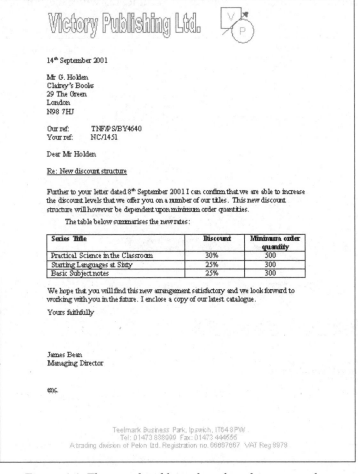

Figure 4.4: The completed letter based on the new template

It is also possible to modify the styles that you have created:

- Select any example of the style and make manual changes to the format.
- Select the name in the **Style** box and press **Enter**.
- In the Modify Style dialogue box select the first option as shown below and click **OK**.

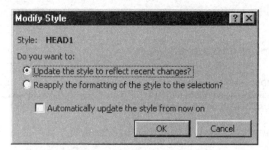

Figure 4.5: Modifying a style.

All the other parts of the document using this style will change to reflect the new formatting.

4.4. Inserting fields

To ensure that all staff who use this letter template insert the text in the correct location, it would help if fields were inserted that incorporate *boilerplate* text that indicates where certain text should be entered. (See Figure 4.6 below.)

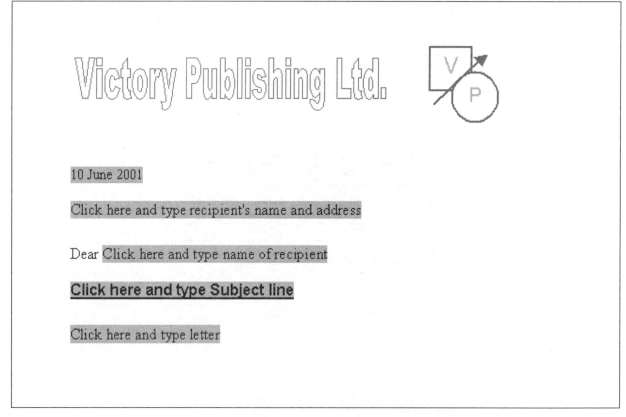

Figure 4.6: The template with boilerplate text shown in fields

- Reopen **Lettertemplate.dot** as a template so that it can be modified.
- Insert a couple of blank lines.
- From the **Insert** menu, click **Field** and select **Date and Time** in **Categories**, **Date** in **Field names** as shown in Figure 4.7 below.

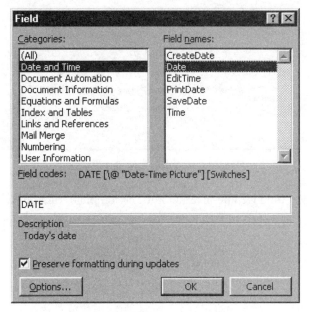

Figure 4.7: Inserting a date field

- Click **Options** and select the format **d MMMM yyyy**.
- Click **Add to Field** and click **OK**.
- Click **OK**. Today's date should be inserted into the template.
- Insert a blank line.
- From the **View** menu, select **Toolbars** and select **Forms**.

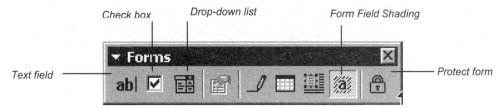

Figure 4.8: The Forms toolbar

- Click on the **Text Field** button and drag across the screen at the insertion point.
- Right-click the field and select **Properties**.
- In the **Text Form Field Options** dialogue box (see Figure 4.9 below) set unlimited length and type in the following default text:

    Click here and type recipient's name and address

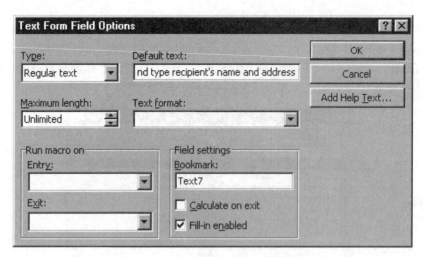

Figure 4.9: Setting text field options

- Click **OK**. The shaded field will be inserted into the template together with the default text.
- Enter the other fields as shown in Figure 4.6 above. Be sure to assign the correct style to each line of the letter.
- Save the template.
- Create a new letter using the template, clicking in the fields and overwriting the boilerplate text as appropriate.

4.5. Building your portfolio

Produce one of the six original documents required for your portfolio demonstrating some of the skills you have learned in this chapter.

- Produce a template for a standard document such as a letter, fax header or memo incorporating styles and fields for data entry.
- Experiment with different layouts and keep copies of your different attempts as evidence.
- Print out draft copies showing hand-written annotation marks and/or revision marks inserted with Microsoft Word.
- Provide evidence that you have run the spell checker and have proofread the document carefully.

Chapter 5 – Combining Information

Objectives

✓ Standardise the styles of presentation
✓ Blend existing and original information
✓ Combine text, sound, graphics and number information

Chapter 4 showed how document templates may be used in Microsoft Word to maintain consistency. You can also use a template to create an impressive slide presentation combining text, sound and graphics. One of the software packages most commonly used for this purpose is Microsoft PowerPoint.

Task 5.1: Prepare a PowerPoint presentation for the Sales Department of Victory Publishing

Victory Publishing often produces this type of presentation to introduce prospective customers (wholesalers or large booksellers) to their company. The Sales staff know from experience that it is much easier to keep the listener's interest and to get their message home if they include some graphics, sound and animations. To create maximum effectiveness, the speaker normally connects the PC screen to an overhead projector and provides the audience with printouts of the slides and a copy of their notes.

5.1. Planning the presentation

In designing and planning a presentation you need to take into account how long the presentation is to be, where and how it is to be delivered, and to whom. The contents of each slide can then be planned and special effects such as sound and animation added to spice it up and keep your audience riveted. Drawing out some rough sketches of the slides by hand before you start using PowerPoint is also a good idea.

Here are a few basic tips for designing a presentation:

* Start with a title screen showing what the project is about.
* Do not put more than 4 or 5 points on each slide. People cannot absorb too much information at once.
* Keep each point short and simple. You can expand on the points shown during your presentation – the text on the slide acts as a reminder of what you want to cover.
* Use sound, animation and graphics to maintain interest – but don't overdo them!

5.2. Starting PowerPoint

* To load PowerPoint, you can either double-click the PowerPoint icon, *or*
* Click **Start**, **Programs**, then select **Microsoft PowerPoint.**

The following screen appears:

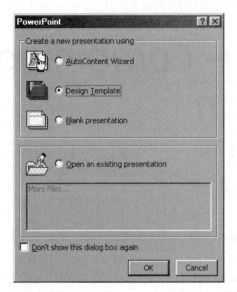

Figure 5.1: The opening Window in PowerPoint 2000

- Leave **Design Template** selected and click **OK**.

You will now be asked to select a template. You can browse through to select a suitable one.

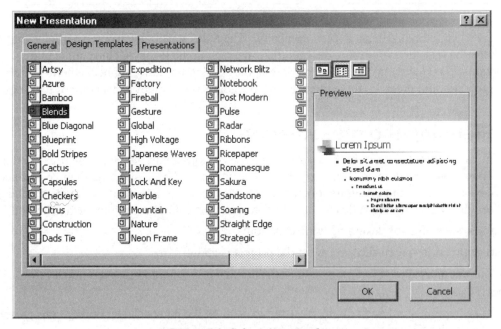

Figure 5.2: Selecting a template

- Select the **Blends** template and click **OK**.
- In the New Slide dialogue box, choose the first **AutoLayout** from the selection. This is the most suitable layout for the title page of your presentation.

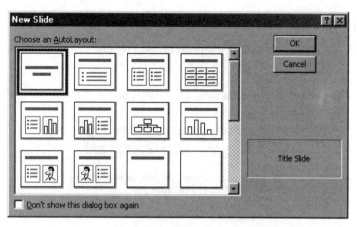

Figure 5.3: Choosing a layout for the first slide

Each slide layout has 'placeholders' in appropriate places.

- Click the **Title** placeholder and insert the Victory Publishing logo that you created in WordArt in Chapter 2.

- Click where indicated and type the sub-title *Educational textbooks and software* as shown below.

- You can edit or format the text in a text box by highlighting it and then using the tools on the Formatting toolbar. The text font in the sub-title below has been changed to **Comic Sans MS**.

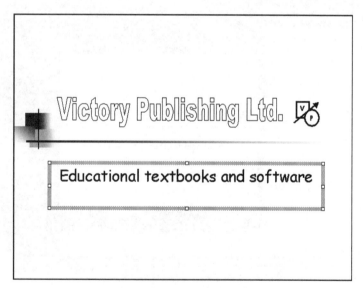

Figure 5.4: Adding text to the title screen

5.3.   Changing the view

You can alternate between various views of the presentation by clicking on the icons at the bottom of the screen.

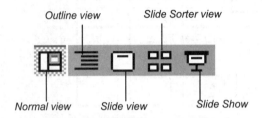

Figure 5.5: Presentation views

At the moment, **Normal View** is highlighted and the screen looks like Figure 5.6. (If it does not, click the **Normal View** icon.)

Normal View also displays the outline on the left and the Notes Pane at the bottom right. (This is a new feature of PowerPoint 2000.) You can make changes to a slide either by altering it in the slide itself or in the outline on the left.

You can browse through the other views – we will examine them again later when you have more slides to look at.

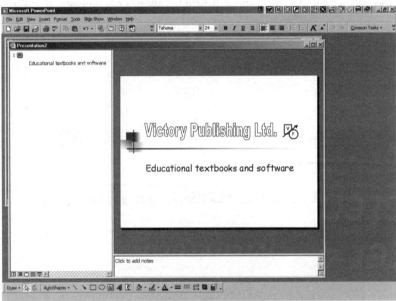

Figure 5.6: Normal view

5.4.   Adding a new slide

Now you can create the second slide of the presentation.

- Click the **New Slide** icon on the Standard toolbar.
- The second layout, **Bulleted List**, is already selected for you. Click **OK**.
- Click the **Slide View** button at the bottom of the screen to go to Slide view (see Figure 5.5).
- From the menu you can select **View, Zoom** to make the slide bigger or smaller.
- Enter the text in the bulleted list as shown in Figure 5.7.

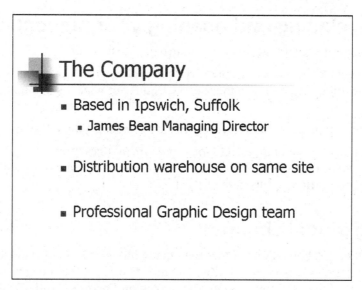

Figure 5.7: Slide 2 – A bulleted list

- You may need to reduce the default text size to fit all the text in. You can do this by highlighting the text and using the **Font Size** button on the Formatting toolbar. Alternatively, you can use the **Increase Font Size** and **Decrease Font Size** buttons to alter the size of the text to fit into a given space.

- Check the spelling in each box by clicking somewhere in the text and then clicking the **Spelling** tool on the Standard toolbar.

- Add one more slide. Make sure the slide shown in Figure 5.7 is on the screen, and then click the **New Slide** icon to insert a new slide after the current one.

- Select the first **Autolayout** again.

- Insert the slide title as for slide 1 and add the text **The End** as the sub-title.

- Switch to **Slide Sorter** view and your slides should look something like this:

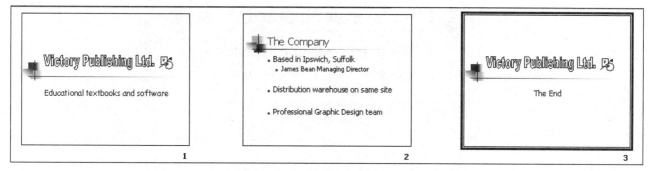

Figure 5.8: Slide Sorter view

5.5. Viewing the presentation

You can view your slide show by clicking the **Slide Show** icon at the bottom of the screen.

- On the left of the screen, click the **Slide 1** icon.
- Click the **Slide Show** icon.
- Click the mouse to go to the next slide.

5.6. Saving, closing and opening your presentation

Don't forget to save your presentation every few minutes.

- Select **File**, **Save** from the menu bar. Save your presentation as *VPpresentation.ppt* or some suitable title. You don't need to type the file extension **.ppt** which is automatically added by PowerPoint.

- You can now close your presentation if you wish by selecting **File**, **Close** from the menu.

- To open an existing presentation, select **Open an existing presentation** on PowerPoint's opening window (as shown in Figure 5.1). Your most recently saved presentations will be listed and you can select **VPpresentation.ppt** from the list.

5.7. Making global changes

As you can see in Figure 5.2, PowerPoint comes with many professionally-created designs that you can apply to your presentations. We selected the **Blends** template earlier, but you can apply a different template to your presentation at any time. You simply click on **Format**, **Apply Design Template** and choose a different template in the dialogue box.

When you apply a design template to your presentation it applies its formatting to the **Slide Master**. This looks like a slide but is just a design grid that you can make changes to that will affect every slide in the presentation. When you apply a template you are actually applying it to the Slide Master, which in turn applies it to each slide.

You can make global changes to a presentation by editing the Slide Master manually. For example, Victory Publishing want to include the date at the bottom of each slide and number the slides.

5.8. Editing the Slide Master

- Select **View**, **Master**, **Slide Master**. The Slide Master appears as shown below:

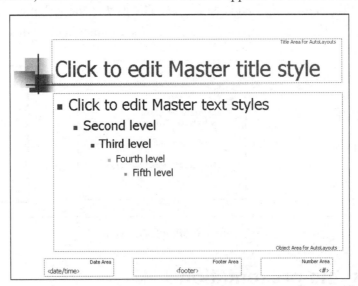

Figure 5.9: The Slide Master

The bullet points show the default styles of text that have been defined on the Slide Master, but you can change these at this stage if you wish.

- Click in each line as instructed and change the font to **Comic Sans MS**.
- Now add the date and page numbers in the Master Slide footer.
- With the Slide Master still displayed, select **View**, **Header and Footer**.

The Header and Footer dialogue box appears:

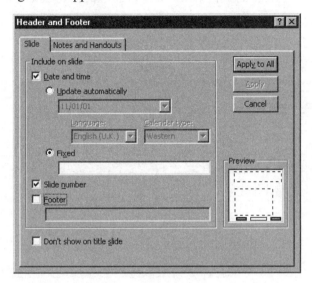

Figure 5.10: Setting up the Slide Master footer

- Select the options shown in Figure 5.10 and click **Apply to All**.
- In the Slide Master highlight the Date/Time field and replace with a date e.g. January 2001.
- Click on Slide View and check the changes to the slides. The Title slides (i.e. slides 1 and 3) will only show the page number – it has a different Slide Master which can be edited by selecting **View**, **Master**, **Title Master**.

Slide 2 should look something like this:

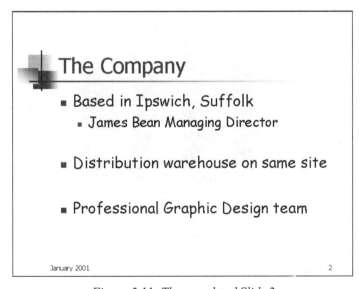

Figure 5.11: The completed Slide 2

5.9. Adding charts

On another slide you will add a chart that gives some information about Victory Publishing's book sales by market sector for two consecutive years.

- Click the Slide 2 icon and the second slide will appear on the screen.
- With the second slide on the screen click the **New Slide** icon to insert a new slide after Slide 2.
- Select the **Chart** layout. Click **OK**.

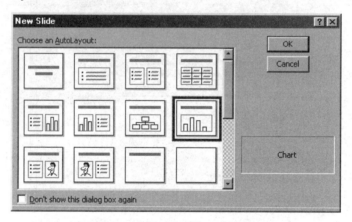

Figure 5.12: The Chart layout

- Enter a slide title: **Sales by Market Sector (%ge)**.
- Double-click the **Chart** placeholder that PowerPoint has created on the slide. The following chart will appear:

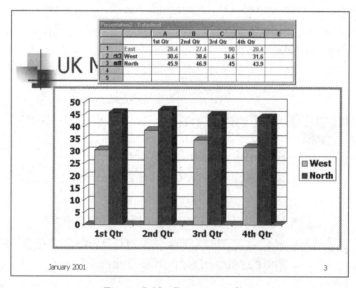

Figure 5.12: Creating a chart

To make your own chart you need to add your own information into the table.

- Edit the table and enter the figures as shown in Figure 5.13.

		A	B	C	D
		1999	2000		
1	Schools/Colleges	67	66		
2	Wholesalers	22	23		
3	Bookshops	9	9		
4	Other direct	2	2		

Figure 5.13: Entering the chart data

- Click the **Slide Show** icon to see what your slide looks like.
- Press **Esc** to return to Normal view.
- To edit a chart, simply double-click it and the spreadsheet appears ready for you to edit. You can look at **Chart, Chart Options** on the menu bar for other features.
- Click the **By Column** button.
- Right click the X-axis label and select **Format axis** and click the **Alignment** tab.
- Set the text orientation to *45* degrees.
- Remember to save your work regularly.

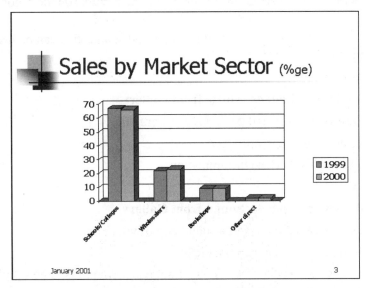

Figure 5.14: The completed slide 3

5.10. Inserting Clip Art pictures, animation and sound

On the next slide we will insert a clip art image.

- Return to Normal view.
- Click the Slide 3 icon to select it and then click the **New Slide** icon to insert a slide after this one.
- Select the **Text and Clip Art** layout.
- Type the text as shown in Figure 5.15.

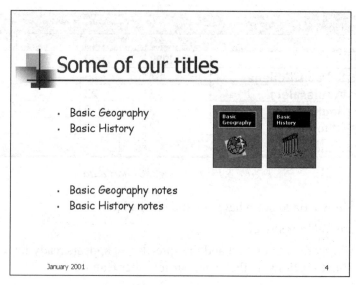

Figure 5.15: Text and Clip Art layout

- Use the Drawing toolbar to draw boxes to represent the books. Enter the titles in small text boxes as shown above.

- Select **Insert**, **Picture**, **Clip Art** and insert some suitable pictures on the 'book covers' (resizing them to fit).

The Clip Art gallery also includes some animated graphics and sounds that can be inserted into your slide show. Try these out on slide 1.

- Click on the icon for slide 1.

- Select **Insert, Movies and Sounds, Movie from Gallery**.

- Click on the **Business** category and the Sales chart graphic.

- Insert the graphic and size it appropriately.

- Change to **Slide Show View** to see the animation.

- Return to **Slide View**.

- Select **Insert, Movies and Sounds, Sound from Gallery**.

- Click on the **Music** category and insert a sound clip of your choice.

- Select the option to play the sound automatically.

A sound icon will be inserted onto your slide. You do not really want this to be visible so hide it behind the animated graphic as follows:

- Drag the speaker icon on top of the animated graphic.

- With the speaker icon still selected click on **Draw, Order, Send to Back** from the Drawing toolbar.

- Return to **Slide Show View** to hear the sound.

A very limited number of clips are supplied with PowerPoint but if you have access to the Internet you can select **Clips Online** and gain access to hundreds of suitable clips for almost any presentation.

5.11. Adding autoshapes

- Return to **Slide View** and display slide 4.

- In the bottom right-hand corner of the slide add an autoshape from the Drawing toolbar similar to the one shown below.

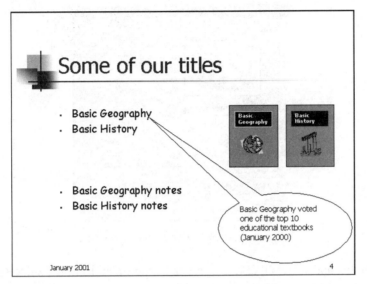

Figure 5.16: Adding an autoshape

- Use the **Rotate** button on the Drawing toolbar and the sizing handles around the shape to create the effect shown in Figure 5.16.

- Right-click the autoshape and select **Edit Text** to add the text to the shape.

5.12. Adding slide transitions

Transitions change the way that a slide opens. You can make the next slide open like a blind or a curtain, for example.

- Click the **Slide Sorter View** button at the bottom left of the screen.

You will notice that an extra Slide Sorter toolbar appears at the top of the screen. This has all the tools for adding transitions and effects to your slides.

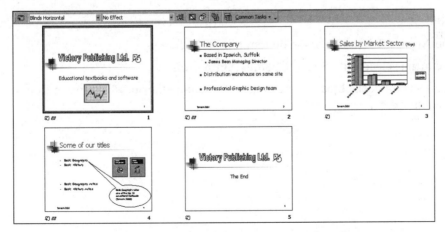

Figure 5.17: Slide Sorter view with toolbar

- First select the slides to which you want to apply the transition effect. Select Slide 1, then hold down **Ctrl** while you select the other slides.
- Click the **Slide Transition** icon at the left-hand end of the toolbar.

A Slide Transition window opens:

Figure 5.18: Selecting a slide transition

- Scroll down the list and select an effect – you can experiment to find a suitable one. (You can choose a sound too if you wish.)
- Click **Apply**. This will apply the effect to your selected slides.
- Change to **Slide Show view** and try out the result.

5.13. Adding animation to text and objects

- In Slide Sorter view select Slide 2.
- From the **Text Preset Animation** list on the Slide Sorter toolbar, select **Fly from Bottom**.
- Switch to Slide Show View to test the effect. You have to click the mouse button to make each picture or line of text appear.

You can apply custom animation to individual objects on a slide. To do this, you have to change to Normal view.

- Select Slide 4.
- Click the **Normal View** icon at the bottom left of the screen.
- From the menu select **Slide Show, Custom Animation**.
- Choose effects for each object. For example try making the autoshape fly in from bottom right when you click the mouse.

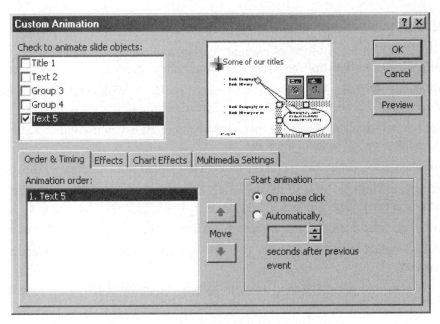

Figure 5.19: Adding custom animation

- Test out the effects. You may find the animation order seems wrong – if so, go back and alter it using the **Move** buttons in the Custom Animation dialogue box. (You need to have the **Order and Timing** tab selected.)
- Save your presentation.
- EXPERIMENT!

5.14. Printing your slides

You will need to print out your slides to put in your portfolio. You may also want to give hard copy of a presentation to the audience.

You can print several slides to a page by selecting **Handouts**.

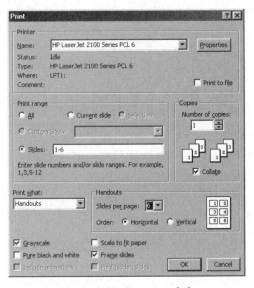

Figure 5.20: Printing slides

5.15. Delivery

Presentation skills are an important form of communication, and once learned will stand you in good stead all your life. Here are a few tips for a successful presentation:

- If you are giving the presentation using an overhead projector, make sure that you have set it up so that you can face the audience and refer to the screen behind or beside you.
- Double-check before the presentation that all the equipment is functioning correctly, and that the screen is visible from all seats in the room.
- Make sure the text on each screen is large enough to be read from all parts of the room.
- Introduce yourself and the topic to the audience. Keep your voice bright and enthusiastic, and try to look as if you are enjoying yourself.
- Don't rush – give the audience time to absorb what is on the screen, and what you are saying.
- Maintain eye contact with the audience. You can stop and ask a question now and then, to keep them involved.
- Always rehearse your presentation in advance so that you know exactly how long it will take.

5.16. Building your portfolio

Create the final original document required for your portfolio. Produce a PowerPoint presentation about a topic that interests you, for example: facilities at a Sports Centre, a local attraction, a music or film genre or a foreign country. Research the subject thoroughly so that the content is relevant, current, accurate and above all interesting! Choose a subject that will allow you to incorporate features such as bullets, clip art, charts, sounds, animation and slide transition effects.

- Consider your likely audience and tailor the content accordingly.
- Experiment with different layouts and keep copies of your different attempts as evidence.
- Provide evidence of the use of a master template into which you have inserted variable data (print out or take screenshots of master slide layouts).
- Provide evidence that you have run the spell checker and proofread the slides.
- Be prepared to present the presentation on-screen and to print out slides for an audience.

Chapter 6 – Managing Information

Objectives

✓ Understand how organisations collect their information.

✓ Understand the flow of information into and out of the company.

✓ Learn the commonly accepted standards for document layouts.

All organisations have to communicate both internally (i.e. between different departments) and externally (i.e. with other organisations such as suppliers and customers). The documents that are used for communication will vary depending on the type and size of the organisation, but there are some commonly accepted standards. These include the following:

❑ Methods for gathering information such as written questionnaires, on-line forms for customers to complete, requests for quotations from suppliers and specifications for work.

❑ Internal communications within the company such as memos, e-mails, agendas, minutes, reports, itineraries, budgets and sales results.

❑ External communication from the company such as invoices, delivery notes, letters and advertising flyers.

We have already looked at some of these documents earlier in the unit so you should refer back to these sections to refresh your memory. Other types of documents used by organisations are described in this chapter, including several produced by Victory Publishing leading up to and following their attendance at a large Book Fair.

Remember the importance of consistency between documents and the creation of a corporate image or house style that was discussed in Chapter 4. See if you think Victory Publishing have achieved this in their documents.

6.1. Printed Questionnaires

Organisations often need to conduct some market research – perhaps to plan which products to introduce in the future, to find out more about their competitors or, like Victory Publishing, to determine if their customer service can be improved in any way.

Questionnaires are a useful research method, especially where the information to be gathered is quantitative (i.e. facts and figures) rather than qualitative (i.e. opinions, attitudes, behaviour patterns etc.). They tend to be a relatively cheap and easy method especially if, like Victory, the questionnaire is to be posted along with a delivery. However the response rate is normally quite low so you need to think of ways of encouraging people to complete them. The chance of winning a holiday for two in Barbados would be enough to tempt most people!

❑ Start a questionnaire with a brief sentence to explain its purpose.

❑ Where possible use multiple-choice questions with tick boxes.

❑ If it is not immediately obvious, give brief instructions on how to complete the form.

- ❑ Keep the questionnaires anonymous - people are likely to be more honest.
- ❑ Don't ask leading questions (e.g. how many times a week do you kick the dog?)
- ❑ Don't ask biased questions (e.g. would you agree that advertisements influence weak people?)
- ❑ Don't make assumptions about people (e.g. how often do you and your partner holiday abroad?)
- ❑ Don't ask hypothetical questions (e.g. Suppose you won a million pounds…)

The simpler you keep the questionnaire the more likely people are to complete it and the easier the results will be to analyse.

Victory Publishing have recently been analysing how much of their business comes from existing customers and how much is from new customers. During this process they decided to survey customers about their level of service. They have asked customers to return the questionnaire in a prepaid envelope.

Victory Publishing Ltd.

CUSTOMER SATISFACTION SURVEY
QUESTIONNAIRE

We always strive to improve our customer service. Please help us by taking a few moments to complete these questions.

Have you bought from us before?	YES ☐	NO ☐
Did you order by telephone?	YES ☐	NO ☐
Were our staff helpful and polite?	YES ☐	NO ☐
Were the books you required in stock?	YES ☐	NO ☐
Was your order delivered on time?	YES ☐	NO ☐
Have you called our help line?	YES ☐	NO ☐
Were you satisfied with the help line service?	YES ☐	NO ☐
Would you recommend our books to others?	YES ☐	NO ☐

Figure 6.1: A simple questionnaire

6.2. Web sites

Most companies now have a presence on the World Wide Web. Victory Publishing is no exception – its web site is used to publicise its list of books, any forthcoming titles and any special offers. It also offers downloadable resources for teachers such as answers to the questions in textbooks, OHP masters and further tips and advice. The company has found that this facility is very popular with teachers and has helped to increase sales.

Many companies specialising in web site design have sprung up over recent years. The IT department within Victory Publishing has developed a company site using Microsoft FrontPage, a web authoring package.

One of the most important aspects of web design to consider is how easy it will be for users to navigate around the site – a navigation bar is normally incorporated running either vertically or horizontally across each page. It is best not to cram too much information onto each page – try not to make visitors scroll down more than two screens for each page. Pictures and graphics, especially animations, can liven up a web page but remember that they can make the page much slower to load and your visitors may not be patient enough to wait!

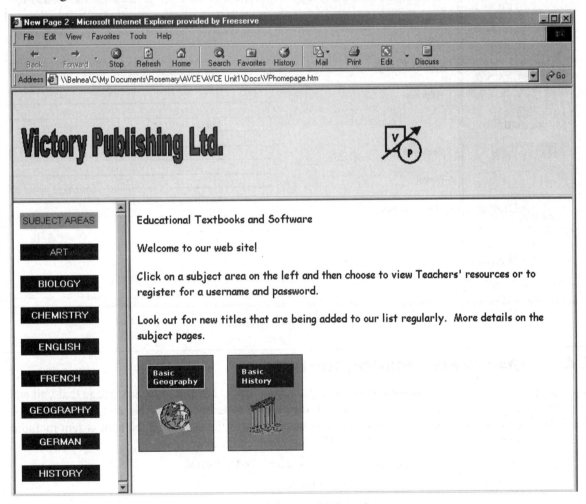

Figure 6.2: The Victory Publishing homepage

6.3. On-line forms

In order to access the resources, teachers are required to register using an on-line form from the web site – this is shown below. When the teacher clicks the **Send** button an e-mail is transmitted to the marketing department of Victory Publishing, where a clerk records the details in a customer database and sends the teacher a return e-mail with a username and password giving them access to the resources.

On-line forms must use simple, clear language and the layout should be easy to understand so that users can complete it correctly. Validation of certain fields and drop-down boxes offering options can help reduce data entry errors and make the form quicker to complete. Once the SEND button has been pressed the user should receive confirmation that their form has been accepted or a clear error message returned.

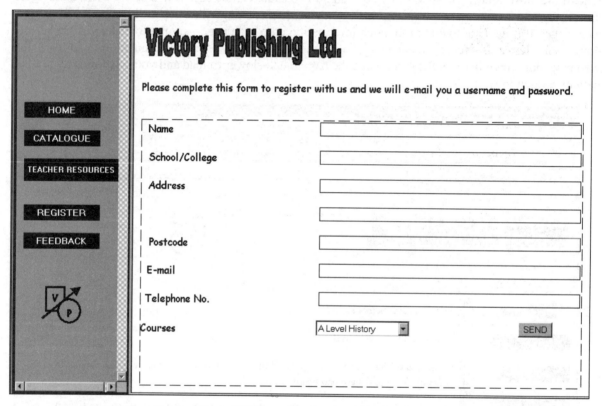

Figure 6.3: The on-line registration form

6.4. Faxed Specification for flyer

Fax (short for 'facsimile') is extensively used by organisations. It has the great advantage that you can transmit hand-written documents or drawings and they arrive instantly at the other end. In addition to speed the main advantage of faxing information is that a copy of the original document is sent including any handwritten or drawn details. Victory Publishing receives faxes such as:

- ❑ orders from Schools and Colleges on official school order forms;
- ❑ requests from bookshops to return unsold books;
- ❑ faxes from other companies selling services/products.

The company also sends faxes to various suppliers. For example the marketing staff often send amendments to draft documents back to their graphic designers. In the example shown below they have faxed a header sheet (created from a document template) together with amendments to an advertising flyer that the designers have been working on. The fax header sheet should include contact details, the date and the number of pages in the fax so that the recipient can be sure they have received the complete communication.

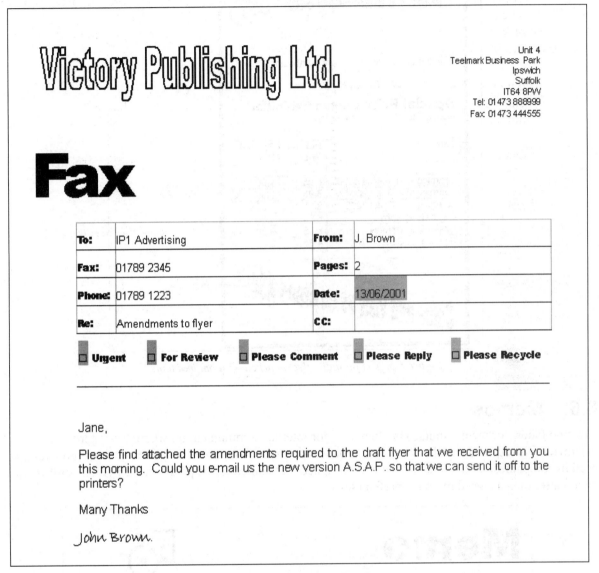

Figure 6.4: The fax header sheet

6.5. Publicity flyers

Companies wanting to advertise products, services or events often use flyers printed on A5 paper (or smaller). You may have had a flyer advertising a new shop or something similar thrust into your hand whilst walking along the street.

Victory Publishing often uses these for promotions at exhibitions. The flyer shown below will be used at the forthcoming book fair. The sales people manning the stand will hand them out to people as they walk along the aisles. The flyer is A5 portrait layout with large bold headlines and a simple message to attract people to the Victory Publishing stand.

The flyer has been designed by the graphic design team who have sent a draft to John Brown. He has marked up some corrections by hand and faxed it back to the graphic designers.

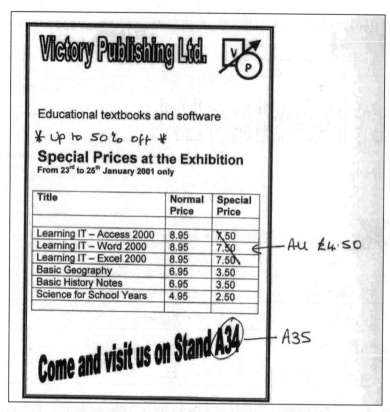

Figure 6.5: The publicity flyer marked with amendments

6.6. Memos

A memo (short for memorandum) is often used for internal communication where less address information is required and the wording can be less formal. First names as formal titles are now rarely used in companies. Memos do not have to be signed, but sometimes if people need written confirmation on a matter then a signed memo is preferable.

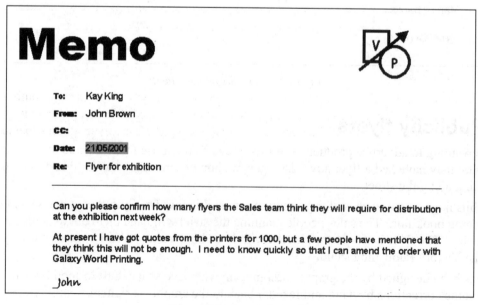

Figure 6.6: A sample memo

6.7. E-mails

E-mails are now one of the most popular ways of communicating both within an organisation and with the outside world. They are relatively cheap, quick and secure, and the user can keep an electronic file of previous messages. Additional files can be attached to e-mails as shown in the example below. Victory Publishing has received the updated file containing the flyer from IP1 Advertising and John Brown now needs to get this to the printers as quickly as possible. He decides to e-mail the file to Dave Cox at Galaxy World Printers. Victory Publishing uses Microsoft Outlook Express, an e-mail package which is supplied with Internet Explorer. John needs only to enter Dave's name and his e-mail address will be picked up from the Outlook address book. If anyone else needs to be sent a copy of the e-mail, then John needs to enter their name on the **Courtesy copy** (Cc:) line – if they are in the address book they will automatically be sent a copy.

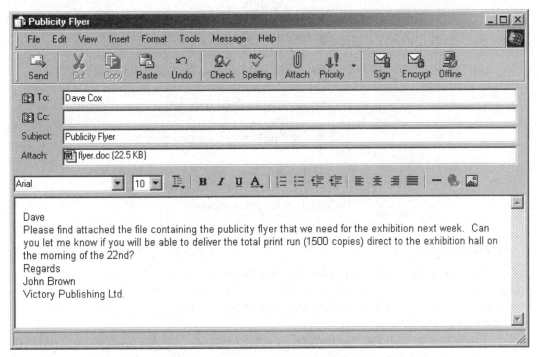

Figure 6.7: Sending an e-mail with an attachment

6.8. Agendas

An agenda is a document which is used to inform people of the date and time of a forthcoming meeting, the topics for discussion and the order in which topics will be discussed. The person who is going to chair the meeting normally produces the agenda. There are some standard agenda items that are normally included at the beginning of the meeting, such as:

❑ Apologies for absence

❑ Minutes of the last meeting

❑ Matters arising from the last meeting.

The following items usually appear at the end of the agenda:

❑ Any other business

❑ Date of next meeting.

The management team of Victory Publishing has organised a meeting with representatives from a number of departments to confirm arrangements for the Book Fair.

Victory Publishing Ltd.

The next Sales and Marketing meeting will take place on Monday 9th January at 13.30 in the Board Room.

Agenda

1.   Apologies for absence.

2.   Minutes of last meeting (please have these with you).

3.   Matters arising from minutes.

4.   Sales & Marketing budget report.

5.   Advertising.

6.   Stand set up arrangements.

7.   Stand break down arrangements.

8.   Customer meetings.

9.   Any other business.

10.   Date of next meeting.

Figure 6.8: A typical agenda

6.9. Minutes

The secretary of the meeting keeps the *minutes* – sometimes a specific minutes secretary is elected. He or she records all the matters that were discussed at the meeting, any decisions that were made and any actions that result, noting what is to be done and by whom. Standard items on the minutes include:

- ❑ The date of the meeting
- ❑ A list of attendees
- ❑ The points discussed.

It is usual to include a heading for each item and to right-align any action points. The minutes of the meeting held about the forthcoming Book Fair are shown below.

Victory Publishing Ltd.

Minutes of the Sales and Marketing meeting held on Monday 9th January 2001.

Present: James Bean (Chair), Jake Hughes (Secretary), John Brown, Kay King, Denise Raymond

Apologies for absence were received from Victor Green.

1. MINUTES OF THE LAST MEETING
The minutes of the last meeting were agreed.

2. MATTERS ARISING
None.

3. SALES AND MARKETING BUDGET REPORT
John Brown presented the projected budget report for the forthcoming book fair. The meeting agreed with these figures. It was suggested that more advertising flyers should be ordered from the printers this year.

ACTION: John Brown

4. ADVERTISING
The content of the advertising posters was agreed. It was decided to place an advertisement in the show guide.

ACTION: John Brown

5. STAND SET UP ARRANGEMENTS
The number of books to be delivered was decided together with catalogues and stationery. Distribution to organise the delivery of all items.

ACTION: Denise Raymond

6. STAND BREAK DOWN ARRANGEMENTS
Distribution requested that the sales team should remain after the exhibition to assist with break down.

ACTION: Kay King

7. CUSTOMER MEETINGS
It was confirmed that a meeting area had been incorporated into this years stand. James Bean already has this booked for several customer meetings.

ACTION: John Brown

8. ANY OTHER BUSINESS
None.

Figure 6.9: Typical minutes

6.10. Itineraries

An *itinerary* is a schedule of times and places to visit during a trip (business or holiday), or possibly during an event. At the Book Fair, Andrea McGregor the Foreign Rights Manager has organised a number of meetings both within the exhibition hall and in other locations. She prepares the following itinerary so that colleagues will know her whereabouts.

Victory Publishing Ltd.

Itinerary for A. Mc Gregor 23rd – 25th January 2001

Date/time	Meeting	Location	Notes
23.01.01 - 10.00	New book series launch	Stand	Short speech required
23.01 01 – 12.30	Lunch with Mr P. Ghandira	Quayles Restaurant	Translation rights
24.01.01 – 10.30	Meeting with J. Van Helm	Stand	Distribution rights
24.01.01 – 14.30	Meeting with K. Helmer	Stand	Advice on USA markets
24.01.01 – 19.30	Dinner with N. Danes	Not yet known	
25.01.01 – 11.00	Presentation to potential authors	Seminar room A1	S. Simons will also be in attendance

Figure 6.10: An Itinerary

6.11. Sales and Marketing Budgets

Several departments at Victory Publishing use Microsoft Excel to produce spreadsheets, for example:

- **Sales and Marketing** produce budgets, customer lists and sales targets.
- **Editorial** prepare book lists.
- **Foreign Rights** calculate deals with distributors or publishers overseas.
- **Distribution** record stock levels.
- **Production** keep records of print runs.

Before the exhibition the Managing Director asks John Brown to provide him with an estimated budget for the book fair.

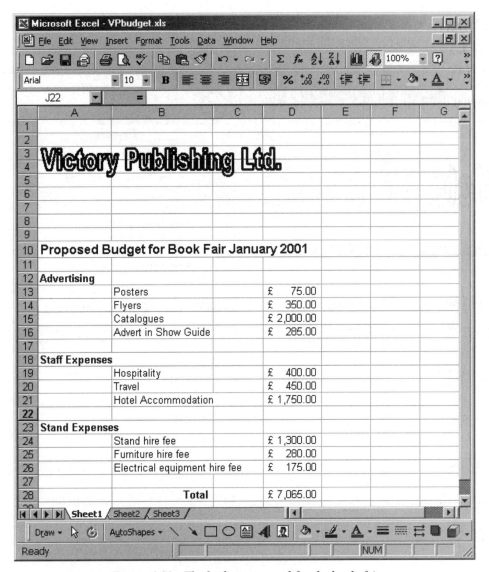

Figure 6.11: The budget proposal for the book fair

6.12. Invoices and Delivery notes

Invoices are used to request payment from customers for goods or services. The exhibition caused a surge in sales as schools and colleges phoned and faxed orders in for books they had seen at the book fair. The Distribution department sends an invoice to the customer with the books. Sometimes the invoice address is different to the delivery address for the books. For example in a school or college the invoice will often be sent to the Finance department for payment but the books will be sent direct to the teacher. A delivery note will be enclosed with the books.

Invoices and delivery notes should include the following information.

- ❑ The date and some type of unique invoice number.
- ❑ The name and address of the company requesting payment. If the company has a logo this is normally incorporated to help customers identify at a glance who the invoice is from.
- ❑ The name and address of the recipient of the invoice.
- ❑ The address to which the goods should be delivered.

❑ Details of the items purchased including price, delivery and VAT.

❑ The payment terms (i.e. when the invoice has to be paid).

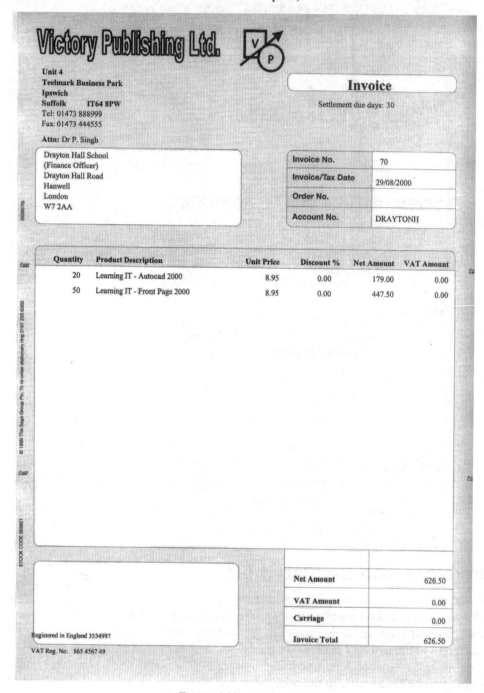

Figure 6.12: An invoice

Discussion: How would a delivery note differ from the invoice shown above?

6.13. Building your portfolio

This chapter has identified the writing style, presentation style and common standards for layouts in different types of documents used by organisations.

In earlier chapters of this unit you have produced original documents using different styles of writing and presentation. Now you should collect six different documents created by other people for your portfolio. You need two standard documents from each of three different organisations. It may help if you choose three very different organisations – for example a letter and an advertisement for a brownie pack, a bank and a charity. They all have different categories of reader and should therefore use different styles and levels of language. Write a report about these documents in which you must:

- Provide detailed descriptions of the content, layout and purpose of the six collected documents.
- Accurately evaluate the good and bad points about the writing and presentation styles of similar items.
- Comment on the suitability for purpose of the documents.
- Identify common elements of similar documents.

Carefully check the accuracy and layout of this report before submission with your portfolio.

Unit 2

ICT Serving Organisations

This unit is about different types of organisation and how they use Information and Communication Technology (ICT). You will see how a typical organisation is organised into departments each with its own specific function. ICT is used in countless different ways – it is almost impossible to imagine how a modern organisation could function at all without computers. So whatever career you end up in, you will almost inevitably be using ICT in some shape or form. Having a working knowledge of how organisations are structured and the way that ICT is used will help you to choose a job you will enjoy, and become a valued member of a team when you land it!

This unit is assessed by an external examination. You will be given a case study in advance of the exam for which you have to make notes and draw charts. You will take these into the exam with you to help answer the questions. You will hand in these notes with your answer paper.

Doing the exercises given in each chapter of this unit will give you practice in drawing charts, making notes and answering questions similar to those you will see in the exam. Two sample case studies are used in the unit, and these are at the end of the book in Appendices A and B.

Chapter 7 – Organisational Structure

Objectives

✓ To learn about different types of organisation

✓ To study a typical organisational structure

✓ To understand the external pressures on an organisation

7.1. How organisations work

Very few people live their lives in isolation. From the moment we are born, (probably in a hospital, a good example of an organisation), through our school and college careers, into various types of work, shipped off to a 'retirement home' and finally cremated or buried, we are in the hands of organisations. **Organisations** are entities comprising a group of people and resources which are managed, organised and coordinated to accomplish goals. The goal of a business organisation is usually to generate a profit; other types of organisation may have quite different objectives such as the preservation of the environment, military conquest or gaining religious converts.

> **Discussion: What are the goals of the following organisations? A College of Further Education, a hospital, the BBC, McDonald's, Virgin, Greenpeace?**

The three fundamental resources of any organisation are

- ❑ People;
- ❑ Organisation;
- ❑ Technology.

The success of an organisation is determined by how well it manages and controls these three resources (the 'pillars' of an organisation), the components of which include the following:

People	*Organisation*	*ICT*
Career	Strategy	Hardware
Education	Policy	Software
Training	Mission Statement	Telecommunications
Employee Attitudes	Culture	Information Systems
Employee Participation	Management	
Employee Monitoring	Competition	
Work Environment	Environment	

Figure 7.1: The three pillars of an organisation

7.2.   Ingredients for success

A survey commissioned by the Department of Trade and Industry in 1997 came to the following conclusions about the most successful UK companies.

Winning UK companies:

- Are led by visionary, enthusiastic champions of change;
- Unlock the potential of their people
  - creating a culture in which employees are genuinely empowered and focused on the customer;
  - investing in people through good communications, teamwork and training;
- Know their customers
  - constantly learning from others;
  - welcoming the challenge of demanding customers to drive innovation and competitiveness;
- Constantly introduce new, differentiated products and services
  - by deep knowledge of their competitors;
  - encouraging innovation to successfully exploit new ideas;
  - focusing on core businesses complemented by strategic alliances;
- Exceed their customers' expectations with new products and services.

Nine out of ten of the winning UK companies studied exhibited these characteristics of innovation best practice.

Source: DTI 'Winning' Report 1997

7.3.   The people in an organisation

Successful companies view people as a key resource rather than simply as a cost – the competition may copy the product but it cannot copy the people. One of the main tasks of management, therefore, is to enable each person in an organisation to fulfil his or her full potential.

As one MD puts it, "motivated staff will be ten times more productive than unmotivated staff". There is a clear recognition that it is employees who most often meet with the company's customers and that "when customers meet an employee they meet the whole organisation and often judge the whole on that basis".

Training is seen as a key component in achieving empowerment of the individual and in maintaining focus on the customer in order to remain competitive. Not only is training "the epicentre of empowerment", with as much as 100% of employees' time spent on it, but successful companies "use education as a competitive weapon".

7.4.   The functions of an organisation

Business organisations have four basic internal functions which they must manage and control:

- The **Production** group produces the goods or services;
- The **Sales and Marketing** group sells the product;
- The **Personnel** or **Human Resources** group hires and trains workers;
- The **Finance and Accounting** group seeks funds to pay for all these activities and keeps track of the accounts.

Traditionally, an organisation is structured in a pyramid fashion, as in Figure 7.2.

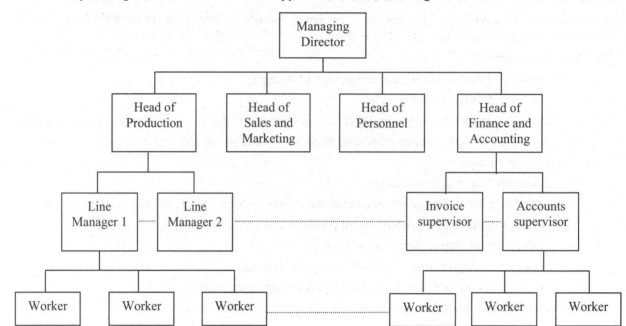

Figure 7.2: The traditional organisational structure

In the late 1990s, changes in working practices resulted in 'flatter' organisations, with layers of middle management disappearing in an effort to eliminate the stifling effects of hierarchy and bureaucracy. As the DTI 'Winning' report says:

"Five years ago the corporate structure was like a pyramid with very steep sides, in fact one could say a stalactite. Now it is more like a plate of peas. The number of levels in an organisation is cut to as few as possible. In some instances there are only three levels within the organisation: Directors, Managers and People".

Discussion: How is the school or college where you are studying structured? How many layers of management are there?

7.5. External pressures on an organisation

Surrounding the organisation is an environment of customers, competitors, government regulators, pressure groups and other interested parties, all of which have an influence on how the business is run and what policy decisions are made. (See Figure 7.3.)

Case study: Preservation vs. the people

In November 1997 the Guardian carried an article describing the four-year battle over local authority plans to replace the chairlift serving the ski centre of Aviemore with a funicular railway. Conservationists compare it with driving a motorway through Stonehenge while local people say it will bring much-needed jobs and money to the area. The RSPB together with the World Wide Fund for Nature (WWF) have fought the plan to develop a glen that offers one of the most breathtaking views in Scotland, home to the rare black grouse and scene of Landseer's famous tribute to the stag, "Monarch of the Glen". For the people of Strathspey, the funicular railway holds the key to their economic future, and the Government is prepared to contribute £9 million to the £17 million scheme.

Discussion: This is a good illustration of the external pressures that can be brought to bear on the decision-making process within an organisation. Anyone with an interest in a business is called a "stakeholder". Who are the stakeholders in this case?

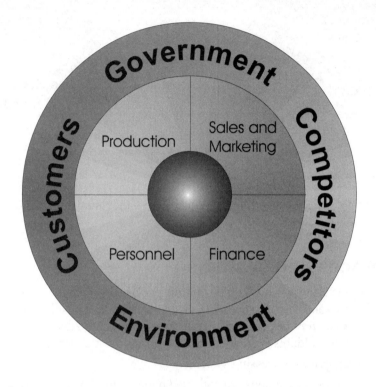

Figure 7.3: The activities of a business organisation

7.6. ICT in organisations

In this module, you'll learn how technology can be used in building and using information systems in organisations. ICT is the third 'pillar' of a successful organisation.

7.7. Organisations and information systems

Most organisations are hierarchical; they are arranged in ascending order of power, pay and privilege. The three major levels in an organisation are production workers, information workers and management workers.

Each level in an organisation has its unique class of information system:

- ❑ Data or transaction processing systems serve the needs of production workers who must deal with thousands, or even millions, of transactions with customers and suppliers.

- ❑ Knowledge work systems serve the needs of clerical and professional people to process and create information and knowledge.

- ❑ Management information systems serve management's needs to control and plan the organisation.

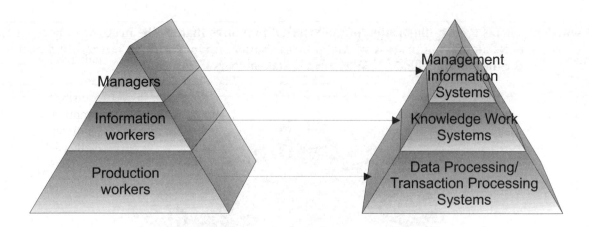

Figure 7.4: Organisations and Information Systems

Organisations, then, do not have just one information system – they may have hundreds. Each of the basic types of systems is described below.

7.8.   Data processing systems

A data processing system is also known as a **transaction processing system**. Every time you buy an item in a supermarket, withdraw some cash from your bank account, make a hospital appointment or sign up for a college course, a **transaction** has occurred. Transactions are all the events that are recorded when goods or services are bought, sold, distributed or dealt with in some manner.

There are two kinds of transaction processing system:

- ❑ Batch systems, whereby transactions are collected over a period of time (say a day or a week) and processed together;
- ❑ On-line systems where the data is processed as soon as it is collected.

When there is no immediate urgency for a response or up-to-the-minute information, a batch processing system is often suitable. The TV Licensing Authority, for example, may collect requests for TV licences and process them in batches of 50 or 100 at a time. An airline reservation system, on the other hand, requires up-to-date information on what seats are available, so an on-line system must be used. Such a system is also known as a 'pseudo real-time' system. The word 'pseudo' indicates that processing takes place effectively but not absolutely immediately: a delay of a couple of minutes is normally acceptable.

> **Discussion: What type of transaction processing (batch or on-line) would be suitable for the following?**
>   **A mail-order company taking orders by telephone or mail;**
>   **A credit-card company processing sales transactions;**
>   **A bookshop using electronic point-of-sale tills to keep track of sales and stock;**
>   **A hospital appointment system.**

7.9. Knowledge work systems

'Information workers' are of two general types: office clerical workers and sales personnel, and behind-the-scenes professionals such as accountants, lawyers, doctors and engineers.

Knowledge work systems are used by information workers to help deal with problems requiring knowledge or technical expertise. Word processing programs, spreadsheets, databases, computer-aided design packages and project management software all fall into this category. In addition, software and hardware that enables groups of people to find out information, communicate or work together as a team, even though they are geographically separated, is of vital importance in large organisations. Networks, web browsers, e-mail facilities and the use of video conferencing are examples of such technology.

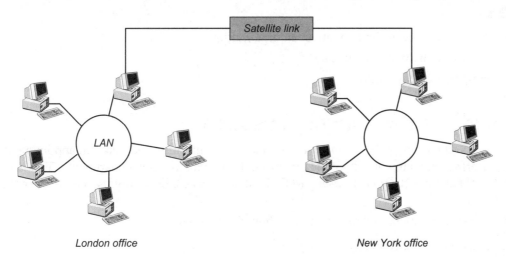

Figure 7.5: Global communications network

7.10. Management information systems

Management information systems are designed to help managers monitor and control organisational performance and plan for the future. This type of information system is discussed in more detail in Chapter 13.

7.11. Questions

1. Think of an organisation where you have worked or with which you are familiar. What are the major functions and levels in the organisation? How might the information systems used in the organisation relate to those functions and levels?

2. The major functions of a business organisation are **Production, Sales and Marketing, Personnel** or **Human Resources**, and **Finance and Accounting**. However, there may be other functions and departments specific to a particular organisation, such as Research and Development. Name 2 other departments that you would expect to find in a particular organisation such as, for example, Ford Motor Company, a large College, an educational publishers or any organisation with which you are familiar.

3. For a specified product (e.g. a car, a new brand of toothpaste or a textbook, or a product of your choice) suggest at least 6 ways in which a manufacturing company could market the product. Would Information Technology be used in any or all of these ways? How?

Chapter 8 – Studying an Organisation

Objectives

✓ To prepare for an interview to find out about an organisation

✓ To write up a case study of an organisation

✓ To study a pre-prepared case study

8.1. Finding out about an organisation

As part of this course you may have the opportunity to select an organisation and make an appointment with a member of staff to find out more about the organisation, its functions and departments. You need to have a clear idea of exactly what you are trying to find out, and make a list of points that you want to address.

You might start by asking questions and making notes about the following:

❑ The main functions of the company

❑ A brief history of the company

❑ The company location

❑ Who are the customers?

❑ Who are the suppliers?

❑ The structure of the organisation

You then need to find out more detail about the many different departments and job functions that an organisation of any size will have. These may include:

❑ Accounts or Finance

❑ Sales

❑ Distribution

❑ Marketing

❑ Research and Development

❑ Human Resources

❑ Design

❑ Production (or service provision)

❑ ICT services

❑ Administration

Your notes then need to be structured into a logical order and written up. Two sample case studies are given in Appendices A and B. In addition, you will be given a case study by the Examination Board on which you will be expected to make notes. These notes may be taken into the examination and should be very helpful to you in answering the questions, so be sure to complete the notes, which are themselves to be handed in for extra marks (Edexcel Board).

8.2.   The function of each department

Accounts (Finance)

The Accounts Department is usually subdivided into Purchase and Sales Ledger accounting. The people dealing with the Purchase Ledger process purchase invoices from the company's suppliers for goods that the company needs. These may be raw materials or general purchases such as stationery, services such as gas, electricity, phones etc. They also arrange payment for these purchases either by direct debit, BACS or by sending a cheque.

The people dealing with the Sales Ledger send out monthly statements, receive and record payments from customers who have purchased goods or services. They also have to perform a credit control function, chasing up customers who are late in paying their invoices.

Sales

The sales order processing team receive and process customer orders. The orders may come in by mail, e-mail, fax, phone or electronic means. For example, an order may be placed via the company web site. (Perhaps you have ordered a book, CD or other item over the Internet yourself.) This is a form of electronic data interchange (EDI), whereby the order placed electronically by the customer is saved directly into the Sales Order Processing system with no need for re-keying. It has the great advantage that the customer receives an order acknowledgement very quickly and the order is processed more speedily.

 The Sales Department staff also answer customer queries about, for example, the price or availability of goods. There may be a team of sales people in the same department who go out to customers and show them what is available, take orders from regular customers and attempt to find new customers.

Marketing

The function of the Marketing Department is both to find out what people want and to find new and better ways of selling the product to the customer by advertising, producing catalogues, etc. For example, in a publishing company the cycle might look something like Figure 8.1:

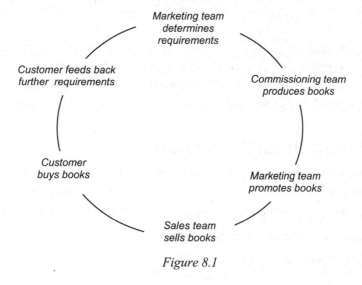

Figure 8.1

Distribution

The distribution of goods generally takes place in a warehouse. The functions include:

- ❑ picking the goods off the shelf;
- ❑ packing the goods safely and securely;
- ❑ arranging for collection by courier, air freight, shipping agent etc. or posting the goods;
- ❑ attaching a delivery note (and/or an invoice) to the goods.

Research and Development

The functions of this department are self-explanatory – whether the company is producing cars, drugs, washing powder or packaging materials, the personnel are working on, inventing and trying out new and improved products.

Human Resources (Personnel)

The Personnel Department is in charge of all the employees. Functions include hiring and firing, caring for, appraising, nurturing, and training and development of employees. They will maintain records relating to each employee and may agree a training or development program with them.

Design

The Design department also has a self-explanatory role. They may be designing the details of a new product, the style of the text and cover of a new book, patterns for upholstery fabric, packaging for cereal boxes, the position of the cigarette lighter in the latest model of car or whatever the requirements of the company are.

Production

This department is where the products are actually made.

ICT services

The ICT department will be responsible for installing, maintaining and customising hardware and software. They will be called upon to put things right when a problem with the computer system occurs, and they will have an important role to play when a new system is being considered.

Administration

This department is responsible for the day-to-day running of the company. They will implement changes such as restructuring or a change of office premises. They will look after general office maintenance such as having the gas boiler serviced or a new telephone system installed. An important function is to keep the whole company informed of what is going on – how the information is circulated will depend on the nature of the information.

> **Discussion: A manufacturing company has 100 employees. What would be the best way of informing staff of: the date of the Christmas party; the retirement of the Managing Director; a forthcoming downsizing resulting in redundancies; the date that a new computer system will go live?**

8.3. Researching in further detail

In the next few chapters, we will be looking at various aspects of the organisations in the case studies given in the Appendices and discovering how the systems in each department work.

Read the **ShoeShock** case study in Appendix C carefully and see if you can answer the questions below.

1. How many main departments does ShoeShock have?

2. Why is there no IT or Personnel department?

3. What does it mean to say that the company's *turnover* is over £15,000,000? How much is spent on marketing each year?

4. Why is there no Production Department? Where are the shoes made? Why do you think this is?

5. What is the function of a Credit Controller?

6. What is the function of a Pick and Pack Warehouse?

7. What is a Pick Note?

8. Several marketing methods are used by the company. Suggest one other way the shoes could be marketed in the UK.

9. Are shoes ordered direct from the company by individuals? Who are the ShoeShock's major customers?

10. From reading the case study, how do you think customers place their orders?

11. Name 5 different expenses that the company has to budget for, excluding the direct cost of purchasing the shoes.

12. Does the company use an online or a batch system for processing sales orders?

8.4. Information in organisations

A huge amount of time is spent by employees in most organisations simply exchanging information with other people inside and outside the company. Walk into a shop, a bank, a travel agent or a school and observe what the employees are doing. For a large proportion of their time, they are getting information from or entering information into a computer, talking on the telephone, giving advice to customers, receiving and noting information about payments, writing memos or letters, sending faxes and so on.

A delivery note, an invoice or a party invitation?

In an organisation such as ShoeShock Ltd, consider what type of information is exchanged between the people described below.

1. **Customers and sales representatives**
   The sales reps will tell the customers about products, prices, availability, special offers, special marketing or advertising efforts taking place. The customer will tell the sales reps what is and is not selling well, what orders they want to place, any problems they are having for example with quality, returned goods, etc.

2. **Customers and Finance Department**
   The Finance Department will send the customer an invoice for each order placed, and a monthly statement listing all unpaid invoices. Reminders will be sent or telephoned if bills go unpaid. The

customer will send notification if a payment is paid straight into the supplier's bank account. They may ask for additional discounts or for a longer credit period, or ask why goods ordered have not been received.

3.   Import/Distribution department and P&P, the warehouse.

Invoices for goods to be sent out from the warehouse are sent to P&P. P&P send the delivery note with the goods and send information back to ShoeShock about what has been sent out.

> **Discussion: Think what information is exchanged between managers and employees, between the Marketing Department and a magazine with whom ShoeShock wishes to book advertising space, between the Import/Distribution Department and Head Office in New York.**

8.5. Exercises

Each week you need to add to the notes that you will take into the examination and practise answering questions of the type that you will be faced with.

1.   Describe briefly **two** uses of an organisation chart.   (2 marks)

2.   List 4 ways in which modern technology has improved or speeded up communication between on an organisation and its customers.   (4 marks)

3.   For the case study provided by the examination board:

Draw an organisation chart similar to the one given for ShoeShock Ltd.   (5 marks)

- Use Word with drawing tools for this. Open a new document and set the Page Layout (accessed from the **File**, **Page Setup**) to landscape. With the **Text Box** tool, draw the first box and put the text inside it. Then copy and paste the box as many times as you need to by keeping your finger on the **Ctrl** key while you drag the box. Edit the text in each box, and add lines using the line tool. Keeping your finger on the **Shift** key while you draw a line will keep it horizontal or vertical.

4.   Referring to the case study provided by the examination board, or to an organisation you have studied:

What is the main function of the company?

5.   Use PowerPoint to start a presentation on the above company. Create slides that cover its main function and organisation.

Chapter 9 – Information Flows

Objectives

- ✓ To study how information is communicated internally and externally
- ✓ To distinguish between formal and informal information systems
- ✓ To draw a diagram showing the relationship between departments and external agencies

9.1. Internal and external information

Much of the information used by management concerns the **internal** operations of the company. However, **external** information about the environment in which an organisation exists is crucial to all organisations. This may include

- ❑ Intelligence gathering about competitors' activities;
- ❑ Information about population shifts;
- ❑ Economic and social factors;
- ❑ Government legislation.

This type of information is of great importance to managers who are trying to shave production costs, find new markets, develop new products, or make strategic decisions about the future direction of the company. Information is collected in many ways – through conversations and interpersonal 'networking', reading newspapers, trade reviews and magazines, attending conferences and meetings, browsing the Internet. A **formal information system** relies on procedures for the collecting, storing, processing and accessing of data in order to obtain information.

> **Discussion: What methods could the management of ShoeShock use to decide what types of shoe are likely to be popular in the new season?**

9.2. Formal and informal information systems

Information flows through an organisation through both formal and informal information systems. Informal ways of gathering information include face-to-face conversations, meetings, telephone conversations, reading newspapers and magazines, listening to radio and television and surfing the Internet.

Information is also circulated through company newsletters, memos and notice boards. The problem with newsletters and memos is that readers often have so much information to absorb, they quickly forget it.

Figure 9.1: Informal information gathering may take place anywhere...

Informal information gathering is a very important tool at all levels of a company from top management downwards. You probably find yourself that you sometimes learn more about a subject from chatting to your classmates in break times than you do from reading a textbook or attending a lecture – which is not to say you should skip lectures! For someone in charge of planning company strategy, inspiration may well come from a casual conversation with a colleague or fellow conference delegate rather than from poring over a set of figures.

Formal methods of disseminating information around an organisation include the following:

❑ Computerised information systems which allow users to query databases over a company-wide network. Internal data is often collected in the first instance through transaction processing systems. External data can be collected, for example, through agencies such as Dunn and Bradstreet which produces an on-line electronic data service called 'DataStream' to both business and academic organisations.

❑ Software packages such as Lotus Notes enable people at different locations to have the same document on their screens and work on it together. Appointments can be held on the systems so that meetings can be arranged at a time when everyone is free.

❑ E-mail allows correspondence and files to be transmitted throughout an organisation as well as to others outside the organisation.

Company-wide Intranets are networks which work on the same principle as the Internet but are for use within the organisation. Information can be disseminated throughout an organisation via the Intranet rather than in the form of written memos and newsletters.

9.3. Relationships between departments

We will be examining how data flows in and out of an organisation and between the departments in the organisation. We will take as an example the organisation ShoeShock UK Ltd described in Appendix C.

Look at the case study and make a list of all the departments and external agencies mentioned. You should come up with a list something like the one below:

Departments:
> Sales/Marketing
> Import/Distribution
> Finance/Credit/IT

External Agencies:
> Head Office USA
> Manufacturers in Asia
> P&P 'Pick and Pack' distributors

Customs and Excise
Payroll (Independent supplier)
Axel (IT functions)
Sales Agents
Customers

A chart may be drawn showing the relationship between these departments and external agencies, as shown in Figure 9.2.

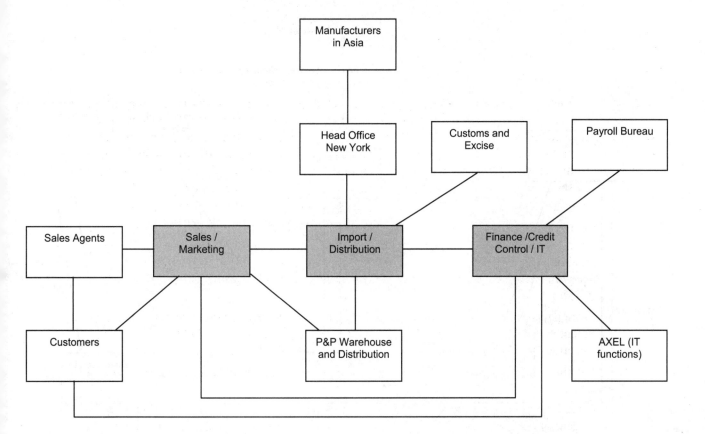

Figure 9.2: Chart showing relationship between departments and external agencies

The internal departments of ShoeShock UK are shown shaded. The diagram shows which departments or agencies have a direct relationship with each other. See if you can deduce from the diagram the answers to the following questions:

- ❑ Who orders goods from the manufacturers?
- ❑ Through which department does the sales department place an order?
- ❑ Who clears imported goods through Customs?
- ❑ How many different departments or agencies deal directly with customers? What is their relationship with each of these?
- ❑ No relationship is shown between P&P Warehouse and the customers. Do you think this is correct? Justify your answer.

9.4. Information flow diagram

An information flow diagram shows the information that flows between departments. The diagram showing the relationships has already been drawn. Now you need to add labels to show what information flows between these departments, and in which direction. This has been done in Figure 9.3.

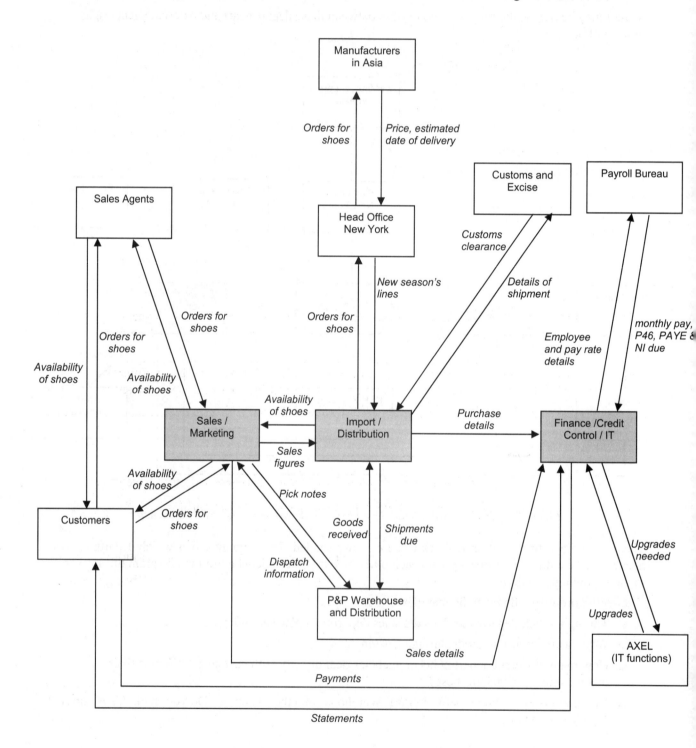

Figure 9.3: Information flow diagram

9.5. Other external agencies

Any company has to deal with many more external agencies than those mentioned in the case study. ShoeShock, for example, will deal with all of the following:

Stationery suppliers

Telephone company

Utilities companies (water, gas, electricity)

Local Council

Accountant

Auditor

Recruitment agency

Inland Revenue

Insurers

Advertising agencies

Bank

VAT office

Training organisations

All these agencies are suppliers of goods and services or, in the case of the Inland Revenue, recipients of tax owed by both the company and its employees. Communication may be by phone, fax, e-mail or regular mail.

Discussion: For selected items in the list given above, decide what type of communication is most efficient. What information passes backwards and forwards between the entities? What form does this information take? What documents are used?

9.6. Exercises

1. For the case study provided by the Examination Board, or for an organisation you have studied:

    (i) Draw a relationship chart showing the main departments in the scenario; (6 marks)

    (ii) Name **three** external agencies that the company deals with; (3 marks)

    (iii) Describe the relationship between the company and each of the external organisations (6 marks)

    (iv) Draw a diagram showing information flows between the main departments, and between those departments and external agencies. (5 marks)

Chapter 10 – Sales Order Processing

Objectives

- ✓ To study how a Sales Order Processing System works
- ✓ To draw an information flow diagram of the subsystems involved
- ✓ To list personnel involved in processing sales
- ✓ To examine the role of ICT in the Sales Order Processing System

10.1. Marketing and sales

Many manufacturing companies sell only to wholesalers or shops, not directly to customers. Others sell to both individuals and to the trade. 'The trade' could include both wholesalers and retailers.

> **Discussion:** Who might the company sell to in each of these cases? Think of some other companies manufacturing goods. Do any of them sell only to the end-user?
>
> i   A small company manufacturing cricket bats
>
> ii   A publisher of educational textbooks
>
> iii   A car manufacturer
>
> iv   A computer manufacturer
>
> v   A knitwear company employing 300 people making a wide range of knitted goods such as sweaters, socks, tops etc.

It is the job of the Sales and Marketing Departments to find new customers and persuade them to buy the company's product. Sales and Marketing are two separate functions. The Marketing Department is concerned with finding out what products and services customers want and promoting these products once they have been produced. The Sales Department is concerned with selling them. There is some overlap in these functions which is why 'Sales and Marketing' are sometimes lumped together.

> **Discussion:** Suggest ways in which the companies listed above could carry out market research and market their products. In each case, describe what role IT plays.

10.2. How is an order processed?

The business of actually processing an order and doing whatever has to be done to get the goods to the customer and getting paid for them is called the Sales Order Processing System. In fact, several different subsystems are involved in the process. These may all be part of one integrated computer system.

Here is a typical scenario for a manufacturing company making bags, cases and rucksacks.

When a customer (typically a High Street store) places an order through the Sales Order Processing subsystem, information about the products and quantity required is passed to the Stock Control subsystem. Assuming there is sufficient quantity to fill the order, the 'free stock' figure is amended on the stock file and the order details are sent to the warehouse. When the goods are packed and ready for despatch, the invoice and despatch note are printed in the Packing and Despatch subsystem. The Accounts subsystem receives the invoice details, such as the date and the amount owed by the customer, from the Sales Order Processing subsystem. Periodically the Marketing Department uses information about who has purchased goods over a period, say the past two years, so that they can post all their customers a new catalogue.

The information flow can be shown in a block diagram as follows:

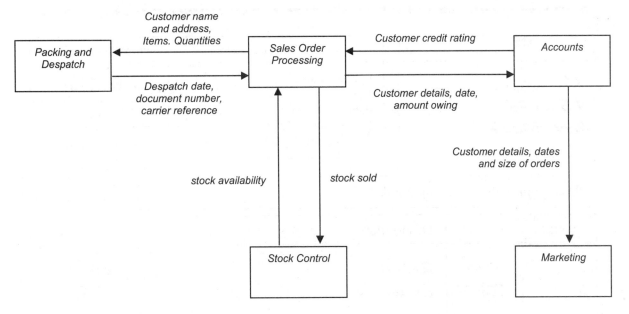

Figure 10.1: Information flow diagram of SOP system and subsystems

10.3. Placing an order

Generally, trade orders (i.e. orders from wholesalers or retailers) are accepted and the customer (the retailer or wholesaler) is given credit. This means that the customer will receive an invoice (a request for payment) and will not have to pay for say, 30, 60 or 90 days. Wholesalers generally ask for a longer credit period and a bigger discount because they order in bulk and have to store the goods until they sell them on.

New customers may have their credit rating checked before goods are supplied, although if the customer is large and well-known, this may not be done. Individuals who order say, a bench from a garden furniture manufacturer may not be given credit, because it is simply too costly to chase up payments that are not made. A cheque or card number has to be sent with the order.

An order from a customer may be placed in one of several ways. For example:

1. The order is telephoned. A clerk in the Sales Order Department can then type the order straight into the computer and there is no paper record of the transaction.

2. The order is posted on the customer's own order form or on a form printed in the manufacturer's catalogue, for example. The order is then typed into the computer.

3. An order may be faxed.

4. A salesman may visit retail stores in his area, take orders on a laptop and transmit them directly to the Sales Order Processing System.

A typical order form is shown on the next page.

The Hadley Group

Head Office: Belair Court, London Road, Tickton DC2 6QY Telephone: (01234) 456789

Supplier	Delivery and Invoice Address	Purchase Order No.
KOC Ltd *4 Severn Rd* *Bristol BR56 4GG*	13 Market Square Tickton Hants DC4 7HJ Tel: (01234) 777888 Fax: (01234) 777889	**GH 53765** Date: *8 April 2001*

Please supply the following goods:

Quantity	Ref No.	Description	Price
6	*M1222*	*Rucksack*	*215.70*
3	*B26654*	*Carrying case*	*53.85*
		Subtotal	*269.55*
		VAT @ 17.5%	*47.17*
		TOTAL	*316.72*

Ordered by: *S. Pickwell*

Proprietors: Hadley Hall Ltd. Registered in England No. 12309876 Registered Office: Belair Court, London Rd, Tickton.
WHITE COPY – SUPPLIER   PINK COPY – ACCOUNTS   BLUE COPY - RETENTION

Figure 10.2: Purchase order form

10.4. Inputting an order

Once the purchase order is received, it is input into a Sales Order screen on the computer. A screen form similar to the one below may be displayed:

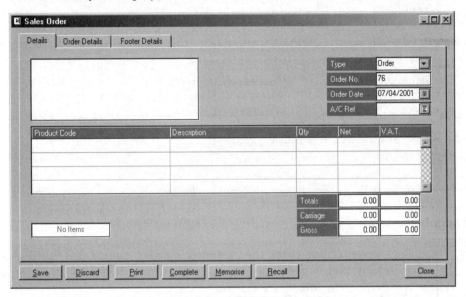

Figure 10.3: Sales Order form

On this form, several fields are entered automatically, including **Type**, **Order No** and **Order Date**. The field **A/C Ref** is the customer's account number. An order cannot be input for a customer who is not already on the system. As soon as the A/C ref is entered, the name and address of the customer will be automatically displayed.

Then, as soon as a product code is entered, the description will be displayed.

Once the quantity is entered, if there is insufficient stock to fill the order, a message will be displayed.

Further details are input by clicking the **Order Details** and **Footer Details** tabs, bringing up the following screens:

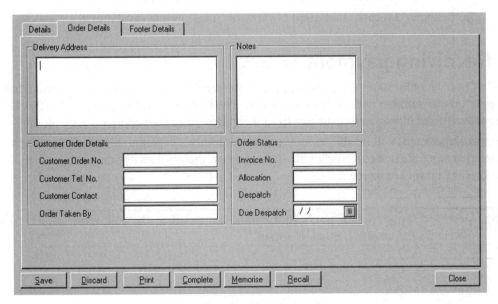

Figure 10.4: Entering Order details

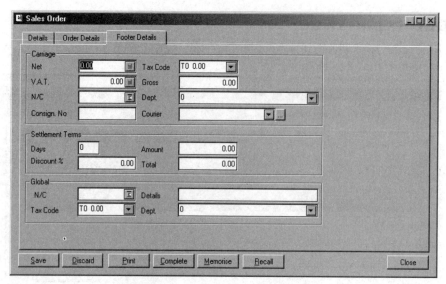

Figure 10.5: Entering Footer details

Discussion: Where does the operator enter the customer's order number? What fields, other than the ones already mentioned, may be entered automatically by the computer system? Where is it getting the information from?

10.5. Processing the order

In a typical system, orders are entered as they come in by mail, phone, fax or e-mail. Then, maybe once or twice a day, a batch of invoices is printed. These are sent to the Packing and Despatch Department who pack the goods and enclose the invoice in a sealed pouch on the outside of the box. Alternatively, a delivery note may be sent with the goods and the invoice posted separately to the Finance or Accounts Department of an organisation buying goods.

Once the invoices are printed

> the stock figures are automatically adjusted by the computer system;

> the customer's record is adjusted to show the total amount outstanding.

10.6. Receiving payment

At the end of every month, statements will be printed for each customer with an outstanding balance, showing each invoice number and the amount owing. The customer will then pay either by cheque or by BACS, transferring the money automatically from their account to the supplier's account.

The Accounts Department will be able to look up any customer's account. A report of overdue accounts can be printed at any time and customers who have not paid their bills will then be chased up. This is the job of the Credit Control Department.

Discussion: Describe some other reports that would be useful to the following departments: Sales, Marketing, Accounts, Stock Control.

10.7. Exercises

1. (i)   Identify one document that would pass from a customer to the Sales Department.   (1 mark)

    (ii) Identify one document that would pass from the Despatch Department to a customer.   (1 mark)

2. (i)   Describe briefly **two** functions of the Marketing Department in a car manufacturing company.
                                                                                         (2 marks)

    (ii) Describe two ways in which each of these functions may be carried out.   (4 marks)

3. Name three functions of each of the following departments in a company.

    (i)   Sales Department   (3 marks)

    (ii) Despatch Department   (3 marks)

    (iii) Research and Development Department   (3 marks)

    (iv) Human Resources Department   (3 marks)

4. Using the case study ShoeShock Ltd (Appendix C) explain, using diagrams where appropriate, how a customer order, which can be wholly filled from finished goods, is processed from receipt of order to receipt of payment, including:

    (i)   the departments and external agencies involved;   (5 marks)

    (ii) descriptions of the data and how it is captured;   (5 marks)

    (iii) inputs and outputs;   (5 marks)

    (iv) the use of ICT in each departmental area.   (5 marks)

5. Now try the same question (Question 1) for the case study provided for the Examination Board or for an organisation you have studied.

6. Put your findings into the PowerPoint presentation started at the end of Chapter 8.

Chapter 11 – Stock Control

Objectives

- ❏ To learn what is meant by stock control
- ❏ To understand the inputs and outputs to a stock control system
- ❏ To appreciate the role of ICT in maintaining correct stock levels

11.1. Why hold stock?

In the simplest possible manufacturing organisation, all goods are manufactured on demand and there is no need to hold stock. A customer orders a custom-built table or whatever and the manufacturer makes it. The customer then receives it in a few days' or weeks' time.

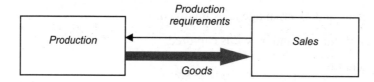

Figure 11.1

However in almost all situations it is necessary to hold some stock so that customers do not have to wait for their goods, and so that the Production Department can be kept working even during slack sales periods. A company cannot simply lay off all its production workers every time orders are not coming in fast enough to keep everyone busy. The Stock Control system acts as a buffer between Production and Sales.

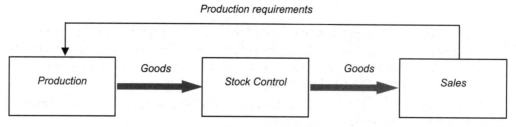

Figure 11.2

There are some advantages to holding quite large stocks of goods, whether they are clothes, cars, books, or anything else.

The advantages of holding large stocks are:

❑ It will be possible to fill even large orders from stock, so there will be no danger of the customer going elsewhere because the items are not in stock.

❑ It is often cheaper to manufacture a large quantity of goods at the same time. There are usually substantial costs involved in setting up machinery for a production run.

❑ It is usually cheaper to buy raw materials in larger quantities from which to manufacture the finished goods.

However, there are disadvantages to holding more stock than necessary:

❑ Capital is tied up in stock instead of earning interest in the bank.

❑ It costs money to store both raw materials and finished goods – warehouse space and shelving have to be bought or rented and maintained.

❑ The goods could go out of fashion, be superseded by a better product or not be popular any more for various reasons after a period of time, so it is unwise to hold stocks which you do not anticipate selling within say, 6 months or a year. They may have to be sold very cheaply or even thrown away.

11.2. The function of a stock control system

The main functions of a stock control system are to

❑ keep track of how much of each item is in stock;

❑ record the **reorder level** and **reorder quantity** for each item in stock (whether this is raw materials stock or stock of finished goods);

❑ generate a reorder report when more stock is required.

Each item manufactured will have a different reorder level. When stock falls below this level, it will be reordered or more goods manufactured. This is called the reorder level.

In a manufacturing company, someone has to make sure that there are enough raw materials in stock to make the necessary quantity of finished goods. The reorder level will depend on how much raw material is used every week and how many weeks it takes for new stock to be delivered.

Example: A particular type of aluminium tubing used in the manufacture of rucksack frames is sold by the metre. A company uses 200 metres of this tubing every week. They like to reorder stock sufficient for 6 weeks' manufacture, and it takes 1 week from the date of placing the order for the tubing to be delivered. Calculate the reorder level and the reorder quantity.

Answer: Since it takes one week for tubing to be delivered, they need to reorder when they have one week's supply left. So the reorder level is 200 metres.

They need to order 6 weeks supply, i.e. 1,200 metres. That is the reorder quantity.

The calculation may be much more complex than this. For example, sales may vary according to the time of year, and the reorder quantity and reorder level will then have to take this into account. Also, there may be random factors like a special offer on 2,000 metres of tubing which makes it more economical to order more than usual.

11.3. Inputs to a stock control system

Different types of input will automatically update the stock file.

Addition of new items

When a new item is ordered that has not previously been held in stock, details have to be entered. A typical input screen is shown below.

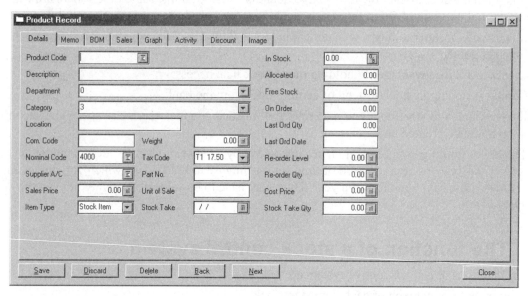

Figure 11.3: Inputting a new stock record

Customer order

When a customer order is entered and posted to the system, the **Free Stock** figure will be automatically updated. If there is insufficient quantity in stock to fill the order, the customer order is added to a Back Orders file and the **Allocated** field is updated.

Returns

If a customer returns stock, the **In Stock** and **Free Stock** figures will be updated.

Adjustments

When a physical stock-take is done, if the number of items counted does not exactly match the computer's figure, a stock adjustment (either In or Out) can be entered.

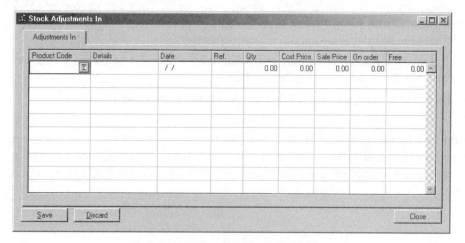

Figure 11.4: Entering stock adjustments

Purchase orders

When new stock is ordered, the **On Order** figure is automatically updated.

11.4. Outputs from the stock control system

A typical stock control system will be able to produce dozens of reports to keep management informed of stock quantities, values, movements, and so on. Part of a list of reports available in Sage Financial Controller is shown below:

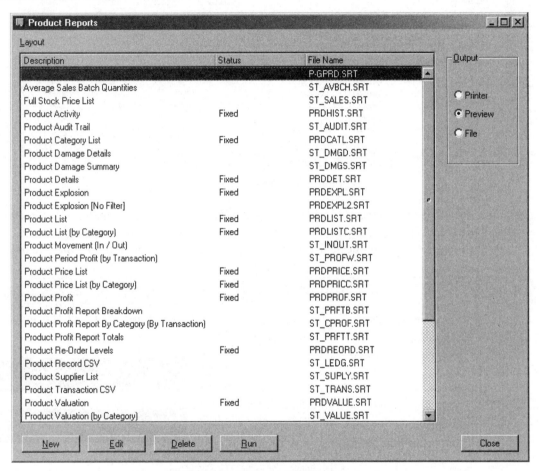

Figure 11.5: Typical Stock reports

For example, the Editorial Department at Victory Publishers may want to know how well a particular title is selling, and how profitable the title is. They could print out a Product Profit report.

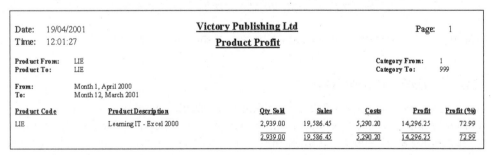

Figure 11.6: A Product Profit report

The Sales Manager may want to know how many of each title is in stock, and what stock movements there have been. The Product movement list can be printed out:

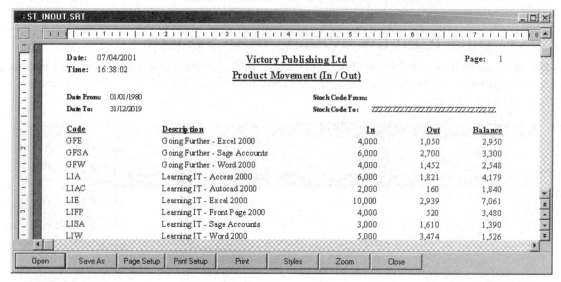

Figure 11.7: A product report

An organisation may have tailor-made reports for its particular products. For example, ShoeShock needs to give its sales force a weekly report before they go out on the road to inform them of any stock shortages. A report may be specially designed for this purpose, looking something like the one below.

Code	Product	Colour	Size	Comments
	WINTER			ANY MAJOR CHANGES TO STOCK SITUATION HIGHLIGHTED
M9483	Winter Mule	Black	7-12M 4-8W	good stocks
M9484	Winter Mule	Grey	7-12M 4-8W	good stocks
M9485	Winter Mule	Blue	7-12M 4-8W	Sold out until May
M9486	Winter Mule	Black	7-12M 4-8W	Sold out 10, 11 until May, rest good stocks
M7651	Monterey	Cloud	7-12M 4-7W	Sold out Wms 6,7
M7652	Monterey	Natural	7-12M 4-7W	Sold out until May
M7653	Monterey	Taupe	7-12M 4-7W	Good stocks
M7654	Monterey	Black	7-12M 4-7W	good stocks
M 6666	Polar Extreme	Natural	7-12M 4-8W	good stocks
M 6667	Polar Extreme	Natural	7-12M 4-8W	good stocks
M 6667	Polar Extreme	Natural	7-12M 4-8W	Sold out Mens 12 until April
etc				

Figure11.8: Customised report for ShoeShock Ltd

This report can be e-mailed or faxed to each salesperson at the start of each week.

11.5. Purchase ordering

The Purchasing Department is responsible for making sure that the company does not run out of stock of any item. In order to do this it needs reports from the stock control department showing which items have fallen below the reorder level, and how much should be reordered. However, personal experience and knowledge of particular circumstances will be crucial in composing purchase orders. The manager may be aware that a large customer is closing down and will not be ordering any more items. A TV commercial may have been made which is having a marked effect on sales and extra raw materials need to be ordered to satisfy expected demand.

In the Sage Line 50 screen shown below, only the supplier's name and the Product code need to be entered. The computer system holds the supplier's details and the product details such as description, unit cost and reorder quantity. The Order number and today's date are entered automatically. Any of these fields can be manually overridden.

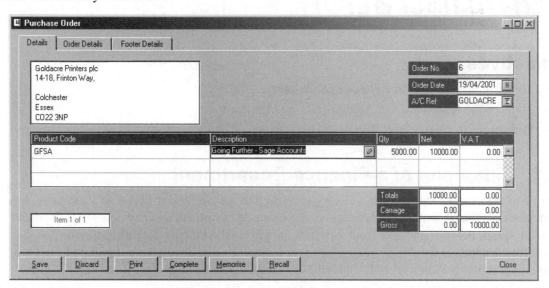

Figure 11.9: Entering a Purchase Order

Discussion: Suppose you are in charge of deciding how many of a particular textbook to reprint. What factors would you take into consideration?

11.6. Exercises

1. Describe briefly:

   (i) Two advantages to a manufacturing company of ordering large quantities, say enough for 1 year, of raw materials when they place an order. (2 marks)

   (ii) Two disadvantages of ordering large quantities of raw materials. (2 marks)

2. Describe what is meant by:

   (i) A reorder level (1 mark)

   (ii) A reorder quantity (1 mark)

3. Refer to the ShoeShock case study in your answer to this question.

   Ian Bertram is in charge of placing the weekly order with Head Office for shoes. He relies on information from the Stock Control system as well as his own experience.

   (i) What information does he need from the Stock Control system? (3 marks)

   (ii) Draw up an example of a possible report which may be useful in assisting with making purchase orders. (5 marks)

   (iii) Give two reasons why Ian may decide to use his own judgement rather than going by the figures on this report in placing his stock order. (2 marks)

Chapter 12 – Finance and Administration

Objectives

✓ To learn the functions of a Finance Department
✓ To learn the functions of an Administration Department
✓ To appreciate the role of ICT in these departments

12.1. Functions of a Finance Department

The role of the Finance Department will vary according to the size and structure of a company. It is from this department that statements and reminders are issued to customers and payment is received and recorded. Invoices and statements from suppliers are sent to the Finance Department, which is in charge of making payments at the proper time. These two functions – dealing with the **Sales** and **Purchase** Ledgers – are usually separated and dealt with by different teams within the Finance Department.

In addition to these operational tasks, one of the main functions of the Finance Department is to be able to provide, at any time, a picture of the financial health of the organisation. It must be able to answer questions such as:

- ❑ Is the company making money?
- ❑ Is it making more or less than last year?
- ❑ What are the major expenses?
- ❑ How much does the company owe its creditors?
- ❑ How much is owed to the company by its debtors?
- ❑ Will there be enough cash available for the purchase of say, a new building, new machinery or an advertising campaign?
- ❑ If not, will the company be able to raise funds?

> **Discussion: Think of some other questions relating to the company finances that the Managing Director of a company may want answered.**

The tasks of the Finance Department may be broken down to include any or all of the following:

- ❑ Producing budgets
- ❑ Producing a Cash Flow forecast
- ❑ Looking after the Sales ledger
- ❑ Looking after the Purchase and Nominal ledgers
- ❑ Credit control
- ❑ Administering and recording payments in and out
- ❑ Producing the monthly and annual accounts
- ❑ Payroll

12.2. A budget for a new product

When a company is planning to launch, say, a new product, someone has to work out what price to charge in order to make an acceptable profit. A lot of budgeting will involve guesswork as no one can predict for certain how many will sell, what unexpected expenses will occur, and so on.

Example: Victory Publishers publish a range of educational computing textbooks. Before they commit themselves to publishing a new book, a budget is drawn up showing the costs and expenses. They will not proceed unless the gross margin is 35% or over.

Below is a budget for a new book that Victory Publishers are contemplating publishing.

	A	B	C	D	E	F
1	Victory Publishers Limited				08-Apr-01	
2	New Publishing Proposal		Title:	Computers in Business		
3			Extent:	208		
4	SALES REVENUE					
5	Published price	£ 9.95				
6						
7		Discount	Quantity	Revenue		
8	Home sales	25%	4000	£ 29,850		
9	Gratis	100%	1000	£ -		
10			Total	£ 29,850		
11						
12	FIXED (PLANT) COSTS			VARIABLE (PPB) COSTS		
13	Artwork (Manual)	£ 500		Print Quantity	5000	
14	Cover (Manual)	£ 250		Print cost	£ 15,000	
15	Typesetting (calculated)	£ 2,080		Royalties (10% of gross)	£ 3,980	
16	Contingency (manual)	£ 200		Distribution	£ 8,480	
17						
18	Total (calculated)	£ 3,030		Total	£ 18,980	
19						
20	UNIT COST					
21	Fixed cost	£ 3,030				
22	Variable cost	£ 18,980				
23	Total cost	£ 22,010				
24	Unit cost	£ 4.402				
25						
26	MARGIN					
27	Sales revenue	£ 29,850				
28	Cost of sales	£ 22,010				
29	Gross Margin	£ 7,840				
30	Gross Margin %	26.3%				
31						

Figure 12.1

> **Discussion: Some of the costs are calculated according to a set formula. For example, the printing costs are £3.00 per copy for 5,000 copies. This reduces by 20p per copy for 6,000 copies, and by a further 20p for each extra thousand copies printed. Typesetting costs £10.00 per page. The distribution costs are calculated as 10% of the gross sales value plus £4.50 for every gratis (free) copy sent out. Gratis copies are promotional copies sent out to lecturers to encourage them to recommend the book to their students. The figure also includes books that have to be pulped because they are returned damaged or after they have gone out of print.**
>
> **What changes to the budget would you suggest to help Victory Publishers reach their 35% gross margin?**

12.3. Cash flow forecast

A month-by-month cash flow forecast enables the management of a company to predict how much actual cash they will have in the bank at any time. If the balance goes negative, they will probably need to ask the bank for a loan. The bank will ask to see the cash flow forecast before giving the loan because they will want to ensure that the company is making a profit and will be able to repay the money within a specified period.

Successful companies often experience cash flow difficulties. Some possible reasons are:

❏ The business is extremely successful and needs to expand. However, expansion has to be funded up front before any returns on the investment are received.

❏ The business has manufactured too many of a particular product, which is now not selling well and is tying up capital and warehouse space.

❏ Overheads have increased – this includes salaries, rent and rates, utilities and so on.

❏ A customer owing a large amount of money has gone bankrupt and the debt cannot be recovered.

The Victory Publishers Cash Flow forecast below shows that they are going to have difficulties between June and October even though by the end of the year they will have made a good profit.

	A	B	C	D	E	F	G	H	I	J	K	L	M
1	Victory Publishers Ltd												
2													
3	Cash Flow Statement for the period of 12 months ending March 31												
4													
5		Apr	May	Jun	Jul	Aug	Sep	Oct	Nov	Dec	Jan	Feb	Mar
6													
7	Actual cash received in bank	310,000	300,700	294,000	310,000	520,000	400,000	620,000	600,000	900,000	450,000	200,000	150,000
8													
9	Actual cash paid out of bank												
10	Printing costs	100,000	87,000	88,000	166,000	75,000	42,000	195,000	18,856	49,562	8,500	20,635	8,000
11	Distribution						0	26,739	80,000	32,000	20,000	6,000	10,000
12	Salaries	140,000	140,000	140,000	140,000	140,000	140,000	140,000	140,000	140,000	140,000	140,000	140,000
13	Royalties			500,000					700,000				
14	Marketing	50,000	3,015		477	53,000	70,000	200,000	60,000				150,000
15	New hardware/software		3000	200	20,000	2,000						2,500	
16	Overheads	20,000	20,000	20,000	20,000	20,000	20,000	20,000	20,000	20,000	20,000	20,000	20,000
17	Corporation tax								120,000				
18	Total cash paid out	310,000	253,015	748,200	346,477	290,000	272,000	581,739	438,856	941,562	188,500	189,135	328,000
19													
20	Net cash flow (Cash In - Cash Out)												
21													
22	Opening Bank Balance	37,000	37,000	84,685	-369,515	-405,992	-175,992	-47,992	-9,731	151,413	109,851	371,351	382,216
23	Plus or Minus net cash flow	0	47,685	-454,200	-36,477	230,000	128,000	38,261	161,144	-41,562	261,500	10,865	-178,000
24	Closing bank balance	37,000	84,685	-369,515	-405,992	-175,992	-47,992	-9,731	151,413	109,851	371,351	382,216	204,216
25													

Figure 12.2: A cash flow forecast

> **Discussion: Victory's biggest sales are made in September. Why do the cash receipts not peak in September?**

In preparing a cash flow forecast many assumptions have to be made and although it will give an indication of the likely situation it is unlikely to be completely accurate.

12.4. The Sales Ledger

The Sales ledger keeps track of all invoices, credit notes and discounts sent to customers and all receipts received from customers. This is a vital tool in **Credit Control** – which is, in other words, making sure you get paid for goods supplied.

When a new customer makes an order, their details are entered into the computer using a screen similar to the following:

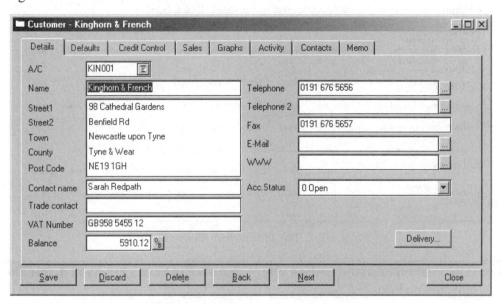

Figure 12.3: Entering a new customer

Further details can be entered on other screens, for example by clicking the Defaults tab or the Credit Control tab.

A customer's activity can be viewed by clicking the Activity tab:

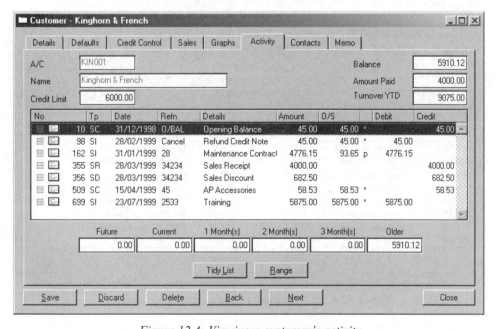

Figure 12.4: Viewing a customer's activity

A number of reports can be printed showing overdue invoices in different amounts of detail or in different sequences – for example by customer account number or in descending order of outstanding balance. These customers can then be phoned and reminded to pay. Customers who fail to pay up even after being reminded are usually put on 'stop' – no more goods issued to them – until the bill is paid.

An extract from a report is shown below:

| Date: 08/04/2001 | | | **DEMONSTRATION** | | | | | Page: 1 | | |
| Time: 11:47:24 | | | **Aged Debtors Analysis (Contacts) - By A/C Name** | | | | | | | |

Report Date:	30/12/1999						Customer From:			
Include future transactions:	No						Customer To:	ZZZZZZZZ		
Exclude later payments:	No									

A/C	Name	Crd Limit	Turnover	Balance	Future	Current	Period 1	Period 2	Period 3	Older
ABS001	ABS Garages Ltd Kerry Stagg 0191 254 5909	4,000.00	1,032.50	1,208.67	0.00	0.00	0.00	0.00	0.00	1,208.67
BRO001	Bronson Inc Susan Armstrong 001 214 248 8924	4,000.00	10,000.00	230.00	0.00	0.00	0.00	0.00	0.00	230.00
BUS001	Business Exhibitions Fiona Hewison 017684 30707	4,000.00	11,610.00	1,791.75	0.00	0.00	0.00	0.00	0.00	1,791.75
FGL001	F G Landscape & Design Mike Hall 01603 354564	100.00	409.50	182.13	0.00	0.00	0.00	182.13	0.00	0.00
KIN001	Kingham & French Sarah Redpath 0191 676 5656	6,000.00	9,075.00	5,910.12	0.00	0.00	0.00	0.00	0.00	5,910.12
MOR001	Morley Solicitors Angela Haworth 01789 656 556	4,000.00	5,009.30	4,327.71	0.00	210.71	210.71	732.03	210.71	2,963.55
PIC001	Picture Frame Ltd 01249 265 9874	9,000.00	12,734.75	4,189.89	0.00	0.00	0.00	2,330.31	1,929.31	-69.73
ROB001	Robertson Joinery	8,000.00	2,000.00	2,350.00	0.00	0.00	0.00	0.00	0.00	2,350.00

Figure 12.5: The Aged Debtor Analysis report

Discussion: Why would it be useful to the Credit Controller to have a report in descending order of outstanding balance?

12.5. The Purchase Ledger

The Purchase Ledger records all the company's suppliers and transactions with these suppliers. When an invoice from a supplier is received it is entered and in due course a payment is made and recorded. A list of all outstanding payments can be viewed to assist in this task:

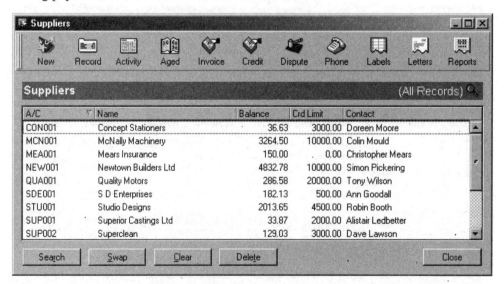

Figure 12.6: List of suppliers and outstanding balances

If the clerk then decides to make a payment to, say, McNally Machinery, the appropriate option brings up a payment screen and the clerk can choose which invoices to pay:

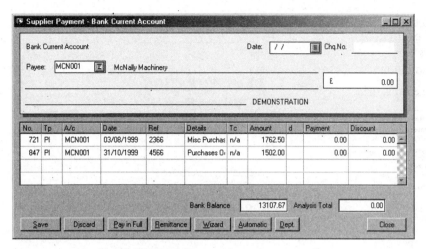

Figure 12.7: Making a payment to a supplier

12.6. The Nominal Ledger

The Nominal Ledger is affected by all transactions posted in all ledgers. It is the heart of the accounting system, and the balances on the Nominal Ledger accounts form the Trial Balance, Balance Sheet and Profit and Loss statements. These documents show the state of the business, and without these the Managing Director would have very little idea of how well or badly the business is doing.

Date: 08/04/2001	**DEMONSTRATION**	**Page:** 1
Time: 12:16:32	**Profit & Loss**	

From: Month 12, December 1999
To: Month 12, December 1999

Chart of Accounts: Default Layout of Accounts

	Period		Year to Date
Sales			
Sales South	5,952.00		58,135.00
Sales North	2,180.00		47,629.80
Sales Midlands	1,523.00		20,741.26
Other Sales	0.00		40,512.33
Miscellaneous Sales	0.00		60.03
		9,655.00	167,078.42
Purchases			
Raw Materials	155.00		32,353.99
Misc Purchases	212.77		11,270.85
Stock	0.00		37,210.00
		367.77	80,834.84
Direct Expenses			
Sales Promotion	0.00		674.00
		0.00	674.00
Gross Profit/(Loss):		9,287.23	85,569.58
Overheads			
Gross Wages	9,027.61		108,382.83
Rent and Rates	1,200.00		17,000.00
Heat, Light and Power	150.00		1,852.00
Motor Expenses	0.00		424.04
Travelling and Entertainment	550.00		1,096.50
Printing and Stationery	0.00		773.60
Maintenance	0.00		50.00
Bank Charges and Interest	11.10		122.11
Depreciation	0.00		2,777.28
Bad Debts	0.00		(0.02)
General Expenses	0.00		(2.50)
		10,938.71	132,475.84
Net Profit/(Loss):		(1,651.48)	(46,906.26)

Figure 12.8: Sample Profit and Loss report

A sample balance sheet is shown below:

Date: 08/04/2001	**DEMONSTRATION**	Page: 1
Time: 12:19:27	**Balance Sheet**	

From: Month 12, December 1999
To: Month 12, December 1999

Chart of Account: Default Layout of Accounts

	Period		**Year to Date**	
Fixed Assets				
Plant and Machinery	0.00		46,515.00	
Furniture and Fixtures	0.00		16,807.00	
Motor Vehicles	0.00		16,440.72	
		0.00		79,762.72
Current Assets				
Stock	0.00		3,500.00	
Debtors	1,264.27		34,419.66	
Deposits and Cash	(550.00)		955.93	
Bank Account	8,052.53		11,555.33	
		8,766.80		50,430.92
Current Liabilities				
Creditors : Short Term	432.13		22,029.04	
Taxation	3,055.32		17,481.22	
Wages	5,972.29		18,236.90	
Creditors : Long Term	(300.00)		12,755.00	
VAT Liability	1,258.54		10,265.74	
		10,418.28		80,767.90
Current Assets less Current Liabilities:		(1,651.48)		(30,336.98)
Total Assets less Current Liabilities:		(1,651.48)		49,425.74
Capital & Reserves				
Share Capital	0.00		96,332.00	
P&L Account	(1,651.48)		(46,906.26)	
		(1,651.48)		49,425.74

Figure 12.9: A sample Balance Sheet

A general Accounts package such as Sage Line 50 integrates the functions of Sales Order Processing (SOP), Purchase Order Processing (POP), Stock Control and Nominal Ledger. By clicking the appropriate option button, the operator can enter or edit a customer, supplier or Nominal account. Bank payments and receipts can be recorded, invoices and sales or purchase orders entered and reports printed.

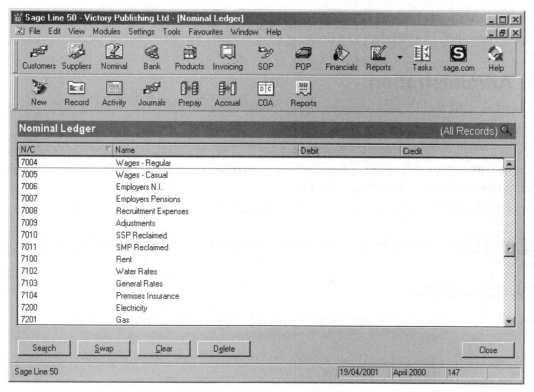

Figure 12.10: The functions of a standard accounting package

12.7. Payroll

Payroll is generally handled by a Payroll package which may interface directly with the Accounts system. Many smaller companies outsource their payroll to a Payroll Bureau which keeps the records and ensures that the correct deductions are made.

Payroll is a complex application ideally suited to computerisation because it involves time-consuming and repetitive calculations. The reports which have to be sent to the Inland Revenue at the end of each financial year can be quickly produced by the system.

12.8. Human Resources (Personnel)

Small companies will not have a separate Personnel Department and these functions will be carried out by the Administration Department or by individual managers. In a large company, the functions may include:

- ❑ liaising with other departments regarding staffing requirements;
- ❑ designing and placing advertisements for new staff;
- ❑ sending out application forms to people requesting them;
- ❑ processing applications;
- ❑ obtaining references;
- ❑ interviewing applicants;
- ❑ preparing induction materials, courses, etc;
- ❑ keeping personnel records;
- ❑ dealing with grievances;
- ❑ dealing with disciplinary matters;

❑ liaising with Trade Unions;

❑ supervising personal development (training programmes) for individuals .

12.9. Administration

Administration tasks may include a number of functions such as:

❑ general day-to-day running of the company;

❑ building and office equipment maintenance;

❑ implementing and coordinating changes such as change of office layout, change of offices for individuals, change of company logo, etc;

❑ keeping people throughout the organisation informed of changes, events, etc.

Discussion: What other tasks would come under the general heading of Administration?

12.10. Exercises

1. Describe three ways in which the Administration Department of a company may use IT to communicate important information to the employees of the company. (6 marks)

2. Describe briefly 3 tasks of the Human Resource Department of a large company. Describe how IT will be used to assist each of these tasks. (6 marks)

3. Name or describe briefly a report that would be useful to a credit controller. Describe 5 fields that you would expect to find on this report. (6 marks)

Chapter 13 – Management Information Systems

Objectives

✓ To understand the difference between a data processing system and a management information system (MIS)

✓ To see how a MIS can assist management in decision-making

✓ To study the factors influencing the success or failure of a MIS

13.1. Introduction

Over the past two decades, a transformation to an information society has been taking place, and computers and telecommunications technologies have revolutionised the way that organisations operate. We live in an information age, and no business of any size can survive and compete without embracing information technology. Information has come to be recognised as a resource of fundamental importance to an organisation, in the same way as the more traditional resources of people, materials and finance.

It is not enough to be merely 'computer-literate' in order to become an expert in information systems. It is also necessary to understand how to apply modern technology in a business, commercial or other environment to achieve the goals of the organisation.

13.2. Information systems v. data processing systems

In Chapter 7 we looked at the different levels of information system in an organisation.

Remember that a data processing system is simply one which records the day-to-day transactions taking place within an organisation. An information system is one which uses this data and turns it into useful information. For example:

❑ Data on items sold is collected by the **data processing system** and stored on a computer file;

❑ An **operational information system** then reads this data and produces a list of items that need reordering;

❑ A **management information system** may analyse the sales data to highlight sales trends and use this information to plan a new marketing campaign, adjust price levels or plan an increase or reduction in production facilities.

13.3. The purpose of a management information system

The purpose of a management information system is:

❑ to help managers with decision-making;

❑ to warn managers when something needs action – for example, stock levels are low, the number of faulty products being produced is higher than expected, etc;

❑ to produce summary reports showing for example actual vs. budget sales;

- to analyse and report on data over a period of time – for example to show sales trends over a period of months or years;

- to enable a manager to perform 'what if' calculations to forecast the likely effect of policy decisions such as price changes, extra production, additional staff, introduction of new products or services.

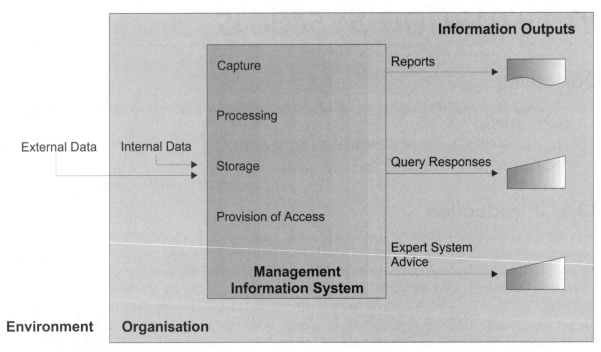

Figure 13.1: The role of a Management Information System

13.4. What managers do

To understand how information systems can benefit managers, we first need to examine what the functions of management are and the kind of information they need for decision-making.

The five classical functions of managers (described more than 70 years ago) are:

1. **Planning.** Managers plan the direction a company is to take, whether to diversify, which areas of the world to operate in, how to maximise profit.

2. **Organising**. Resources such as people, space, equipment and services must be organised.

3. **Coordinating**. Managers coordinate the activities of various departments.

4. **Decision-making**. Managers make decisions about the organisation, the products or services made or sold, the employees, the use of information technology.

5. **Controlling**. This involves monitoring and supervising the activities of others.

Management information systems must be designed to support managers in as many of these functions as possible, at different levels (operational, tactical, strategic) of an organisation.

Discussion: How could a MIS help the managers at various levels of ShoeShock carry out activities of planning, organising, coordinating, decision-making and controlling?

A study in 1973 by Henry Mintzberg found that managers divided up their time as shown in the pie chart below. He described the work of a manager as consisting of hundreds of brief activities of great variety, requiring rapid shifts of attention from one issue to another, very often initiated by emerging problems. Half of the activities of chief executives lasted less than 9 minutes.

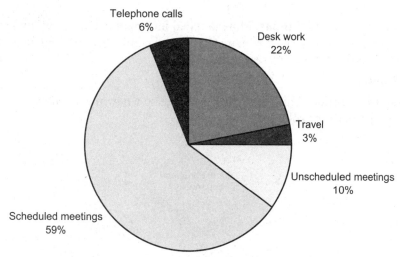

Figure 13.2: How managers spent their time in 1973

Discussion: Today's managers still spend their time divided between many activities. Do you think there are any activities which managers spend more time on than they did in 1973?

13.5. Types of decision

Management decisions can be classified into two types – *structured* and *unstructured*. Structured decisions are repetitive, routine and involve a definite procedure for handling them. Unstructured decisions on the other hand are decisions which require judgement, insight and evaluation. They are often important decisions and there is no set procedure for making them.

Discussion: Categorise the following decisions to be made by a department store manager as structured or unstructured:

In which town shall we open the next branch?

How many extra staff shall we hire to cope with the Christmas rush?

What shall we do about an employee who has had 30 sick days in the last 6 months?

Should we try and increase the number of customers who hold a store card?

13.6. Stages of decision-making

Making unstructured, non-routine decisions is a process that takes place over a period of time, and consists of several stages. Think of any important decision that you may have to make, like whether to go on to University or get a job, which college or University to attend, what course or career to follow. You will probably reach any of these decisions over a period of time, having gathered together information from various sources and listened to friends, parents or careers advisers.

The manager who has non-routine decisions to make typically goes through the following stages:

1. **Recognition that there is a problem.** An information system is useful at this stage to keep managers informed of how well the department or organisation is performing and to let them know where problems exist. The principle of exception reporting is especially important in this stage – in other words, only situations which need some action are reported. (For example, customers with outstanding accounts, a sudden drop or increase in sales compared with the same period last year or a rash of staff resignations.)

2. **Consideration of possible solutions.** More detailed information may be needed at this stage, or possibly tools such as a spreadsheet which can model the effect of different solutions such as price increases or decreases, staff pay increases etc.

3. **Choosing a solution.**

4. **Implementing the solution**. This may involve setting up a new management information system to report on the progress of the solution.

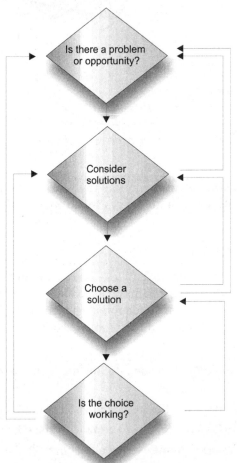

Figure 13.3: The decision-making process

Most decisions do not proceed smoothly from one stage to the next, and backtracking to a previous stage is often required if a chosen solution turns out to be impossible or new information comes to light which offers alternative choices.

Making structured decisions – often of an operational nature – is made easier by having an information system which provides the information necessary to make the correct decisions.

Discussion: A car company gathers information about its customer base through many sources, including market research surveys. One company has discovered that it has relatively few customers in the 18-30 age range. How can this information be used by the company to improve its sales?

If you want to purchase a new car from a Ford dealer, chances are that the make and model you want, in the right colour with the right accessories, is not in stock. It's just too expensive to have cars with every possible combination of options sitting in the parking lot waiting for a customer. In the past, it's been almost impossible for dealers to track down exactly the model that a customer wants.

With the new information system, the dealer can type the details of the required car into a terminal connected to the main Ford plant at Dagenham. The information will then come back to tell the dealer whether there are any cars available of that specification, and exactly where they are. They may be on the Ford parking lot, or there may be only two available, one at a dealers in Perth and the other in Bournemouth. There may be none available – in which case Ford will make one for you, though this may take some time.

Plant production managers are also connected to the system, and so they know exactly what cars have been ordered and can adjust production to reflect demand every day.

Discussion: This is an example of a management information system. How does it help

– the dealer?

– the customer?

– the manufacturer?

13.7. The benefits of a management information system

Many companies have a computer system which allows them to set up new products, customers and suppliers, enter sales and purchase orders, and perform stock control and accounting functions. It can still be difficult for management to extract information useful for making executive decisions.

Additional software is often available as an add-on to extract management information from an operational system. The software compiles reports by extracting information from the database.

For example, as a rule of thumb, many businesses find that 80% of their revenue comes from 20% of their products. In other words, they have a few items which are very successful and make a large profit, and a lot of items which contribute much less to the overall turnover and/or profit. It is obviously very important for management to be aware of which are their most profitable products, who are their most valuable customers, what the sales trends are.

Discussion: In ShoeShock Ltd, management wants a report on the contribution to turnover and profit from each of their product lines. Design the format of a report that will give them this information.

It is useful to be aware of which customers buy the most goods. If one wholesaler buys 20% of a company's output, it will make an enormous difference to the company's profit if a lower discount can be negotiated with that customer. There is, on the other hand, no point spending a lot of effort negotiating a lower discount with a customer who buys hardly anything.

A management information system may be able to produce graphs showing, for example, the sales of a particular product over a period of 12 months. It will also be able to add a trend line to predict probable sales over the next few months.

Victory Publishers may be able to extract information on the success of a particular promotional or marketing activity. For example, it might be useful to have a report on how many schools who received a free sample copy of a book subsequently ordered it. Or, to find out how many schools who ordered one particular title also ordered another title.

Discussion: How would this sort of information help Victory Publishers to sell more books or make a bigger profit?

13.8. Typical functions of a MIS

A summary of some of the functions of a MIS, examples of which have been discussed, is given below. A typical system could include:

- a comprehensive database holding all the information about products, customers, suppliers and finance that would be needed to provide managers with reports for decision-making;
- the ability to analyse the information in the database to highlight situations that need attention;
- the ability to show figures over a period of time, perhaps in graphical format including production and sales figures;
- ability to show a snapshot of the company's financial situation over a period of time;
- ability to perform 'what-if' calculations to show what the effect would be of raising production levels, hiring more staff, acquiring a new building etc.;
- warning signals to indicate that decisions are required, such as low stock levels, expenditure exceeding information, numbers of faulty products exceeding expectations;
- audio and visual warnings when incoming orders exceed production capacity;
- daily calculation of productivity levels by analysis of costs and output;
- monthly graphs of price comparison with competitor goods or services resulting from regular market research.

13.9. Exercises

1. (i) Explain the purpose of a MIS. (4 marks)

    (ii) Describe three essential features of a MIS. (6 marks)

    (iii) Describe three implications of the decision to implement a fully integrated MIS into an organisation. (3 marks)

2. Refer to the Victory Publishers case study in Appendix B to answer these questions.

    (i) Describe two potential benefits which you believe may derive from the implementation of a full management information system. (4 marks)

    (ii) Describe two examples of how such a system could affect decision-making. (4 marks)

Chapter 14 – E-commerce and Other Applications

Objectives

- ✓ To appreciate the benefits and pitfalls of e-commerce
- ✓ To describe the advantages of e-mail
- ✓ To study other ways in which an organisation uses ICT

14.1. E-commerce

One of the main challenges facing many businesses today is to keep up with the explosion in the use of online commerce – buying and selling over the Internet. Very many different kinds of company realise that the future is interactive, and they cannot afford to ignore the new ways of doing business. Even if in the short term, most sales continue to come from traditional methods, most businesses must offer an online service.

> **Discussion:** **What type of goods and services are available over the Internet? Have you used any of these?**

A typical large mail-order company such as JD Williams produces 16 paper catalogues in a year promoting thousands of product lines to more than three million companies throughout the UK.

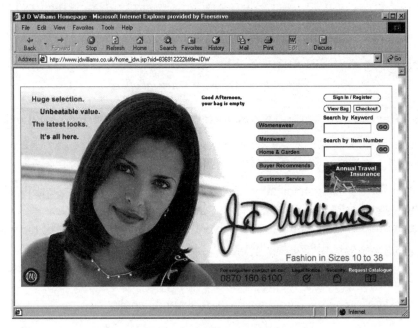

Figure 14.1: The JD Williams home page

What are the benefits of e-commerce for a mail order company such as JD Williams? Some of them are listed below:

❑ They will be able to expand the company's customer base while increasing sales to existing customers.

❑ A paper catalogue takes weeks to prepare and, because of its seasonal nature, is not current for very long. Having an online catalogue enables the company to constantly update its product information.

❑ It can offer new buying opportunities to customers by advertising special offers. This can also be used to reduce slow-moving stock and keep inventory costs down.

❑ The company can monitor, analyse and exploit individual customers' buying habits. It can use online registering, surveys and transaction monitoring to find out all it needs to know about its customers.

❑ It can offer extra services to customers such as a birthday reminder service to prompt customers when to buy birthday presents.

❑ It can advertise and sell other services such as loans and insurance services – once customers are used to buying from an organisation online, they are quite likely to buy other products from them.

Figure 14.2: The week's special offers

Discussion: What would be the advantages to Victory Publishing of using e-commerce?

14.2. Advantages of e-mail

Compared with other forms of communication such as sending letters by post, e-mail has some tremendous advantages.

❑ It is very quick, making it possible to send several letters to the other side of the world and back in a single day. It is also very inexpensive.

❑ It is possible to attach files containing for example text, drawings, photographs etc., to be printed out by the recipient.

❑ The same message can be sent simultaneously to several people.

Discussion: What would be the advantages to Victory Publishing of using e-mail?

14.3. Using Microsoft Outlook

Microsoft Outlook is a package in which you can record information that you might record manually in a number of different places such as an address book, a diary, calendar or Post-it note, as well as handling e-mail both within an organisation or over the Internet.

For a busy manager, these functions help to ensure that important tasks and appointments are not forgotten, e-mails are answered and addresses and telephone numbers are ready to hand when required.

Outlook's functions include:

- ❑ Outlook today. Provides an overview of today's appointments and To-Do list.

- ❑ Inbox. Keeps track of all e-mail and electronic faxes. On a network, you can communicate with co-workers.

- ❑ Calendar. Records appointments. On a network using Microsoft Exchange Server, it is possible to schedule meetings with co-workers.

- ❑ Contacts. All contacts' names, addresses, and other details can be held, and activities with different contacts recorded.

- ❑ Tasks. Maintains a To-Do list, and an alarm can be set to remind you when an appointment is about to come up.

- ❑ Notes. Creates reminders that replace hand-written notes, which can be left open on the Windows Desktop.

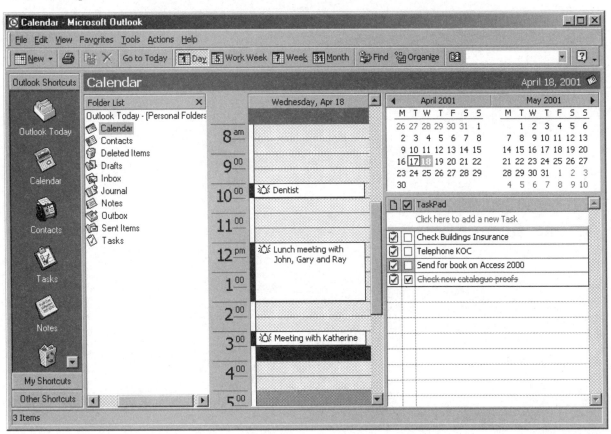

Figure 14.3: Using the Calendar in MS Outlook

14.4. Computer-aided design

Computer-aided design is a very important application in many manufacturing companies. Although a CAD system cannot replace human creativity, it can automate many of the labour-intensive parts of design work. CAD system can accept descriptions of components or processes and display graphical representations. They can then create photorealistic representations that allow the designer to see exactly what an object will look like without ever producing a physical model. Many CAD packages can also evaluate an object for example by testing a circuit or verifying that a structure is strong enough to fulfil its purpose.

A computer-aided manufacturing (CAM) system can be integrated with a CAD system so that a part designed using a CAD system can be automatically manufactured using, for example, a lathe.

14.5. Exercises

1. Referring to the case study ShoeShock Ltd (Appendix C), describe in detail two ways in which the company may benefit from more extensive use of new communication technologies. (6 marks)

2. Give three advantages of e-mail over regular mail. (3 marks)

3. What are the advantages of placing orders over the Internet, rather than by post or fax, to

    (i) the customer; (2 marks)

    (ii) the supplier? (2 marks)

Unit 3

Spreadsheet Design

This unit covers the design and implementation of a spreadsheet system. It covers the process of developing a specification based on the requirements of the end-user, to implementing, testing and documenting the system. For your portfolio you will need to provide evidence that you have worked through these stages for your own project (see Assessment Evidence in Appendix D).

The system specification for this spreadsheet system can be found in Chapter 22 – it would be a good idea to read this first so that you can see what you are trying to achieve.

The unit assumes a very basic knowledge of spreadsheets and in particular Microsoft Excel, so you should be able to start Excel and enter data into a spreadsheet before attempting this unit. By the time you have worked through these chapters you should be well-equipped to design and implement your own system using some of the more complex spreadsheet facilities.

Chapter 15 – Getting Started

Objectives

- ✓ To select a suitable project
- ✓ To set cell formats to match the data format
- ✓ To set cell presentation formats
- ✓ To enter a simple formula
- ✓ To set a conditional format

15.1. Choosing a project

Choosing an appropriate project to develop for this unit is very important. You need to choose something that is a realistic spreadsheet application. It may help to talk to contacts you have (perhaps even your parents) who work in businesses that use spreadsheets. Although those systems may be far too large and complex you might be able to implement a cut-down version. The project developed in the following chapters is in fact similar to a system currently running at a local company. Before developing such a system, it is desirable to visit, chat to employees about the system and see it in operation.

The specification states that your system must use at least six of the more complex spreadsheet facilities. It is better to implement a fairly simple system which meets the specification than to try developing a very complex system which you are unable to get working. Note also that there is a great emphasis on the project documentation in the assessment criteria. You must plan your work carefully and not use all of your time trying to get a very complicated spreadsheet to work, neglecting the other important aspects of the assessment.

Here are a few suggestions for some projects:

- ❑ an accounts system for a club or society
- ❑ an analysis of stock market performance
- ❑ a sales commission system for a company
- ❑ a stock control system with automatic reorder levels
- ❑ a company expenses system
- ❑ a break-even analysis for a manufacturing company
- ❑ an invoicing system for a small company
- ❑ a budget for a major event
- ❑ a record and analysis of experiment results

In the first part of this unit, Chapters 15-21, you will be learning some advanced features of Microsoft Excel that you can use in your own project. Chapters 22-24 show you how to document a project for your portfolio evidence. You should start by reading the Design Specification given in Chapter 22 so that you understand the objectives of this sample project. Before you start on your own project, **read the assessment criteria and follow them!**

15.2. **Starting the sample project**

We are going to set up one of the worksheets for the new ShoeShock system specified in Chapter 22.

- Start Microsoft Excel and open a new workbook.

- Enter the data shown below into **Sheet1**. This may take you a little time but you will need it to complete the rest of the ShoeShock system.

You can speed up some data entry by using the Fill feature. This can be used to copy cell contents into contiguous (adjoining) cells, to enter series of data and to copy formulae.

- In cell A2 enter *101* and in cell A3 enter *102*.

- Highlight the two cells and place the mouse pointer in the lower-right corner of the selected cells. The pointer becomes a small black plus sign. This is called an **AutoFill handle**. Drag the AutoFill handle to cell A21. Excel should complete the series down to Staff No. 120.

- Drag across column headers A to H to select these columns and double-click. This automatically makes all the selected columns wide enough to display the headings and data.

- Save the file as *ShoeShock.xls*.

Column header / *Row header*

	A	B	C	D	E	F	G	H
1	Staff No.	Surname	Forename	Dept.	Start Date	Annual salary	Normal Gross Monthly Salary	Paid Overtime?
2	101	Smith	Jack	Purchasing	1-Dec-86	16500		y
3	102	Brown	Ian	Sales	21-Aug-99	22000		n
4	103	Green	Jill	Distribution	1-Feb-01	12000		y
5	104	Jones	Sally	Sales	23-Jul-95	30000		n
6	105	Jones	Brian	Purchasing	17-Jun-92	15500		y
7	106	James	Alan	Purchasing	18-Mar-98	14000		y
8	107	Williams	Sarah	Accounts	3-Jul-00	13000		y
9	108	Baker	James	Purchasing	12-Dec-95	13000		y
10	109	Lamb	Charles	Sales	14-Apr-99	22000		n
11	110	Gunn	Ben	Purchasing	2-Feb-89	14000		y
12	111	Jackson	Jill	Mgmnt	14-May-93	16000		n
13	112	Shaw	Bill	Mgmnt	1-Mar-86	40000		n
14	113	Little	Sidney	Purchasing	17-Aug-97	18000		y
15	114	Chaplin	Ian	Mgmnt	1-Mar-86	35000		n
16	115	Philips	Marie	Sales	30-Jun-92	22500		n
17	116	Collier	Robin	Distribution	5-Jan-96	14000		y
18	117	Wilson	Harold	Accounts	3-Mar-99	17000		y
19	118	Bottomley	Alice	Sales	14-Jun-95	21000		n
20	119	Kenyon	James	Purchasing	1-Mar-01	14500		y
21	120	Smythe	Gerald	Sales	9-Feb-97	12500		n

Figure 15.1: The data to be input

15.3. **Formatting numbers**

Formatting can improve the presentation of a spreadsheet so that the data can be more easily understood by other people.

When you change a numeric format, you change the *appearance* of a number, not its *value*. The default format for all cells in a new worksheet is the General format, in which leading zeroes and extra zeroes to the right of the decimal place are left out, all decimal places are shown and numbers are aligned to the right of the cell.

You can assign a more appropriate format during or after data entry. There are 12 categories of number formats available in Excel. You can apply any numeric format by accessing the Format Cells dialogue box.

Decimal numbers and currency

By default all text will be left-aligned and all numbers will be right-aligned. If you type the dates as shown, Excel recognises the date format and right-aligns them. We will format the columns containing numbers using the Format Cells dialogue box and the toolbar buttons.

Staff No. has a numeric value but would never be represented with decimal places – it will always be an integer (i.e. no decimal places).

- Highlight column A by clicking in the column header. Select **Format**, **Cells** from the menu.

You will see the following dialogue box:

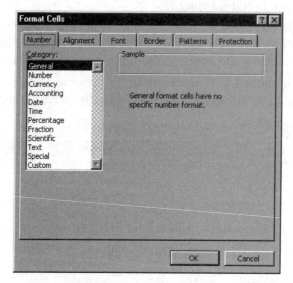

Figure 15.2: The Format Cells dialogue box

- Click on **Number** and set **Decimal places** to **0**. Click **OK**.
- To test this, change the value in cell A2 to *101.13*.
- Tab out of the cell and the value that you have just entered will be rounded to the nearest whole number – 101 in this case.
- Change the contents of cell A2 back to *101*.

The most commonly used numeric formats are also represented by buttons on the Formatting toolbar.

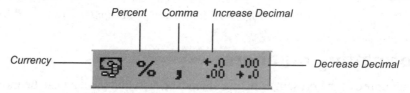

Figure 15.3: The numeric formatting buttons

Columns F and G contain monetary values which are normally shown to two decimal places with a comma as a thousand separator.

- Highlight cells F2:F21 and click the **Increase Decimal** button twice (see Figure 15.3). The figures should automatically be displayed to 2 decimal places.
- With the column still highlighted practise using the **Increase Decimal** and **Decrease Decimal** buttons. Leave the column formatted to 1 decimal place.
- With the column still highlighted click the **Comma style** button.

- To display a £ sign click the Currency button. This automatically displays two decimal places, thousand separators and a currency symbol all vertically aligned – this is often called an Accounting format.

> **Note:** If a different currency symbol is displayed (e.g. $) your system settings may not have been set correctly. Check this from the Control Panel.
>
> - From the **Start** menu select **Settings**, **Control Panel** and double-click on **Regional Options**.
> - In the Regional Options Settings dialogue box click on the **Currency** tab and then check that the correct currency symbol has been selected.
> - Click **Apply** and then **OK**.

You can also change the currency symbol together with some other currency format options from the Format Cells dialogue box.

- Highlight cells F2:F21 again.
- Select **Format**, **Cells** and make sure the **Number** tab is selected.

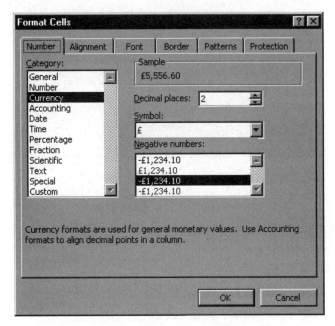

Figure 15.4: Formatting number cells

- In the **Category** list box select **Currency**.

You can now specify the number of decimal places to display, the currency symbol to use and how to display negative numbers.

- Set the options as shown in Figure 15.4 and click **OK**.

Notice that the £ signs are now next to the number entries in the formatted cells.

- Format the empty cells G2:G21 as currency.

Dates

Microsoft Excel treats dates and times as numbers. The way that a time or date is displayed on a worksheet depends on the number format applied to the cell. When you type a date or time that Excel recognises, the cell's format changes from the General number format to a built-in date or time format. By default, dates and times are right-aligned in a cell. If Excel cannot recognise the date or time format, the date or time is entered as text, which is left-aligned in the cell.

Options you select in the **Regional Options** of Control Panel determine the default format for the current date and time and the characters recognized as date and time separators – for example, the slash (/) for dates.

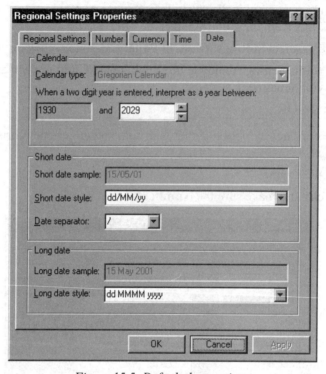

Figure 15.5: Default date settings

Confirm the formatting of the dates in your ShoeShock spreadsheet:

- Click in the column header to highlight column E of the worksheet. Right-justify the column.
- Select **Format**, **Cells** and the **Date** category.
- In the Type list select **14-Mar-98** and click **OK**.
- In cell E22 type *8/7/99* and tab out of the cell.

The date should automatically be formatted as 08-Jul-99.

- Delete the date in cell E22 by pressing the **Delete** key.

Note: When entering dates remember to enter a four-digit year. For example, 09/2002 will be displayed as 01-Sep-02. If you enter only two digits for the year Excel assumes you are specifying a month of the current year, so 09/02 will be displayed as 09-Feb-01 (if the current year is 2001).

Percentages and fractions

You can also format cells to display numbers as percentages with a specified number of decimal places. Either select the **Percentage** type from the **Format cells** dialogue box shown in Figure 15.4 or use the **Percent Style** button on the Formatting toolbar shown in Figure 15.2.

To display a decimal number as a fraction select the **Fraction** type from the Format Cells dialogue box. Try this:

- In cell I3 enter the text *Overtime Rate* and tab out of the cell. Widen cell I3 so that the text is fully displayed.
- In cell J3 enter the number *1.5* and tab out of the cell.

- Click in cell J3 again and select **Format**, **Cells**. Click on Category **Fraction** and then click **OK**.

The number should be displayed as 1½.

- In cell J3 click the **Percent Style** button.

The number should be displayed as 150%.

> **Note:** You can also enter percentages by typing a number followed by the percent symbol (%).

Custom number formats

You can customise formatting to meet your own specific needs. For example in the spreadsheet we can add text to show that the salary is per annum.

- Highlight cells F2 to F21. This time, instead of using the **Format** menu right-click the highlighted range and click **Format Cells**.
- Click the **Custom** Category.
- In the **Type** list select **£ #, # # 0.00**.
- Where the cursor is flashing, click after the last 0 and type a space and *"per annum"* (include the quotation marks) and click **OK**.

The custom number format is applied and saved. (You may have to widen the column to see the contents of the cells.) However, it is superfluous here as the heading says "Annual Salary", so click the **Undo** button to restore the original format.

Format numbers using a conditional format

It can also be useful to format cells only if a certain condition is met. It is easy for operators to make data entry errors in column H. The ShoeShock company rules state that certain departments are never paid overtime (i.e. Sales and Management). We will check the contents of the cells in column H and if they contain the letter **y** we will make it bold and change the font colour to red. This will bring the entries to the attention of the operator who will recheck the entry.

- Highlight column H.
- Select **Format**, **Conditional Formatting**.
- In the Conditional Formatting dialogue box ensure that **Cell Value Is** is selected in the box on the left. In the middle drop-down list select **Equal To**. In the box on the right type *y*.
- Click the **Format** button and the Format Cells dialogue box should appear.
- Select a bold font style and a red colour and click **OK**. Click **OK** to close the Conditional Formatting box.

Figure 15.6: Applying conditional formatting to cells

All the cells containing **y** will turn red and bold.

15.4. Entering a formula

The entries for Column G (Normal Gross Monthly Salary) can be inserted using a formula so that they will be calculated automatically for every employee. Formulae in Excel always begin with an equals sign (=) and commonly use mathematical operators +, -, *, / (plus, minus, multiplication, division) in order to perform calculations. Without the equals sign the cell entry is interpreted as ordinary data – that is text, numbers, or a combination of the two.

We need to calculate the annual salary divided by 12.

- In cell G2 enter the formula =F2/12.
- Drag the AutoFill handle at the bottom right-hand corner of the cell to copy this formula down to cell G21.

15.5. Formatting the presentation of cells

Cell alignment and wrapping

Before you take a first printout of your spreadsheet it is a good idea to preview it to see how it will look. This way you get a clear view of the layout of the whole page and can make any adjustments before printing.

- Click on the **Print Preview** button on the Standard toolbar.

Only part of the spreadsheet will be displayed, so the page needs to be set up for landscape orientation (i.e. short and wide).

- Click the **Setup** button.
- Click on the **Page** tab. If it is not already selected, select **Landscape** and click **OK**.

It would look better if columns A and H were centered and the headings above the columns containing numbers were right-aligned.

- Press **Esc** or click the **Close** button to return to Normal View.
- Select column A by clicking in the column header. With your finger on the **Ctrl** key, click in the column header for column H. This selects both columns.
- Click the **Center** button on the Formatting toolbar.
- Highlight cells E1 to G1 and click the **Right Align** button on the Formatting toolbar.

The heading in cell G1 is rather wide. Instead of changing the actual text we will wrap the text in the cell.

- Make column G about half the width.
- Right-click in cell G1 and select **Format Cells**.
- Click the **Alignment** tab and select **Wrap Text**.
- Repeat for cell H1.
- Select cells A1:H1 and make them bold.

Your spreadsheet should now be looking something like this:

	A	B	C	D	E	F	G	H	I	J
1	Staff No.	Surname	Forename	Dept.	Start Date	Annual salary	Normal Gross Monthly Salary	Paid Overtime?		
2	101	Smith	Jack	Purchasing	1-Dec-86	£16,500.00	£1,375.00	y		
3	102	Brown	Ian	Sales	21-Aug-99	£22,000.00	£1,833.33	n	Overtime Rate	150%
4	103	Green	Jill	Distribution	1-Feb-01	£12,000.00	£1,000.00	y		
5	104	Jones	Sally	Sales	23-Jul-95	£30,000.00	£2,500.00	n		
6	105	Jones	Brian	Purchasing	17-Jun-92	£15,500.00	£1,291.67	y		
7	106	James	Alan	Purchasing	18-Mar-98	£14,000.00	£1,166.67	y		
8	107	Williams	Sarah	Accounts	3-Jul-00	£13,000.00	£1,083.33	y		
9	108	Baker	James	Purchasing	12-Dec-95	£13,000.00	£1,083.33	y		
10	109	Lamb	Charles	Sales	14-Apr-99	£22,000.00	£1,833.33	n		
11	110	Gunn	Ben	Purchasing	2-Feb-89	£14,000.00	£1,166.67	y		
12	111	Jackson	Jill	Mgmnt	14-May-93	£16,000.00	£1,333.33	n		
13	112	Shaw	Bill	Mgmnt	1-Mar-86	£40,000.00	£3,333.33	n		
14	113	Little	Sidney	Purchasing	17-Aug-97	£18,000.00	£1,500.00	y		
15	114	Chaplin	Ian	Mgmnt	1-Mar-86	£35,000.00	£2,916.67	n		
16	115	Philips	Marie	Sales	30-Jun-92	£22,500.00	£1,875.00	n		
17	116	Collier	Robin	Distribution	5-Jan-96	£14,000.00	£1,166.67	y		
18	117	Wilson	Harold	Accounts	3-Mar-99	£17,000.00	£1,416.67	y		
19	118	Bottomley	Alice	Sales	14-Jun-95	£21,000.00	£1,750.00	n		
20	119	Kenyon	James	Purchasing	1-Mar-01	£14,500.00	£1,208.33	y		
21	120	Smythe	Gerald	Sales	9-Feb-97	£12,500.00	£1,041.67	n		

Figure 15.7: The spreadsheet so far

> **Note:** You can also use the **Alignment** tab in the **Format Cells** dialogue box to adjust the direction of text. So, for example, selecting 90° orientation would format the headings at right angles to the rest of the column – try it out yourself selecting different angles.

Merging Cells

Sometimes you may want some text spread out over several cells in a spreadsheet. For example we will insert a main heading and centre it across the top of the page.

- Insert a row by right-clicking in row header 1, and selecting **Insert**.
- Highlight cells A1 to H1 and click the **Merge and Center** button on the Formatting toolbar.
- Enter the text *ShoeShock Staff List & Details* and tab out of the cell.

Setting cell presentation formats

Other attributes of a cell can be changed to help make your spreadsheet easy to read and use. You can group data logically using cell borders and cell shading and make headings and labels stand out by changing font styles and colours.

- Click on the main heading that you have just entered.
- On the Formatting toolbar, select **Comic Sans MS** from the **Font** drop-down list.
- In the **Font Size** drop-down list select **24** and click the **Bold** button.
- Change the colour to red using the **Font Color** button.
- Use the **Bold** button to make the label in cell I3 bold.
- Click in the main heading and click the **Fill Color** button drop-down arrow. Choose a pale grey shading.
- Highlight cells A2 to H2 and click the **Borders** drop-down arrow.
- Click the **Thick Box Border** button.

	A	B	C	D	E	F	G	H	I	J
1	ShoeShock Staff List & Details									
2	Staff No.	Surname	Forename	Dept.	Start Date	Annual salary	Normal Gross Monthly Salary	Paid Overtime?		
3	101	Smith	Jack	Purchasing	1-Dec-86	£16,500.00	£1,375.00	y		
4	102	Brown	Ian	Sales	21-Aug-99	£22,000.00	£1,833.33	n	Overtime Rate	150%
5	103	Green	Jill	Distribution	1-Feb-01	£12,000.00	£1,000.00	y		
6	104	Jones	Sally	Sales	23-Jul-95	£30,000.00	£2,500.00	n		
7	105	Jones	Brian	Purchasing	17-Jun-92	£15,500.00	£1,291.67	y		
8	106	James	Alan	Purchasing	18-Mar-98	£14,000.00	£1,166.67	y		
9	107	Williams	Sarah	Accounts	3-Jul-00	£13,000.00	£1,083.33	y		
10	108	Baker	James	Purchasing	12-Dec-95	£13,000.00	£1,083.33	y		
11	109	Lamb	Charles	Sales	14-Apr-99	£22,000.00	£1,833.33	n		
12	110	Gunn	Ben	Purchasing	2-Feb-89	£14,000.00	£1,166.67	y		
13	111	Jackson	Jill	Mgmnt	14-May-93	£16,000.00	£1,333.33	n		
14	112	Shaw	Bill	Mgmnt	1-Mar-86	£40,000.00	£3,333.33	n		
15	113	Little	Sidney	Purchasing	17-Aug-97	£18,000.00	£1,500.00	y		
16	114	Chaplin	Ian	Mgmnt	1-Mar-86	£35,000.00	£2,916.67	n		
17	115	Philips	Marie	Sales	30-Jun-92	£22,500.00	£1,875.00	n		
18	116	Collier	Robin	Distribution	5-Jan-96	£14,000.00	£1,166.67	y		
19	117	Wilson	Harold	Accounts	3-Mar-99	£17,000.00	£1,416.67	y		
20	118	Bottomley	Alice	Sales	14-Jun-95	£21,000.00	£1,750.00	n		
21	119	Kenyon	James	Purchasing	1-Mar-01	£14,500.00	£1,208.33	y		
22	120	Smythe	Gerald	Sales	9-Feb-97	£12,500.00	£1,041.67	n		

Figure 15.8: The formatted spreadsheet

- Save your spreadsheet again as *ShoeShock.xls*.

Chapter 16 – Manipulating Spreadsheet Data

Objectives

- ✓ To find and replace data
- ✓ To add worksheets
- ✓ To cut, copy, paste, and move data
- ✓ To use appropriate cell referencing
- ✓ To name cells

16.1. Finding and replacing data

The spreadsheet that you have created so far represents only a small sample of ShoeShock employees. In a live system records for the entire workforce will be kept. With this in mind it is useful to identify quick ways to move around the spreadsheet and to find certain data.

- Test out for yourself some of the keyboard shortcuts listed below:

Page Up	Moves you up a whole screen
Page Down	Moves you down a whole screen
Ctrl-Home	Moves you to the first cell of the spreadsheet
Ctrl-End	Moves you to the end of the spreadsheet

To go to a specified cell:

- Select **Edit**, **Go To**.

- In the Reference box type the cell reference that you want to go to.

Figure 16.1: Using the Go To feature

Previous **Go To** references are stored in the top box – you can click on these again for speed.

If you want to find some particular data entered into a cell, for example the department **Mgmnt**:

- Press **Ctrl-Home** to go to the start of the spreadsheet.
- Select **Edit**, **Find**.
- In the dialogue box enter the text or number you are looking for e.g. *Mgmnt*.
- Click on **Find Next**.

You should move to the first occurrence of the word. If you keep pressing **Find Next** you will move through all of the occurrences. However, if you want to change all occurrences of Mgmnt to Management, you can do this using the same dialogue box.

- Click on the **Replace** button.
- In the **Replace With** box type *Management*.
- Click the **Replace All** button.

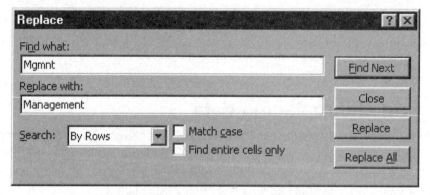

Figure 16.2: Finding and Replacing text

Look through the spreadsheet and the word should have been changed throughout (you might need to widen column D).

16.2. Adding worksheets

So far we have referred to the window in which you have entered data as a *spreadsheet*. However in Microsoft Excel it should strictly be called a *worksheet*. Excel's basic working environment is a *workbook* that contains multiple worksheets that store your data. If you look at the bottom of the Excel screen you should see some tabs called **Sheet1**, **Sheet2** etc. which are the default worksheet names that Excel sets up. You have probably been entering your data into **Sheet1** which needs renaming to reflect its contents.

- Double-click on the name **Sheet1**. Type *Staff List & Details* and press **Enter**.
- Click on **Sheet2**. You should be presented with a blank worksheet. Rename this sheet *Overtime Collection*.

You will also need another worksheet called **Home**.

- Rename **Sheet3** *Home* (remember to press **Enter**) and drag its tab to the left of **Staff List & Details** so that this becomes the first worksheet in the workbook.

Figure 16.3:The worksheet tabs

16.3. Repositioning data

In the **Overtime Collection** worksheet, enter a heading *Overtime Collection* in cell A1 by copying it from the previous worksheet and editing the text. There are several ways of copying and pasting cells – you can choose whichever method you prefer from the alternatives given below.

- Click in cell A1 of the worksheet **Staff List & Details**.

- Select **Edit**, **Copy** *or* right-click in the cell and select **Copy** from the shortcut menu *or* click the **Copy** button on the Standard toolbar.

- Click on the worksheet tab **Overtime Collection** and click in cell A1.

- Select **Edit**, **Paste** *or* right-click in the cell and select **Paste** *or* click the **Paste** button on the Standard toolbar.

> **Note:** Many menu options have shortcut key combinations (e.g. **Ctrl-S** for **File**, **Save**), specified next to the menu item.
>
> Look up the shortcut key combinations for **Edit**, **Copy** and **Edit**, **Paste**.

The formatted heading should be copied to the new worksheet. First you need to clear just the text from the cell, leaving the formatting as it is. To do this:

- Select **Edit**, **Clear**. You will see that there are options to clear everything in the cell, just the contents, just the formatting, or the comments associated with the cell (these will be discussed later).

- Clear just the contents of the cell by selecting **Contents** (Shortcut key **Del**).

- Enter the text *ShoeShock Overtime Collection*.

- Enter the following headings, making them bold, centering column A and right-aligning the others:

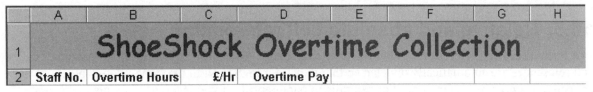

Figure 16.4: The headings for overtime collection

16.4. Linking worksheets

The staff numbers need to be inserted from the previous sheet. We can do this by linking the two worksheets.

- In cell A3 of the **Overtime Collection** sheet type =.

- Return to the **Staff List & Details** worksheet, click in cell A3 and press **Enter**.

You will return to the **Overtime Collection** worksheet. The formula **='Staff List& Details'!A3** will appear in the formula bar and the number **101** will appear in cell A3. This technique is called 3D (three-dimensional) referencing and it will be used again in this project to link worksheets together.

- Fill this formula down to cell A22.

	A3	▼		= ='Staff List & Details'!A3			

The formula bar

	A	B	C	D	E	F	G	H
1			ShoeShock Overtime Collection					
2	Staff No.	Overtime Hours	£/Hr	Overtime Pay				
3	101					Overtime Rate	150%	
4	102							
5	103							
6	104							
7	105							
8	106							
9	107							
10	108							
11	109							
12	110							
13	111							
14	112							
15	113							
16	114							
17	115							
18	116							
19	117							
20	118							
21	119							
22	120							

Figure 16.5: Entering a 3D cell reference

- Enter a label *Overtime Rate* in cell F3. In cell G3, enter *150%*. (This is the overtime rate that will be used in calculations.)

16.5. Relative and absolute cell referencing

In a formula the cell reference is either relative or absolute. When you copy a formula to another cell, any cell references are automatically updated so that they refer to the cell in the same relative position; these are called *relative cell references*. For example in paragraph 15.4 you entered a formula to calculate the **Normal Gross Monthly Salary** for the first employee in the list. You then used the **AutoFill** handle to copy the formula down the column – if you look at the formulae in some of the cells further down the list you will see that Excel has automatically updated these relative cell references for you.

Often though you want a formula to refer to the same cell, regardless of where the formula is copied. For example on the **Overtime Collection** sheet we will use the overtime rate from cell G3. We do not want this to change no matter where it is copied to. To ensure this we precede each part of the cell reference by a $ sign; so that if we use G3 in a formula, the value 150% will always be used. This is an *absolute cell reference*.

First calculate the pay per hour:

- In cell C3 of the **Overtime Collection** worksheet enter a formula that calculates the £/Hr as Annual Salary (from the previous worksheet) divided by [52 (weeks in a year) multiplied by 5 (working days in a week) multiplied by 8 (hours in working day)]. Be careful you get the brackets in the right place! Check the results with Figure 16.6.

    This should be as follows: *='Staff List & Details'!F3/(52*5*8)*.

- Fill this formula down to cell C22 and format the column as currency, using **Format**, **Cells**, **Number**, **Currency**.

Now calculate the overtime pay:

- In cell D3 enter a formula that calculates **Overtime Pay** as **Overtime Hours** multiplied by **£/Hr** multiplied by **Overtime Rate**.

This should be as follows: *=B3*C3*G3*.

> **Note:** You can enter the formula by "pointing" at the cells instead of typing in the cell reference. To turn G3 into an absolute cell reference, enter the first part of the formula *=B3*C3**, click in cell G3, then press function key F4.

- Fill this formula down to cell D22. Because you used an absolute cell reference for the Overtime Rate, the value 150% in cell G3 will be used all the way down the column.

Of course no values will appear in the column because we have not entered the number of overtime hours the employees have worked.

- Enter the **Overtime Hours** as shown in Figure 16.6. Click in the column header and format the cells to 1 decimal place.

To prevent the zero values being displayed in column D:

- Select column D, then select **Tools**, **Options** and click on the **View** tab.
- Deselect the **Zero values** check box.

16.6. Naming cells

Assigning a name to a cell can be an easier way of creating an absolute cell reference. If you use a named cell in a formula it will automatically be an absolute reference. As an example, name cell G3 **OTRate**:

- Click in cell G3.
- Click in the Name box and type the name *OTRate*. Press **Enter**.

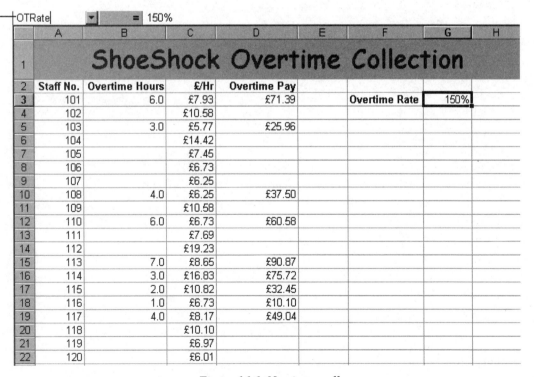

Figure 16.6: Naming a cell

You can now use the name **OTRate** to refer to this cell instead of its cell reference G3. Using an assigned name also means you do not have to remember column and row labels when writing a formula. Another advantage is that a cell name can be used in a formula in any worksheet within the same workbook.

Change the formula in cell D3 to use the new name:

- Click in cell D3 and change the formula to *=B3*C3*OTRate*.

- Fill the formula down to cell D22. You should get the same values as before.

Note: Here are some rules about naming cells:

- ❑   a name must begin with a letter

- ❑   a number can be used so long as it follows a letter or an underscore

- ❑   a space between words is represented as an underscore

- ❑   a name cannot resemble a cell reference e.g. B2

- ❑   single letters can be used except for R and C

  Names can also be attached to ranges of cells in the same way.

Chapter 17 – Formulae and Functions

Objectives

- ✓ To correctly apply and use arithmetic and relational operators in formulae
- ✓ To correctly apply and use logical values in formulae
- ✓ To use common built-in spreadsheet functions

17.1. Operators in formulae

Some simple formulae have already been used to create the ShoeShock spreadsheet. They have been used to perform operations such as multiplication and division. Excel recognises the following numeric operators and does not carry out a calculation simply from left to right, but in the order listed here:

^	raising to the power (e.g. 2^2 is 2^2).
*	multiplication
/	division
+	addition
-	subtraction

You can also use a minus sign (-) in front of a negative number and the percentage sign (%) after a number.

The & sign can be used to combine text strings (sometimes called *concatenation*). Try this out in a blank area of your spreadsheet:

- On the **Overtime Collection** worksheet enter the text *Mon* into cell H16.
- Enter the text *day* into cell H17.
- In cell H18 enter the formula *=H16&H17*.
- Tab out of the cell and the text **Monday** should appear in cell H18.
- Delete the contents of cells H16 to H18.

You can use brackets to change the order of calculation. Anything inside a pair of brackets is calculated first and then the calculation works outwards. Every opening bracket must have a closing bracket or Excel will flag up an error. You can nest up to seven pairs of brackets but mistakes can easily be made if formulae are too complicated. It is best to split a complex formula over several cells as this allows you to find errors more easily.

- Use a calculator to find out what the answer to this formula is.
  =(((500-(8+3)*5)+0.75))/20
- Now enter the formula into a blank cell of your spreadsheet – do your answers agree? Format the cell to 2 decimal places and the answer should be 22.29.
- Delete the contents of the cell.

17.2. The SUM function

Excel also contains many built-in functions. These are predefined formulae that perform special or advanced calculations. They are entered using the function name followed by a pair of brackets containing one or more arguments separated by commas. The arguments are the data that you use in a function to produce a value. For example:

=Function Name (argument1, argument2, etc.)

One of the most commonly-used functions is **SUM** which totals a range of numeric values. We will use this on the **Staff List & Details** worksheet to calculate the total monthly wage bill.

- On the **Staff List & Details** worksheet click in cell G23.

- Enter the formula *=SUM(G3:G22)*. This specifies that we wish to total the range of cells from G3 to G22.

- Tab out of the cell and the answer should be displayed (£31,875.00 if you have entered all the data correctly!).

> **Note:** Instead of typing in the range you can drag the mouse over the cells to be totalled – this method sometimes gives you a better chance of getting it right.

The **SUM** function has a related button on the Standard toolbar called **AutoSum**. This allows you to total rows or columns of numbers quickly.

- Delete the contents of cell G23.

- Click in cell G23 and then click the **AutoSum** button on the Standard toolbar.

The column of numbers above will be highlighted with a dotted line and the SUM function will automatically be inserted for you.

Normal Gross Monthly Salary
£1,375.00
£1,833.33
£1,000.00
£2,500.00
£1,291.67
£1,166.67
£1,083.33
£1,083.33
£1,833.33
£1,166.67
£1,333.33
£3,333.33
£1,500.00
£2,916.67
£1,875.00
£1,166.67
£1,416.67
£1,750.00
£1,208.33
£1,041.67
=SUM(G3:G22)

Figure 17.1: Using AutoSum

- Press **Enter** and the total should appear in cell G23.

> **Note:** AutoSum automatically selects the column of numbers above the current cell. If there are none there it will select the row to the left.

17.3. Functions to calculate averages

You can use the ShoeShock data to try out some Excel functions that calculate averages. The **AVERAGE** function calculates the mean of a range of values (i.e. the total of a range of values divided by the number of values).

The **MODE** function finds the most frequently occurring value in a range of values.

The **MEDIAN** function finds the middle value in a range of values.

- Click in cell G23 of the **Staff List & Details** worksheet and delete the contents.
- Enter the formula *=AVERAGE(G3:G22)* and press **Enter**.

The answer £1,593.75 should be displayed

- Delete the contents of cell G23.
- Enter the formula *=MODE(G3:G22)* and press **Enter**.

The answer £1,166.67 should be displayed (this is the only value that appears more than once).

- Delete the contents of cell G23.
- Enter the formula *=MEDIAN(G3:G22)* and press **Enter**.

The answer £1,354.17 should be displayed.

17.4. MIN and MAX functions

These functions allow you to find the maximum and the minimum values in a range.

- Replace the contents of cell G23 on the **Staff List & Details** worksheet with the formula *=MIN(G3:G22)* and press **Enter**.

The answer £1000.00 should be displayed.

- Now enter a formula into cell G23 to find the maximum monthly salary using the **MAX** function – which employee is the highest paid (before overtime)?
- Delete the contents of cell G23.

17.5. COUNT functions

The COUNT function will count the number of numeric values in a range. For example to count the number of employees on the **Staff List & Details** worksheet we will use the **COUNT** function on the **Staff No.** column as it is a numeric field.

- In cell A23 enter the formula *=COUNT(A3:A22)* and press **Enter**.

You should get 20. This is a fairly simple calculation that you could do in your head, but this function can be useful on more complex spreadsheets that have a large number of rows.

COUNTA and **COUNTBLANK** are variations of the **COUNT** function. **COUNTA** calculates the number of cells in a range that are not empty. **COUNTBLANK** calculates the number of empty cells in a range.

- Try out these two functions at the bottom of the **Overtime Hours** column on the **Overtime Collection** worksheet.

The **COUNTIF** function counts the number of cells within a range that meet a given condition. For example, we will use it on the **Staff List & Details** worksheet to count how many employees are paid overtime.

- Click in cell H23 on the **Staff List & Details** worksheet.
- Enter the formula *=COUNTIF(H3:H22, "y")* and press **Enter**.

The answer 11 should be displayed.

- Delete row 23 by clicking in the row header, right-clicking and selecting **Delete**. All of the results of the functions should have been deleted.

17.6. The Paste Function wizard

So far the functions have been entered in full, but for more complex ones it is often easier to use the **Paste Function** feature. This is a tool that guides you through creating a function and helps reduce errors that can occur when you are typing them in. You can also use the **Paste Function** feature to help you decide which one to use.

- Display the **Staff List & Details** worksheet on the screen.
- Click in cell G24 of the worksheet and click the **Paste Function** button on the Standard toolbar. (Alternatively, select **Insert**, **Function** from the menu.)

The Paste Function dialogue box displays a list of function types in the **Function category** box and a list of associated functions in the **Function name** box.

- Click on some of the categories and have a look at the enormous range of functions that are available.
- From the **All** category scroll down to the **INT** function (this rounds a number to the nearest integer) and click **OK**.

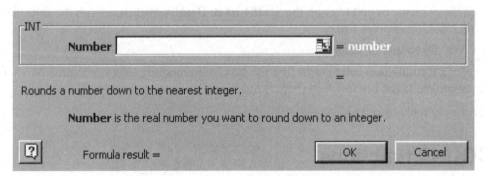

*Figure 17.2: Using **Paste Function***

- In the dialogue box enter the cell reference *G22* and click **OK**.

The value £1,041.00 will be displayed in cell G24.

- Delete the contents of cell G24.

17.7. IF function

One of the most useful of Excel's functions is the IF function. This is a conditional function that compares two values and returns one of two results depending on the outcome of the comparison.

The function has three arguments:

- ❏ The comparison to be performed. The following operators can be used in a comparison:

<	Less than
<=	Less than or equal to
>	Greater than
>=	Greater than or equal to
=	Equal
<>	Not equal

To make the expressions even more complex, comparisons can be combined with the following logical operators:

AND	True if both expressions are true
OR	True if either or both expressions are true
NOT	reverses the result.

❑ The value to be returned if the result of the comparison is true.

❑ The value to be returned if the result of the comparison is false.

In the ShoeShock system we have calculated overtime pay for everyone, whether or not they are paid overtime. We could change the formula in the **Overtime Pay** column of the **Overtime Collection** worksheet so that it tested to see if **Paid Overtime?** column on the **Staff List & Details** worksheet contained a **y**. If it does then their overtime pay will be displayed, otherwise nothing will be displayed.

- Delete the contents of cell D3 in the **Overtime Collection** worksheet.

- Click in cell D3 and click the **Paste Function** button on the Standard toolbar.

- Select the **Logical** category and the **IF** function and click **OK**.

- Click in the **Logical_test** box and then click in cell H3 on the **Staff List & Details** worksheet to insert the cell reference. (You can move the dialogue box out of the way by dragging it.) Type *="y"*.

- Complete the dialogue box as shown below.

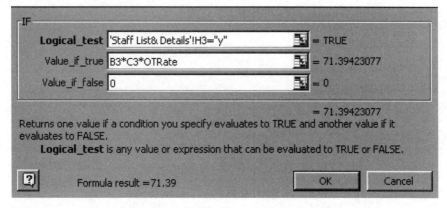

Figure 17.3: Entering the arguments for the IF function

- Fill the formula down to cell D22.

Overtime payments should only be displayed for those people who get paid overtime. You should see 7 entries as shown in Figure 17.4.

	A	B	C	D	E	F	G	H	I
1			ShoeShock Overtime Collection						
2	Staff No.	Overtime Hours	£/Hr	Overtime Pay					
3	101	6.0	£7.93	£71.39		Overtime Rate	150%		
4	102		£10.58						
5	103	3.0	£5.77	£25.96					
6	104		£14.42						
7	105		£7.45						
8	106		£6.73						
9	107		£6.25						
10	108	4.0	£6.25	£37.50					
11	109		£10.58						
12	110	6.0	£6.73	£60.58					
13	111		£7.69						
14	112		£19.23						
15	113	7.0	£8.65						
16	114	3.0	£16.83	£75.72					
17	115	2.0	£10.10						
18	116	1.0	£6.73	£10.10					
19	117	4.0	£8.17	£49.04					
20	118		£10.10						
21	119		£6.97						
22	120		£6.01						
23									

*Figure 17.4: The **Overtime Collection** worksheet*

- Save the spreadsheet.

Chapter 18 – Data Input

Objectives

- ✓ To attach comments to cells
- ✓ To validate input data
- ✓ To create and use data entry forms
- ✓ To provide users with helpful prompts whilst entering data
- ✓ To use macros and command buttons to make the spreadsheet user-friendly

18.1. Comments

Because this system is going to be used by several different people in the ShoeShock Finance department, instructions can be entered in the form of *comments* to ensure that the spreadsheet is used correctly.

The Finance staff will take the overtime figures from the form that employees are requested to complete on a weekly basis (shown in Figure 22.4). The information will be entered into column B on the **Overtime Collection** worksheet. The smallest unit of overtime that is paid is half an hour, but sometimes employees specify some other fraction of an hour on their form. The Finance staff are asked to round this figure to the nearest half hour, but need a prompt to remind them to do this. We will add a comment to help them.

- Click in cell B2 of the **Overtime Collection** worksheet.
- Select **Insert**, **Comment**.

A comment box labelled with your user name appears:

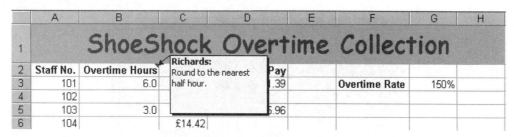

Figure 18.1: Adding a comment

- Type the text *Round to the nearest half hour*.
- Click anywhere outside the comment box and it will close.
- Place the mouse pointer over cell B2 and your comment will appear.

You can make a comment appear permanently by right-clicking and selecting **Show Comment**.

When you want to clear a comment right-click in the cell and select **Delete Comment**. To edit a comment, right-click in the cell and select **Edit Comment**.

18.2. Data Validation

Data validation helps to prevent users from entering inaccurate or invalid data such as text in a cell that should contain a number value. We will validate the overtime hours data to ensure that a numeric value within a specified range is entered.

- Highlight cells B3 to B22 on the **Overtime Collection** worksheet.
- Select **Data**, **Validation** and click on the **Settings** tab of the Data Validation dialogue box.
- The minimum overtime is half an hour and the maximum is 20 hours per week. Enter the settings as shown below.

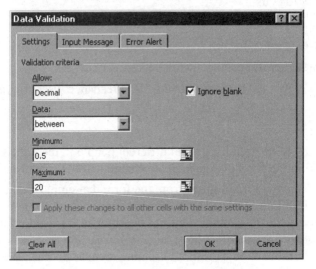

Figure 18.2: Settings for data validation

- Click the **Error Alert** tab and ensure that the **Show Error Alert After Invalid Data Is Entered** check box is selected in the dialogue box. Enter the other settings and the error message as shown below.

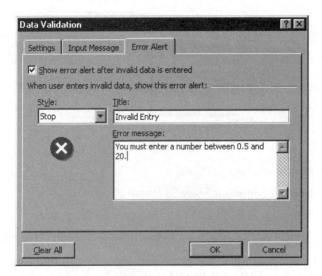

Figure 18.3: Entering an error message

- Click **OK**.
- In cell B4 enter some text and tab out of the cell.

An error message appears containing the warning that you entered into the Data Validation dialogue box.

- Click **Cancel** to delete the entry and then type *3.5*. Tab out of the cell.

This time your entry will be accepted.

18.3. Forms

One way to speed up and simplify data entry is to use forms. For example, if a new employee joins the company their details need to be entered on the **Staff List & Details** worksheet. Similarly if an employee leaves or their details change the **Staff List & Details** worksheet must be updated. It is very simple to create a form for this purpose.

First we must ensure that any new rows that are added to the list are automatically formatted to match the preceding rows. Formulae that repeat in every row must automatically be copied. This feature is called **Extended list formats and formulas**.

> **Note:** To be extended, formats and formulae must appear in at least three of the five list rows preceding the new row.

- Display the **Staff List & Details** worksheet on your screen.
- Select **Tools**, **Options** and click on the **Edit** tab.
- Make sure that **Extend list formats and formulas** is selected and that other options are as shown in Figure 18.4.
- Click **OK**.

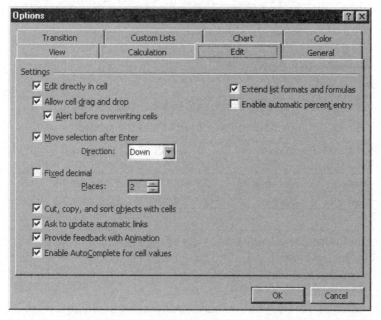

Figure 18.4: Setting Excel options

- Delete the contents of cells I4 and J4. These cell values are not used (the overtime rate is picked up from the **Overtime Collection** worksheet) and Excel gets confused if data is entered to the left or right of a list from which a form is to be created.
- Click anywhere in the list of staff details and then select **Data**, **Form**.

> **Note:** If you get an error message at this point saying that Excel cannot determine which row in your list contains labels, try deselecting the **Merge Cells** option for cell A1 and just left-align the text.

A data form will appear displaying the details of the first employee in the list.

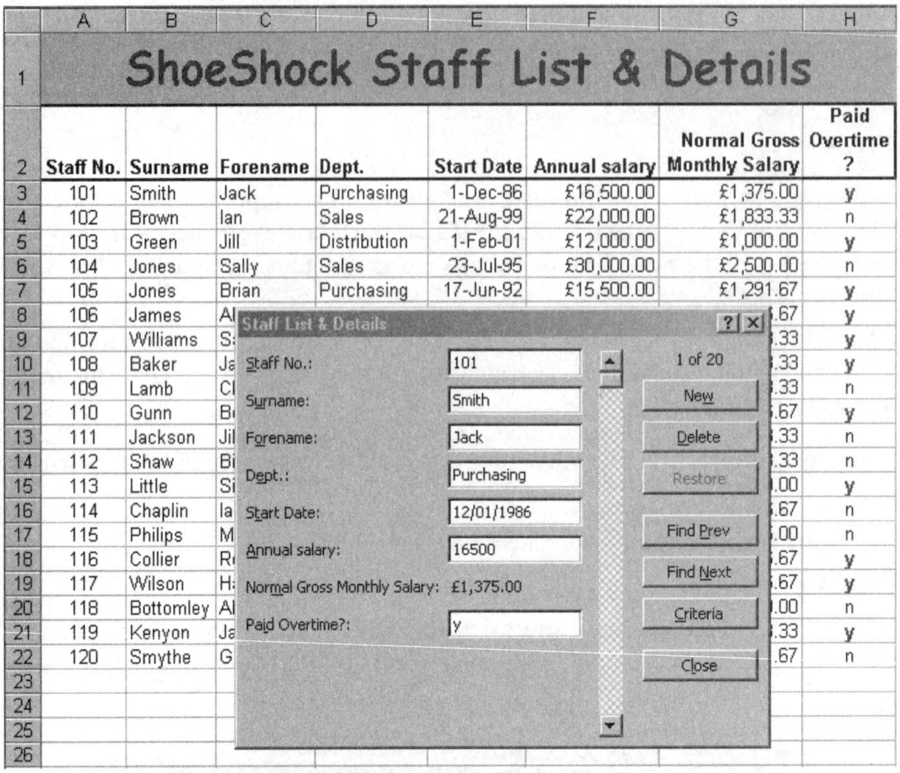

Figure 18.5: Displaying a data entry form

- To add a new employee click the **New** button and the fields will be cleared for you to enter the details of the new person.
- Enter the 2 new records shown below, pressing **Tab** between fields.
- When you have finished typing data, press **Enter** to add the record.
- When you have entered the data for the last record, click Close to add it and close the data form.

| 121 | Farrow | Helen | Purchasing | 22-May-01 | £17,450.00 | | y |
| 122 | Beasley | James | Sales | 22-May-01 | £24,750.00 | | n |

Note:	Fields that contain formulae display the results of the formula as a label (For example **Normal Gross Monthly Salary** in our form). The label cannot be changed in the data form.
	If you add a record that contains a formula, the formula is not calculated until you press **Enter** or click **Close** to add the record.
	While you are adding a record, you can undo changes if you click **Restore** before you press **Enter** or click **Close** to add the record.
	Microsoft Excel adds the record when you move to another record or close the data form.

To update a record in the employee list:

- Click anywhere in the Staff list details and then select **Data**, **Form**.
- To find the record you want to change you can use the **Find Previous** and **Find Next** buttons on the form. To move through records one at a time, use the scroll bar arrows in the dialog box. To move through 10 records at a time, click the scroll bar between the arrows. Also try entering some

criteria to search for a record. Click **Criteria** and enter *115* in the **Staff No.** field. Press **Enter** and the details for employee 115 will automatically be displayed.

- Change the information in the record – Marie Phillips has had a pay rise, change her salary to £24,500 pa.

- When you finish changing the data, press **Enter** to update the record and move to the next record.

- When you finish changing records, click **Close** to update the displayed record and close the data form.

To delete a record using the data form:

- Click a cell in the <u>list</u>.

- On the **Data** menu, click **Form**.

- Find the record you want to delete – James Kenyon has left the company so delete him by clicking **Delete**.

Note: When you delete a record by using a data form, you cannot undo the deletion. The record is permanently deleted.

18.4. Macros

A macro is a set of instructions used to automate a lengthy or frequently-repeated task. It is a program that tells Excel to perform a sequence of commands for you, accomplishing the task much more quickly than you could yourself.

There are two ways to create a macro. You can record the sequential instructions needed to perform a task just as you record music with a tape recorder. You then run the macro to play back the commands and perform the task. Alternatively, you can build the macro using Visual Basic for Applications (VBA) which you enter in a Visual Basic module in the workbook.

To make macros easy to use you can assign a macro to a key combination, to a button on a toolbar or to a command that appears on a menu.

We will record a macro that automatically brings up the data form for the Staff List details when you press **Ctrl-m** on the keyboard.

- Display the **Staff List & Details** worksheet on the screen.

- Select **Tools**, **Macro**, **Record New Macro**.

- Enter the name *EditStaffList*, the shortcut key and a description.

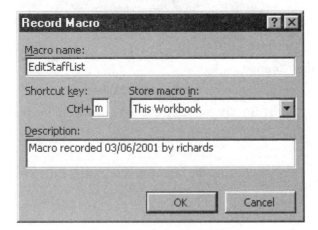

Figure 18.6: Naming a macro

- Click **OK**.

Whatever actions you perform will now be recorded and the Stop Recording toolbar is displayed.

- Click in cell A3.

- Select **Data**, **Form** and click the **Close** button on the form.

- Click the **Stop Recording** button on the Stop Recording toolbar (the button on the left).

- Now try your macro out by pressing **Ctrl-m**.

The data form should be displayed ready for you to edit the list.

Note:	If you get ### displayed on your data form for the Normal Gross Monthly Salary you will need to widen cell G2 so that the text is not wrapped. You may get a $ sign here too – another quirk of Excel!

18.5. Adding command buttons

If you are going to have several macros in a system it can be difficult to remember which key sequence activates which macro. Adding a labelled command button makes the system easier for people to use. We will develop the **Home** worksheet to incorporate buttons for different activities.

- Open the **Home** worksheet.

- Select the entire worksheet by clicking in the top left-hand corner (to the left of the column A header) and shade it in light grey.

- In cell A1 enter the company name *ShoeShock* in Comic Sans MS, 48pt, bold, red. In cell A2 enter the heading *Finance Department* and in A3 *Overtime Collection*, both in Comic Sans MS, 14pt, bold, black.

- Centre these headings across the screen.

- From the **View** menu, select **Toolbars**, **Forms**.

The Forms toolbar will be displayed.

Command button

Figure 18.7: The Forms toolbar

- Click the **Command button** icon.

- Mark out the position for the button on the **Home** worksheet.

- Assign the macro **EditStaffList**. (If you have clicked away from the button, right-click it and select **Assign Macro**.)

- Click **OK**.

- Edit the button name by right-clicking the button and selecting **Edit Text**. At the cursor type in **Edit Staff**.

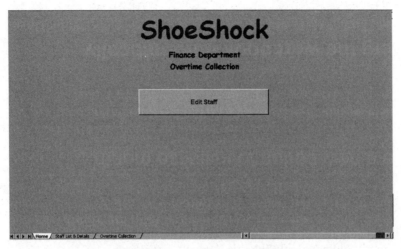

Figure 18.8: The Home worksheet

- Try out your new command button.

It either displays an error message or the wrong form! Can you see what is wrong? We have not told the macro to start on the **Staff List & Details** sheet.

We will edit the Visual Basic code to do this.

- Close the form that has been displayed.
- Select **Tools, Macro, Macros**.
- Click on the **EditStaffList** macro and then on the **Edit** button.
- The Visual Basic Editor will be displayed and you will see the code for your macro. Add the line *Sheets("Staff List& Details").Select* as shown below.
- Add the following line at the end:
  Sheets("Home").Select
  This will return you to the **Home** worksheet.

```
Sub EditStaffList()
'
' EditStaffList Macro
' Macro recorded 14/06/2001 by richards
'


'
    Sheets("Staff List & Details").Select
    Range("A3").Select
    ActiveSheet.ShowDataForm
    Sheets("Home").Select
End Sub
```

Figure 18.9: Editing Visual Basic code

- Close the Visual Basic Editor and try out your command button again – it should work correctly this time.

Task: Create a macro and a command button.

Now it's your turn – create a macro that moves the user to the **Overtime Collection** worksheet so that they can enter the overtime hours. Then create another button on the **Home** worksheet and assign your new macro to it. The Visual Basic code for your new macro should read something like Figure 18.10.

```
Sub Overtime()
'
' Overtime Macro
' Macro recorded 14/06/2001 by richards
'


'

    Sheets("Overtime Collection").Select
    Range("B3").Select



End Sub
```

Figure 18.10: The overtime macro

Your Home worksheet should now look like this:

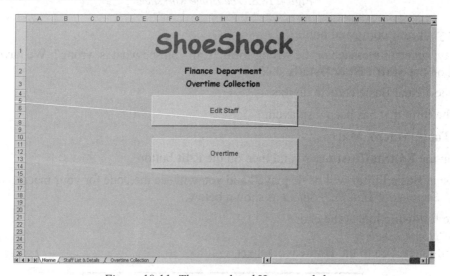

Figure 18.11: The completed Home worksheet

However there is a problem with the spreadsheet as we have developed it so far; if you add a new member of staff their details do not appear on the **Overtime Collection** worksheet. This can be fixed quite easily by filling down the rows in the **Overtime Collection** worksheet. In order to cater for a maximum number of 48 staff, it is necessary to copy all formulae down to row 50.

- Click the **Overtime Collection** worksheet tab.
- Highlight cells A3, C3 and D3.
- Use the AutoFill handle to fill these rows down to row 50.

Try the spreadsheet out again as follows:

- Return to the **Home** worksheet and try out the **Edit Staff** button again, adding a new employee whose details are as follows:

123	Kingsley	David	Accounts	25-May-01	£16,500.00		y

- You can now click the **Overtime** button to take you to the **Overtime Collection** worksheet, enter his overtime claim of *3* hours and tab out of the cell to see his overtime payment.

Chapter 19 – Creating Reports

Objectives

- ✓ To create a report from a worksheet
- ✓ To design an appropriate page layout for the report
- ✓ To use sorting and subtotalling for a summary report
- ✓ To create a macro which runs automatically on opening the workbook

19.1. Creating the monthly pay report

We now need to create a worksheet which lists and adds the normal basic salary and overtime pay for employees to arrive at a list of gross salaries for that particular month. This is the worksheet that will be printed as a report and sent to the Payroll Bureau.

- Open **ShoeShock.xls** and insert another worksheet by selecting **Insert, Worksheet**.
- Move the worksheet to after the **Overtime Collection** sheet by dragging the name tab.
- Double-click the name tab and rename the sheet *Gross Monthly Pay*.
- Type in the following headings (format them as shown):

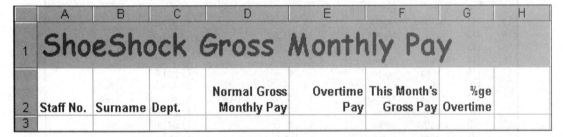

*Figure 19.1: The **Gross Monthly Pay** worksheet headings*

- In cell A3 enter the = sign, click in cell A3 of the **Staff List & Details** worksheet and press **Enter**.
- In the same way link cell B3 in the new worksheet to cell B3 on the **Staff List & Details** worksheet.
- Link cell C3 in the new worksheet to cell D3 on the **Staff List & Details** worksheet.
- Link cell D3 in the new worksheet to cell G3 on the **Staff List & Details** worksheet.
- Link cell E3 in the new worksheet to cell D3 on the **Overtime Collection** worksheet.
- In cell F3 enter a formula to add the **Overtime payment** to the **Normal Gross Monthly Salary**.

In order to cater for a maximum number of 48 staff, it is necessary to copy all formulae down to row 50.

- Fill cells A3 to F3 down to row 50.
- Highlight columns A to G and choose to suppress the display of zero values by selecting **Tools, Options** and deselecting zero values on the **View** tab.

- Centre column A and format columns D-F as currency.

- In cell **G3** enter a formula *=E3/F3* to calculate what percentage of this month's gross pay is overtime. Fill the formula down to cell G50.

- Format column G as percentage, 2 decimal places.

A problem arises because copying down the rows causes an error message to be displayed in column G. Excel knows you have copied a formula which will try to divide a number by zero. We can cure this by using an **IF** function in column G to test whether the cell in column F contains zero: if so then enter a zero otherwise the formula.

- On the **Gross Monthly Pay** worksheet click in cell G3 and edit the formula to read as follows: *=IF(F3=0,0,E3/F3)*

- Fill this down to G50.

If you managed to keep a clear head and follow all that, your last worksheet should now be looking something like this:

	A	B	C	D	E	F	G	H
1	ShoeShock Gross Monthly Pay							
2	Staff No.	Surname	Dept.	Normal Gross Monthly Pay	Overtime Pay	This Month's Gross Pay	%ge Overtime	
3	101	Smith	Purchasing	£1,375.00	£71.39	£1,446.39	4.94%	
4	102	Brown	Sales	£1,833.33		£1,833.33		
5	103	Green	Distribution	£1,000.00	£25.96	£1,025.96	2.53%	
6	104	Jones	Sales	£2,500.00		£2,500.00		
7	105	Jones	Purchasing	£1,291.67		£1,291.67		
8	106	James	Purchasing	£1,166.67		£1,166.67		
9	107	Williams	Accounts	£1,083.33		£1,083.33		
10	108	Baker	Purchasing	£1,083.33	£37.50	£1,120.83	3.35%	
11	109	Lamb	Sales	£1,833.33		£1,833.33		
12	110	Gunn	Purchasing	£1,166.67	£60.58	£1,227.24	4.94%	
13	111	Jackson	Mgmnt	£1,333.33		£1,333.33		
14	112	Shaw	Mgmnt	£3,333.33		£3,333.33		
15	113	Little	Purchasing	£1,500.00	£90.87	£1,590.87	5.71%	
16	114	Chaplin	Mgmnt	£2,916.67		£2,916.67		
17	115	Philips	Sales	£2,041.67		£2,041.67		
18	116	Collier	Distribution	£1,166.67	£10.10	£1,176.76	0.86%	
19	117	Wilson	Accounts	£1,416.67	£49.04	£1,465.71	3.35%	
20	118	Bottomley	Sales	£1,750.00		£1,750.00		
21	120	Smythe	Sales	£1,041.67		£1,041.67		
22	121	Farrow	Purchasing	£1,454.17		£1,454.17		
23	122	Beasley	Sales	£2,062.50		£2,062.50		
24	123	Kingsley	Accounts	£1,375.00	£35.70	£1,410.70	2.53%	
25								

Figure 19.2: The completed Gross Monthly Pay worksheet

19.2. Page Layout

Although this is basically an electronic system, parts of it sometimes need to be printed. For example, the **Gross Monthly Pay** worksheet is either e-mailed or sent through the post to the Payroll Bureau. ShoeShock management is sent regular printouts from the system so that they can monitor the overall expenditure on overtime over a period of time. This means that the printed presentation of the worksheets is just as important as the screen presentation.

The **Page Setup** option in the Excel **File** menu allows you to set options to determine the way in which a particular worksheet will be printed.

- Select **File, Page Setup** and have a look at the different options available.
- Click the **Page** tab.

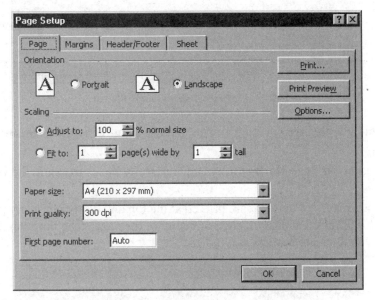

Figure 19.3: Setting page options

- ❑ **Orientation** gives you either tall, narrow pages (portrait) or pages printed sideways (landscape).
- ❑ **Scaling** is either a fixed percentage (e.g. 25% to reduce everything to quarter size) or the largest possible for the sheets to fit the page. To achieve the best-fit scaling you should choose the number of pages to be printed.
- ❑ **Paper size** allows you to choose from a range of standard paper sizes.
- ❑ **Print quality** is available only for certain types of printer so generally do not bother with this setting.
- ❑ **First page number** determines the page number for the first page – Auto defaults to 1.

- Set the orientation of the **Staff List & Details** worksheet in the ShoeShock system to landscape orientation. Click the **Print Preview** button in either the dialogue box or on the Standard toolbar to see what it will look like.

The next tab in the **Page Setup** dialogue box allows you to set margins (i.e. the blank space at the top, bottom and sides of the worksheets).

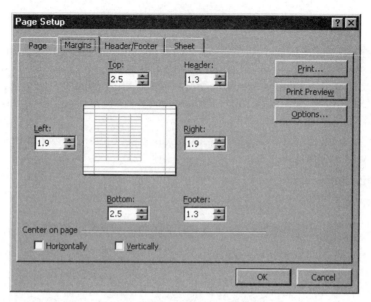

Figure 19.4: Setting margins

- Try experimenting with different margin sizes and use **Print Preview** to see the effect of your changes.

- Click in the **Center on Page Horizontally** and **Vertically** boxes to centre the worksheets on the page.

Headers and footers are pieces of text that are printed at the top and bottom of every page. They both have three sections: for printing on the left, right or centre of the page. The third tab on the Page Setup dialogue box allows you to create headers and footers.

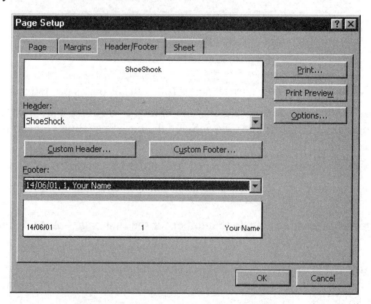

Figure 19.5: Inserting a header and footer

- Create a header and footer for your ShoeShock worksheets as shown above. The header is selected from the drop-down list. Click on **Custom Footer** and choose to insert the date in the left-hand section and the page number in the middle section. Put your name in the right-hand section. Check out the settings in **Print Preview**.

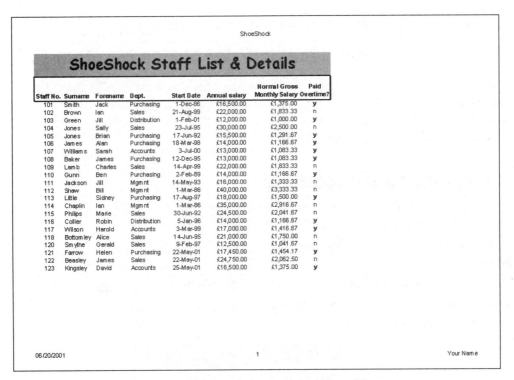

ShoeShock

Staff No.	Surname	Forename	Dept.	Start Date	Annual salary	Normal Gross Monthly Salary	Paid Overtime?
101	Smith	Jack	Purchasing	1-Dec-86	£16,500.00	£1,375.00	y
102	Brown	Ian	Sales	21-Aug-99	£22,000.00	£1,833.33	n
103	Green	Jill	Distribution	1-Feb-01	£12,000.00	£1,000.00	y
104	Jones	Sally	Sales	23-Jul-95	£30,000.00	£2,500.00	n
105	Jones	Brian	Purchasing	17-Jun-92	£15,500.00	£1,291.67	y
106	James	Alan	Purchasing	18-Mar-98	£14,000.00	£1,166.67	y
107	Williams	Sarah	Accounts	3-Jul-00	£13,000.00	£1,083.33	y
108	Baker	James	Purchasing	12-Dec-95	£13,000.00	£1,083.33	y
109	Lamb	Charles	Sales	14-Apr-99	£22,000.00	£1,833.33	n
110	Gunn	Ben	Purchasing	2-Feb-89	£14,000.00	£1,166.67	y
111	Jackson	Jill	Mgmnt	14-May-93	£16,000.00	£1,333.33	n
112	Shaw	Bill	Mgmnt	1-Mar-86	£40,000.00	£3,333.33	n
113	Little	Sidney	Purchasing	17-Aug-97	£18,000.00	£1,500.00	y
114	Chaplin	Ian	Mgmnt	1-Mar-86	£35,000.00	£2,916.67	n
115	Philips	Marie	Sales	30-Jun-92	£24,500.00	£2,041.67	n
116	Collier	Robin	Distribution	5-Jan-96	£14,000.00	£1,166.67	y
117	Wilson	Harold	Accounts	3-Mar-99	£17,000.00	£1,416.67	y
118	Bottomley	Alice	Sales	14-Jun-95	£21,000.00	£1,750.00	n
120	Smythe	Gerald	Sales	9-Feb-97	£12,500.00	£1,041.67	n
121	Farrow	Helen	Purchasing	22-May-01	£17,450.00	£1,454.17	y
122	Beasley	James	Sales	22-May-01	£24,750.00	£2,062.50	n
123	Kingsley	David	Accounts	25-May-01	£16,500.00	£1,375.00	y

06/20/2001   1   Your Name

Figure 19.6: The worksheet with header and footer

The final tab on the Page Setup dialogue box allows you to set up options for the way in which the worksheet will be printed.

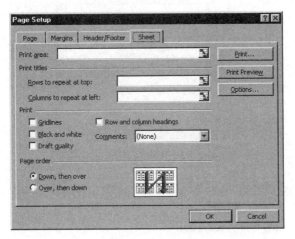

Figure 19.7: Setting print options

- ❑ The **Print Area** is the default range of cells to be printed.
- ❑ **Print Titles** are rows and columns that are to be repeated on every page of a worksheet (for large sheets that will not fit on one page).
- ❑ **Print options** allow you to specify which optional features will be printed.
- ❑ **Page order** is for when you are working with large worksheets that will not fit on one page and specifies how the printing should be done.

- • Try setting the print area to print just the first three columns of the **Staff List & Details** worksheet. Also select to print gridlines. Don't actually print it, just look at the effects in **Print Preview**.

- Set the print area A1 to G50 on the **Gross Monthly Pay** worksheet.

Task: Create a command button **Print Gross Monthly Pay**.

First you need to create a macro that shows the **Gross Monthly Pay** worksheet in **Print Preview** mode. Then on the **Home** worksheet, create a command button which runs the macro. It will save a lot of paper to use Print Preview while testing and the user may prefer it too – they can press the **Print** button when they have done a visual check to confirm that everything is correct.

19.3. Sorting and subtotalling

Amongst the requirements that ShoeShock management specified at the design stage was the ability to find totals of overtime pay and gross monthly pay for each department.

To do this we need to sort the **Gross Monthly Pay** worksheet by department and then create subtotals for each department.

- Copy the **Gross Monthly Pay** worksheet by selecting **Edit, Move or Copy Sheet**.

- In the dialogue box check the **Create a copy** box and select the options to have the new sheet at the end of **ShoeShock.xls** as shown below.

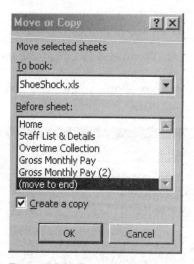

Figure 19.8: Copying a worksheet

- Rename this sheet *Department Summary*. Change the main heading to read *ShoeShock Department Summary*.

- On the new worksheet highlight A2:G24.

- Select **Data, Sort** and choose to sort on **Dept**. Click **OK**.

Note: The data must be sorted into the correct order (in this case Department order) before you create subtotals.

- Select **Data, Subtotals** and enter the details below.

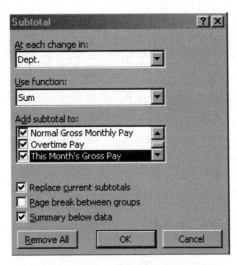

Figure 19.9: Creating subtotals

The worksheet should now display subtotals for overtime and gross monthly pay for each department.

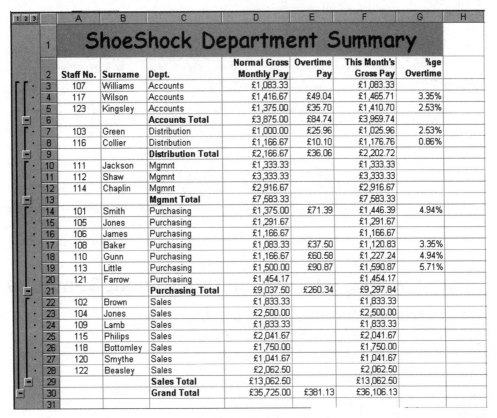

	Staff No.	Surname	Dept.	Normal Gross Monthly Pay	Overtime Pay	This Month's Gross Pay	%ge Overtime
107	Williams	Accounts	£1,083.33		£1,083.33	
117	Wilson	Accounts	£1,416.67	£49.04	£1,465.71	3.35%
123	Kingsley	Accounts	£1,375.00	£35.70	£1,410.70	2.53%
		Accounts Total	£3,875.00	£84.74	£3,959.74	
103	Green	Distribution	£1,000.00	£25.96	£1,025.96	2.53%
116	Collier	Distribution	£1,166.67	£10.10	£1,176.76	0.86%
		Distribution Total	£2,166.67	£36.06	£2,202.72	
111	Jackson	Mgmnt	£1,333.33		£1,333.33	
112	Shaw	Mgmnt	£3,333.33		£3,333.33	
114	Chaplin	Mgmnt	£2,916.67		£2,916.67	
		Mgmnt Total	£7,583.33		£7,583.33	
101	Smith	Purchasing	£1,375.00	£71.39	£1,446.39	4.94%
105	Jones	Purchasing	£1,291.67		£1,291.67	
106	James	Purchasing	£1,166.67		£1,166.67	
108	Baker	Purchasing	£1,083.33	£37.50	£1,120.83	3.35%
110	Gunn	Purchasing	£1,166.67	£60.58	£1,227.24	4.94%
113	Little	Purchasing	£1,500.00	£90.87	£1,590.87	5.71%
121	Farrow	Purchasing	£1,454.17		£1,454.17	
		Purchasing Total	£9,037.50	£260.34	£9,297.84	
102	Brown	Sales	£1,833.33		£1,833.33	
104	Jones	Sales	£2,500.00		£2,500.00	
109	Lamb	Sales	£1,833.33		£1,833.33	
115	Philips	Sales	£2,041.67		£2,041.67	
118	Bottomley	Sales	£1,750.00		£1,750.00	
120	Smythe	Sales	£1,041.67		£1,041.67	
122	Beasley	Sales	£2,062.50		£2,062.50	
		Sales Total	£13,062.50		£13,062.50	
		Grand Total	£35,725.00	£381.13	£36,106.13	

Figure 19.10: Subtotals

- Click the small 2 to the left of the column headers. This will display just the totals.

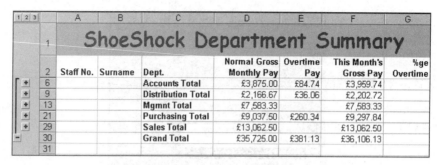

1 2 3		A	B	C	D	E	F	G
	1			*ShoeShock Department Summary*				
	2	Staff No.	Surname	Dept.	Normal Gross Monthly Pay	Overtime Pay	This Month's Gross Pay	%ge Overtime
+	6			Accounts Total	£3,875.00	£84.74	£3,959.74	
+	9			Distribution Total	£2,166.67	£36.06	£2,202.72	
+	13			Mgmnt Total	£7,583.33		£7,583.33	
+	21			Purchasing Total	£9,037.50	£260.34	£9,297.84	
+	29			Sales Total	£13,062.50		£13,062.50	
-	30			Grand Total	£35,725.00	£381.13	£36,106.13	
	31							

Figure 19.11: The summary management report

You should test your procedures as you go. What happens, for example, if:

❏ Jack Smith's salary increases to £20,000? Does the Management Summary automatically update the totals? (It should do.)

❏ Another employee Greg Grey, Staff No.124 joins the Purchasing Department on 1st June at an annual salary of £20,000. Does the Management Summary update correctly?

You will find that in fact it does not. The management summary will look like this:

1 2 3		A	B	C	D	E	F	G
	1			*ShoeShock Department Summary*				
	2	Staff No.	Surname	Dept.	Normal Gross Monthly Pay	Overtime Pay	This Month's Gross Pay	%ge Overtime
+	6			Accounts Total	£3,875.00	£84.74	£3,959.74	
+	9			Distribution Total	£2,166.67	£36.06	£2,202.72	
+	13			Mgmnt Total	£7,583.33		£7,583.33	
+	21			Purchasing Total	£9,329.17	£275.48	£9,604.65	
+	29			Sales Total	£13,062.50		£13,062.50	
-	30			Grand Total	£36,016.67	£396.27	£36,412.94	
	31	124	Grey	Purchasing	£1,666.67		£1,666.67	
	32							

Figure 19.12: A new employee has been added

The list needs to be resorted, taking into account the new employee. The subtotals will be correctly recalculated. Unless you use Visual Basic programming, you will have to get the user to sort the data and create the subtotals on this sheet manually whenever a new employee joins, which will probably be rarely.

19.4. Creating a macro to update Department Summary

Record the following steps as a macro.

- Select **Tools**, **Macro**, **Record New Macro**.
- Type the name *ManagementSummary* and click **OK**.
- Go to the **Department Summary** worksheet.
- Highlight cells A2 to G50.
- Select **Data**, **Subtotals** and click on the **Remove All** button to remove all subtotals.
- Go to the **Gross Monthly Pay** worksheet.
- Highlight cells A3 to G50 and copy these cells.
- Go back to the **Department Summary** worksheet.
- Click in cell A3 and paste the cells.
- Click in cell A2.
- Click the **Stop Recording** button.

- Assign this macro to a command button called **Print Management Summary** on the **Home** worksheet menu.

19.5. Create a routine to print the Management Summary

Before you do this, add a header or a footer giving the current date, which needs to be printed on the report. Do a **Print Preview** to make sure the report will print as you want it and make any necessary adjustments.

The user will have to select the correct range on the **Department Summary** worksheet. We will place a message telling the user to do this.

- Merge and centre cells I2 to K2. Colour them pale blue.
- Enter the text *Please select the range to be sorted, starting in A2, and then click the button below to print the summary.*
- Select **Format**, **Cells**, click the **Alignment** tab and select **Wrap text**.

Now you should highlight the range A2 to G25 as if you were the user. A new macro now needs to be recorded that sorts the data by department, creates the subtotals and displays the summary totals in **Print Preview**. This will be assigned to another command button called **Print Summary** on the **Department Summary** worksheet, we will create this button first.

- Create a large command button covering cells I5 to K25 (you will see later why it has to be this big). Name it *Print Summary*.

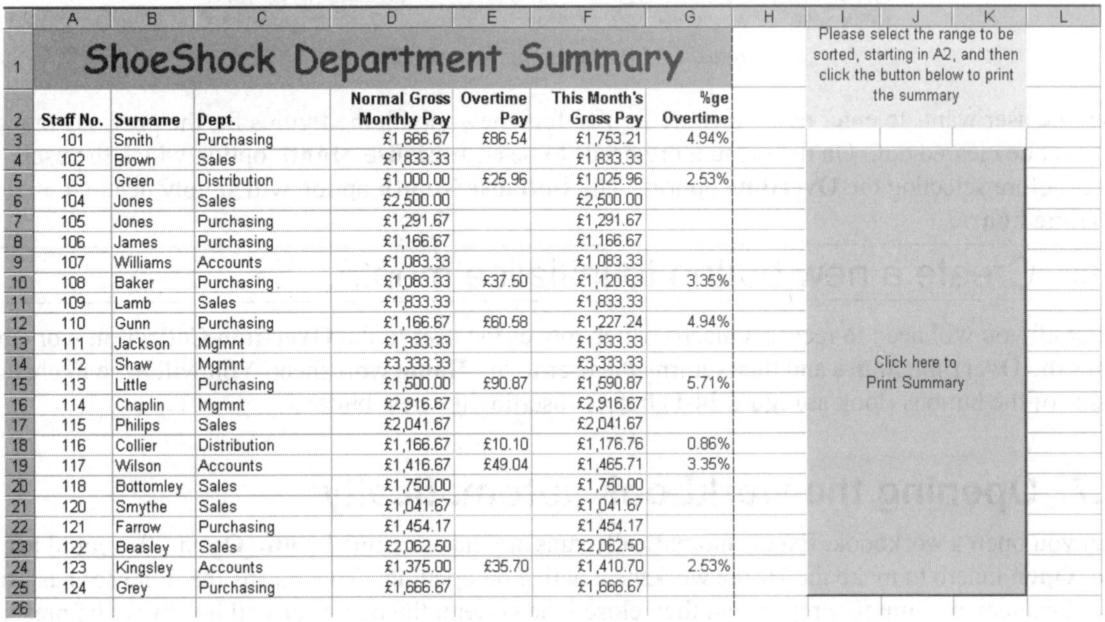

ShoeShock Department Summary

Staff No.	Surname	Dept.	Normal Gross Monthly Pay	Overtime Pay	This Month's Gross Pay	%ge Overtime
101	Smith	Purchasing	£1,666.67	£86.54	£1,753.21	4.94%
102	Brown	Sales	£1,833.33		£1,833.33	
103	Green	Distribution	£1,000.00	£25.96	£1,025.96	2.53%
104	Jones	Sales	£2,500.00		£2,500.00	
105	Jones	Purchasing	£1,291.67		£1,291.67	
106	James	Purchasing	£1,166.67		£1,166.67	
107	Williams	Accounts	£1,083.33		£1,083.33	
108	Baker	Purchasing	£1,083.33	£37.50	£1,120.83	3.35%
109	Lamb	Sales	£1,833.33		£1,833.33	
110	Gunn	Purchasing	£1,166.67	£60.58	£1,227.24	4.94%
111	Jackson	Mgmnt	£1,333.33		£1,333.33	
112	Shaw	Mgmnt	£3,333.33		£3,333.33	
113	Little	Purchasing	£1,500.00	£90.87	£1,590.87	5.71%
114	Chaplin	Mgmnt	£2,916.67		£2,916.67	
115	Philips	Sales	£2,041.67		£2,041.67	
116	Collier	Distribution	£1,166.67	£10.10	£1,176.76	0.86%
117	Wilson	Accounts	£1,416.67	£49.04	£1,465.71	3.35%
118	Bottomley	Sales	£1,750.00		£1,750.00	
120	Smythe	Sales	£1,041.67		£1,041.67	
121	Farrow	Purchasing	£1,454.17		£1,454.17	
122	Beasley	Sales	£2,062.50		£2,062.50	
123	Kingsley	Accounts	£1,375.00	£35.70	£1,410.70	2.53%
124	Grey	Purchasing	£1,666.67		£1,666.67	

Figure 19.13: The Print Summary button

Now record the macro.

- Select **Tools**, **Macro**, **Record New Macro**.
- Type the name *PrintSummary* and click **OK**.
- Select **Data**, **Sort**. Check that **Dept.** is selected as the sort field and click **OK**.
- Select **Data**, **Subtotals**. Check that **Gross Monthly Pay**, **Overtime Pay** and **This month's Gross Pay** are selected and click **OK**.

- Click the small **2** to the left of the column headers to display only the summary totals.
- Click the **Print Preview** button.
- Close the **Print Preview**.
- Click the **Stop Recording** button.
- Assign this macro to the **Print Summary** command button.

19.6. Initialising for a new month

At this point the menu looks like this:

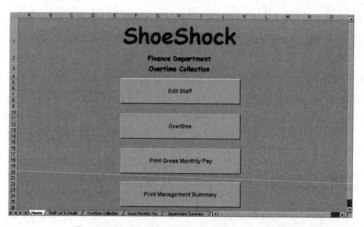

Figure 19.14: The Home worksheet menu

When the user wants to enter new overtime figures for a new month the figures for the previous month must first be cleared out. On the menu there needs to be an **Initialise Month** option which the user selects before selecting the **Overtime** option. The **Initialise Month** option will simply delete the **Overtime hours**.

Task: Create a new button to initialise month.

First of all you will need to record a macro which moves the user to the **Overtime Collection** worksheet, deletes the **Overtime hours** and then returns the user to the **Home** worksheet. You will have to change the size of the buttons (look at Figure 24.1) before inserting the new button.

19.7. Opening the workbook automatically

When you open a workbook, Excel automatically runs any macro named **Auto_Open**. We could use an **Auto_Open** macro to make the **Home** worksheet active on opening. This means that if a user has printed off a Management Summary report and then closed the system, the next user will be always be presented with the **Home** worksheet whenever they reopen the file.

- Select **Tools**, **Macro**, **Record New Macro**.
- Name the new macro *Auto_Open*.
- When the Stop Recording toolbar appears, click the **Home** worksheet tab and then click **Stop Recording**.
- Click on the **Department Summary** tab and close the workbook.
- Reopen the file and you should be presented with the **Home** worksheet.

Chapter 20 – Graphs and Charts

Objectives

✓ To present spreadsheet results in graphical form

✓ To use built-in drawing tools to improve presentation

20.1. Creating a bar chart

Managers love graphs and charts for their notice boards or to use in impressive presentations to the Board! They can also be extremely useful as they often make pages of data easier to understand and can show a trend or be used to forecast figures into the future.

Excel has excellent tools for creating many different types of chart which can be either embedded in an existing worksheet or placed in a separate chart sheet. Once a chart has been created, any aspect of it can be easily modified.

A chart is created using the Chart Wizard, which offers 14 different types of chart falling into three broad categories:

❑ Bar and column charts which have a rectangular bar for each item of data – the height of which is proportional to the data value.

❑ Graphs which plot a series of points usually joined together by a line.

❑ Pie charts which consist of a circle divided into segments. Each item of data is calculated as a percentage of the total and represented by one of the segments.

We will produce some charts for the ShoeShock management team.

As a future enhancement to the system, the Finance department might also want to keep a summary of gross monthly salary details so that management can keep track of how much overtime is being worked throughout the year (this does not form part of the Overtime Collection system).

- Create a new workbook called *Annual Summary*.

- Enter the following headings and data (remember to use the **AutoFill** handle to speed things up – try it on the months).

	A	B	C	D	E	F	G	H	I	J	K	L	M
1					ShoeShock Annual Overtime Summary 2000								
2		January	February	March	April	May	June	July	August	September	October	November	December
3													
4	Total normal monthly pay	£32,833.33	£32,833.33	£32,833.33	£32,833.33	£34,475.00	£34,475.00	£34,475.00	£34,475.00	£24,265.00	£24,265.00	£24,265.00	£24,265.00
5													
6	Total monthly overtime pay	£413.89	£400.56	£589.67	£568.45	£576.34	£403.23	£401.12	£245.89	£189.67	£345.89	£333.78	£356.78
7													
8	Overtime as a %ge of gross pay												

Figure 20.1: The annual summary

We will create a column chart to show the total normal monthly pay.

- Highlight cells A2 to M4.
- Click on the **Chart Wizard** button.

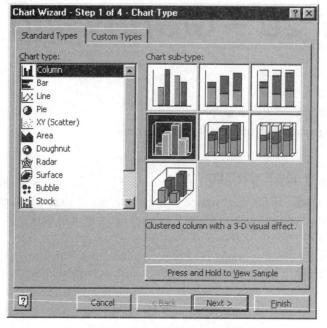

Figure 20.2: Step 1 of the chart wizard

- Choose a chart type and subtype. In the figure above a **clustered column with a 3-D visual effect** has been chosen.
- Click **Next**.

You are presented with a preview of the chart.

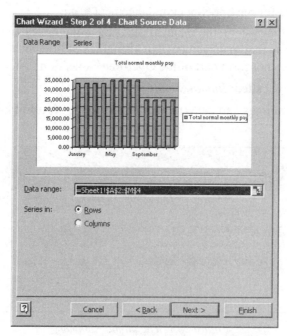

Figure 20.3: A first preview of the chart

- Click **Next**.
- In step 3 of the chart wizard enter some titles as shown below.
- Click the **Legend** tab and deselect the option to display it.

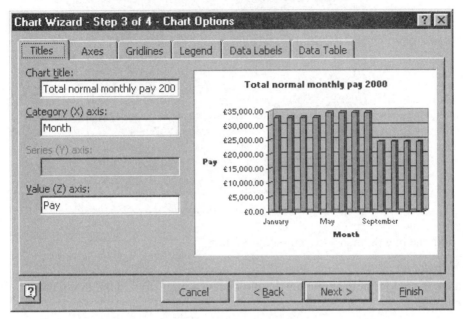

Figure 20.4: Inserting titles

- Click **Next**.
- In step 4 choose to place the chart as a new sheet.

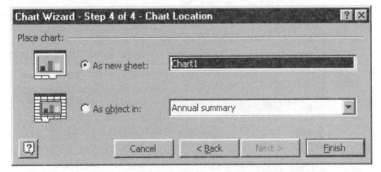

Figure 20.5: Placing the chart as a new sheet

- Click **Finish**.

The chart will appear in a new worksheet called **Chart1**.

20.2. Formatting the bar chart

You will probably find that the chart does not have space to display the months in full. We will change the alignment of these labels so that they can all be seen.

- Double-click on one of the months.
- In the dialogue box that appears click the **Alignment** tab.

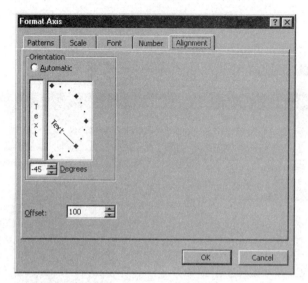

Figure 20.6: Changing the alignment of axis labels

- Either drag the line or enter -45 in the degrees box.
- Click **OK**.
- To change the colour of the columns double-click a column and in the dialogue box click the **Patterns** tab.

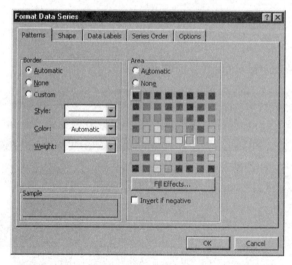

Figure 20.7: Changing the colour of the columns

- Select a different colour and click **OK**.

You will see that you can also change the border style and use special **Fill Effects**. Take some time to try out some of these options.

The **Shape** tab on this dialogue box is also quite good fun allowing you to change the columns to pyramids and cones!

Data labels can be useful if you find it difficult to read values off the chart. These display the values at the top of the columns within the chart.

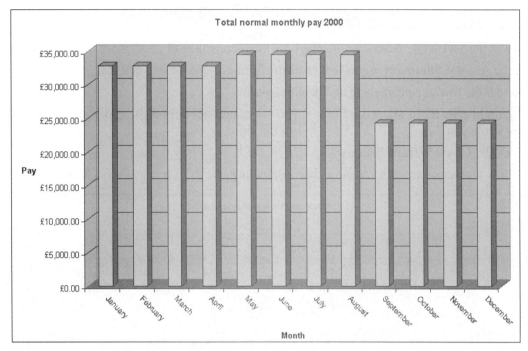

Figure 20.8: The chart so far

20.3. Using drawing tools

There appears to have been a marked reduction in the monthly salary bill from September onwards. This is because several members of staff left the company. We can use the Drawing toolbar in Excel to add lines and text to a worksheet to add comments to explain details such as this.

- Display the Drawing toolbar by selecting **View**, **Toolbars**, **Drawing**.
- Click the **Arrow** tool and draw an arrow pointing to the September column.
- Use the **Text Box** tool to draw a text box above the arrow and enter the text as shown below.

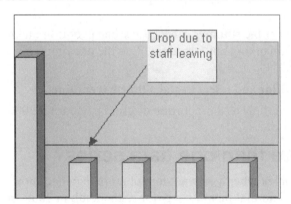

Figure 20.9: Using the drawing tools

- The arrow and text box can be grouped as one object that can be moved or sized. Press the **Shift** key as you select both items, then right-click and select **Grouping**, **Group**.

20.4. Creating a line chart

Now we will produce a line chart to show overtime as a percentage of gross pay.

- In the **Annual Summary** worksheet enter the formula *=B6/B4* into cell B8.
- Format the row as a percentage to 2 decimal places.
- Highlight cells B2 to M2 and B8 to M8. (To select non-adjacent cells hold your finger on the **Ctrl** key while you drag.)
- Click the **Chart Wizard** button.
- Follow the steps through to create a chart something like this on worksheet **Chart2**.

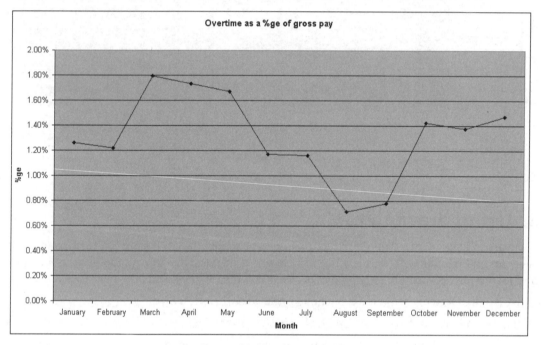

Figure 20.10: A line chart

- The dip in the line chart over the summer is because when people are taking summer holidays they are still being paid but not working any overtime. Use the drawing tools to insert a comment on the worksheet to explain this.
- Select **Chart**, **Add Trendline** and select to add a **linear trendline**.

What was the general trend in overtime as a proportion of gross pay during 2000?

20.5. Charting more than one data series

Charts can get a little more complex when you want to plot more than one series of data. For example suppose we want to plot the total normal monthly pay for each month in 2000 and compare those with the figures for 1999. The X-axis will be the months of the year but we will have two Y-series, one for 1999 and one for 2000.

- Try plotting this type of chart. You will have to modify your worksheet first as follows:

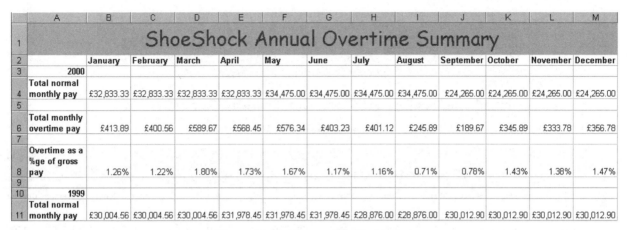

	A	January	February	March	April	May	June	July	August	September	October	November	December
1					**ShoeShock Annual Overtime Summary**								
2		January	February	March	April	May	June	July	August	September	October	November	December
3	2000												
4	Total normal monthly pay	£32,833.33	£32,833.33	£32,833.33	£32,833.33	£34,475.00	£34,475.00	£34,475.00	£34,475.00	£24,265.00	£24,265.00	£24,265.00	£24,265.00
5													
6	Total monthly overtime pay	£413.89	£400.56	£589.67	£568.45	£576.34	£403.23	£401.12	£245.89	£189.67	£345.89	£333.78	£356.78
7													
8	Overtime as a %ge of gross pay	1.26%	1.22%	1.80%	1.73%	1.67%	1.17%	1.16%	0.71%	0.78%	1.43%	1.38%	1.47%
9													
10	1999												
11	Total normal monthly pay	£30,004.56	£30,004.56	£30,004.56	£31,978.45	£31,978.45	£31,978.45	£28,876.00	£28,876.00	£30,012.90	£30,012.90	£30,012.90	£30,012.90

Figure 20.11: The modified worksheet

- Highlight cells B2 to M2, B4 to M4 and cells B11 to M11.
- Click the **Chart Wizard** button and choose to create a column chart.
- In Step 2 click the **Series** tab and name the series *2000* and *1999* so that the legend is labelled correctly, as shown below.

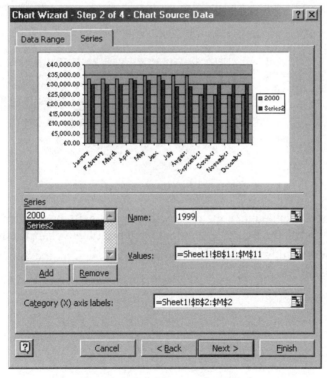

Figure 20.12: Naming the series

The series that we wish to plot have been identified correctly. If, however, you wanted to change the data range that has been selected it is at this point that you have the opportunity to do so. First click the **Data Range** tab. Then either mark the range by dragging the pointer on the worksheet, or edit the range in the dialogue box. To mark a new range, click the icon on the right of the data range. The Chart Wizard will be reduced to a small box allowing you to mark the data range. Click the icon again to return to the dialogue box. (See Figure 20.13.)

Figure 20.13: Editing a data range

- Insert suitable titles and headings and edit the chart format as you wish.
- This time try placing the chart on the **Annual Summary** worksheet.

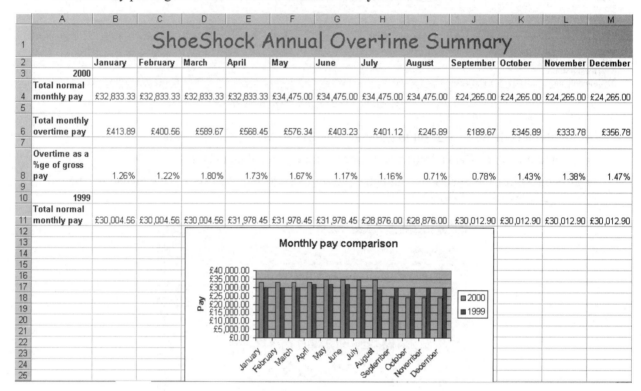

Figure 20.14: An embedded chart

If the data on the worksheet is edited then the chart will automatically be updated. The ShoeShock Finance department will update the figures each month and print out a chart for the management team.

What general points about monthly pay over the two years do you think the ShoeShock management might deduce from this chart?

Chapter 21 – Completing the Application

Objectives

- ✓ To protect workbooks and worksheets
- ✓ To create templates
- ✓ To evaluate your work
- ✓ To consider testing procedures

21.1. Protecting spreadsheet data

It is important that a system such as the ShoeShock overtime system is secure with no unauthorised access allowed. In Excel there are several ways to restrict how users can access, view or change data in workbooks or worksheets. One way is to assign a password that a user must enter in order to open or save a workbook. A password can contain any combination of characters and spaces and it is case-sensitive so *rex* is a different password from *Rex*. Make a note of any password you set up – if you lose it you will not be able to open a password-protected workbook. For this reason it is a good idea to assign a password to a copy of your current workbook.

- Open **ShoeShock.xls**.
- On the **File** menu click **Save As**.
- Locate the folder you wish to save in and in the **File Name** box type *ShoeShockPW*.
- In the Save As dialogue box, click the **Tools** button and then click **General Options**.

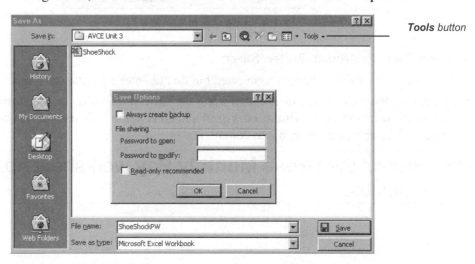

Figure 21.1: Password protecting a workbook

- In the **Password to open** box type a password *abcd* and click **OK**.

- A Confirm Password dialogue box will appear in which you should re-enter your password. Click **OK**.

- In the Save as dialogue box click **Save**.

ShoeShockPW.xls is now password protected. Try closing and reopening it.

> **Note:** You can also password-protect a workbook or individual worksheets from the **Tools**, **Protection** command.

In the case of the ShoeShock system it would also be a good idea to protect certain cells so that they are not accidentally overwritten. All cells that contain headings or formulae should be protected. To do this, you first have to unlock all the cells that users can enter data in, and then protect the whole worksheet. Protect cells on the **Overtime Collection** worksheet as follows:

- Return to **ShoeShock.xls** and display the **Overtime Collection** worksheet on your screen.

- Highlight cells B3:B50.

- Select **Format**, **Cells** and click the **Protection** tab.

- Deselect the **Locked** check box and click **OK**.

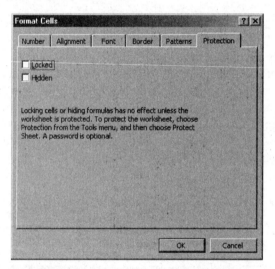

Figure 21.2: Protecting cells

- Select **Tools**, **Protection**, **Protect Sheet**.

- Make sure all the check boxes are selected but do not enter a password. Click **OK**.

Test this out by adding a new member of staff using the **Edit Staff** button on the **Home** worksheet. Then click the **Overtime** button on the **Home** worksheet and enter some overtime for this new member of staff. You should only be able to enter data into column B.

Task: Protect the **Gross Monthly Pay** worksheet from accidental changes.

21.2. Templates

When you have created a workbook that will be used over and over again with different data each time, it is a good idea to save the basic structure as a template. The ShoeShock system does not need a template as each month they need to use the previous month's data. However, a template may be used to set up the system in the first instance. Templates are an advanced feature you may like to include in your own project.

- Make a copy of **ShoeShock.xls** called *ShoeShocktemplate.xls*.
- Delete the data from the columns in the **Staff List & Details** worksheet (row 3 downwards).
- In cell G3 re-enter the formula *=F3/12* and fill down to cell G50. Zero values will be displayed down the column.

Look at the **Overtime Collection** worksheet and the **Gross Monthly Pay** worksheet. All the data will have disappeared, but the formulae will still be there.

- Select **File**, **Save As**.
- In the **Save As Type** box, select **Template (*.xlt)**. The default folder automatically changes to the **Templates** folder. Click **Save**.
- Close the template.

To use the template select **File**, **New** and select the **ShoeShocktemplate** template instead of the general Workbook template which simply contains 3 empty sheets.

Note:	If you are working on a school or college network you may have problems with this as you may not be able to save anything to the Templates folder. The easiest way around this is probably to change the destination drive or save the template onto a floppy disk.
	If you were not able to save the template in the standard Templates folder you will encounter a problem when you come to use it – you are not given the option to use a template stored in any other folder. So, if for example you have saved the template on a floppy disk, try the following method:
	Minimise any documents and applications that you have running and return to the desktop.
	From the desktop double-click on **My Computer**.
	Double-click on **A**:
	Right-click on **ShoeShocktemplate.xlt** and select **New**.
	A new worksheet based on the template will appear on your screen.

21.3. Evaluating your application

When you get to this stage it is a good idea to sit back and consider the application as a whole. Have you met the first part of the assessment specification given in Appendix D – i.e. does your spreadsheet solution meet specified user requirements and does it use at least six of the more complex spreadsheet facilities? The sample project we have just developed appears to meet the requirements of the ShoeShock Finance Department as given in the System Specification. Examples of 'complex spreadsheet facilities' are given in the complete unit specification. We have used the following complex facilities:

- ❏ Named cells for use in formulae
- ❏ Auto-fill lists
- ❏ Data validation
- ❏ Protecting cells
- ❏ Data forms
- ❏ Macros

- ❑ Command buttons
- ❑ Templates
- ❑ Linked worksheets
- ❑ Sorting and subtotals

In your technical documentation you will be describing the use of these complex facilities. You must also specify any limitations of the system that you have identified. For example in the ShoeShock system we have catered for only 48 members of staff (this could easily be increased if necessary).

21.4. Testing

Your Design Specification should detail a test plan. Your testing must be thorough – remember you are actually trying to make your system fail. If you are hoping to achieve a good mark for this unit it is important that you include comprehensive records of testing. These can be included in the Technical Documentation, as you will see in Chapter 23. As you describe the test results you can show how the spreadsheet was refined and developed and how problems were resolved. The following two sections describe some facilities that will help you with your records of testing.

21.5. The Auditing toolbar

Microsoft Excel provides tools that help you track down problems on your worksheets. For example, the value you see in a cell may be the result of a formula, or it may be used by a formula that produces an incorrect result. The auditing tools graphically display, or trace, the relationships between cells and formulas with tracer arrows. These tools are found on the Auditing toolbar. This is not on the shortlist of toolbars that is available from the **View** menu: instead select **Tools**, **Auditing**, **Show Auditing toolbar**.

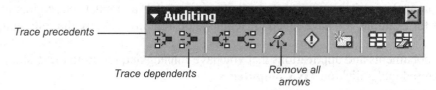

Figure 21.1: The Auditing toolbar

When you audit a worksheet, you can trace the precedents (the cells that provide data to a specific cell) or you can trace the dependents (the cells that depend on the value in a specific cell).

- Display the **Gross Monthly Pay** worksheet.
- Click in cell F5.
- Click the **Trace precedents** button.

A blue arrow appears over cells D5 and E5 showing that this is the data that the formula in F5 needs.

- Click the **Trace dependents** button.

A blue arrow is inserted to cell G5 showing that this cell depends on the value in F5.

- Click the **Remove all arrows** button.

21.6. Displaying formulae

For the technical documentation you need to display the formulae in your worksheets. Try this:

- Display the **Staff List & Details** worksheet.
- From the menu select **Tools**, **Options** and click the **View** tab.
- Select **Formulas** and click **OK**.

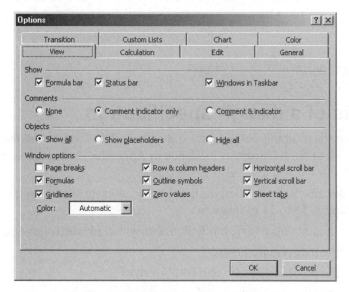

Figure 21.4: Selecting View options

The formulae in the worksheet will now be displayed:

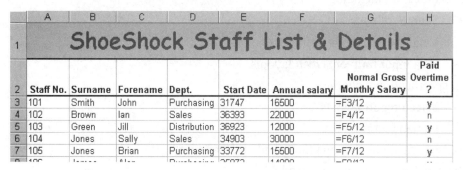

Figure 21.5: Formulae displayed

21.7. Screenshots

Your records of testing should include evidence produced in the form of screenshots. One way of doing this is to press the **PrintScreen** key on the keyboard which will take a screen dump and save it in the clipboard so that you can later paste it into another document. This will only give you a copy of the complete screen, but there are other utilities available which offer more options. For example later releases of CorelDraw are supplied with a utility called **Corel Capture** which allows you to select which part of the screen you want to capture and to save it in various file formats. You can also download a free copy of **Screen Print Gold** from Software labs (www.softwarelabs.com). This user-friendly program also allows you to specify exactly which area of the screen you wish to capture. You can then edit the images and print the result, send it to the clipboard or save it as a graphics file.

Chapter 22 – Design Specification

Objectives

✓ To write a design specification for a project

22.1. Contents of a design specification

For your assessment you must submit design, user and technical documentation for the work you have done, and you should look at the Assessment Evidence in Appendix D to check exactly what you need to produce.

In this chapter we will document the detailed design specification for the ShoeShock Overtime system that is developed in Chapters 15 to 21 of this unit.

The contents of the specification may vary, but will probably include the following:

❑ A description of the user requirements.

❑ A description of the proposed system and its objectives.

❑ Spreadsheet specification including:

    – Workbook structure detailing the individual worksheets and their interconnection.

❑ Input specification including

    – Sources of data

    – Validation methods

    – Data input form or screen layouts

❑ Output specification including

    – Screen report layouts

    – Printed report layouts

❑ Process specifications showing the calculations required

❑ Test Plan and test data with expected results

❑ Conclusion, including a discussion of

    – Software

    – Hardware

A sample design specification is given in the rest of the chapter. You need to include some hand-drawn designs of your worksheets showing their contents, formulae and how they link together. Blank spreadsheets are given at the end of the book for you photocopy and use in your own project.

Design Specification

For ShoeShock Ltd
Overtime Collection System

Written by
N. McNeil
19-02-01

Description of the proposed system

ShoeShock Ltd does not run a payroll system in-house but employs a Payroll Bureau to provide this service. The company's Finance Department supplies details of each employee's gross pay and the Bureau calculates deductions for Income Tax and National Insurance, arranges bank transfers and produces payslips for the employees.

An employee's gross salary can vary from month to month because of pay rises and overtime payments. The Head of Finance would like to set up a new system using a spreadsheet that will help record this information each month. As the department is currently understaffed other administrative members of staff are often drafted in to help, so the system must be simple to use with clear documentation.

Currently a manual system is used to produce a list of gross salaries which is sent by post to the Payroll Bureau. Pay rises and overtime payments are made a month in arrears. The list of gross salaries must reach the Bureau by the 10th of the following month if payments are to be included in that month's pay packet. So for example, if an employee works 6 hours overtime in June, assuming the Bureau get that information by the 10th July he will be paid for that overtime at the end of July.

Not all staff are entitled to overtime payments as their contract may specify that their annual salary includes any necessary out-of-normal hours working. However, all staff are required to complete a weekly overtime form and send it to the Finance Department as management reports are created that show all overtime, either paid or unpaid.

Pay rises are generally negotiated individually with management on the anniversary of an employee's start date with the company. Once agreed, managers are required to complete a form and send it to Finance.

If a member of staff's details change i.e. they change department or change their name they must complete a form and send it to the Finance department.

If a new member of staff joins the company or an employee leaves the company, their line manager must notify the Finance department by completing the appropriate form.

It is planned to maintain this method of data collection so employees and managers will complete the same forms as before. But, as an alternative to completing the forms by hand, electronic versions will be held on the company network and the facility to e-mail these forms to the Finance Department will be introduced. Initially the Finance staff will have to transfer the details from these forms into the new system manually.

Objectives

The new system must

- allow the data entry of staff details, regular and overtime pay each month;
- have built-in controls to ensure accuracy and completeness of data input;
- calculate the overtime payments and total gross salary for each employee each month;
- produce a monthly summary by department showing gross pay, overtime pay and overtime as a percentage of total gross pay.

Data capture

The Finance department staff will receive input information on the following forms:

<table>
<tr><td colspan="3">

Time sheet

V / P
</td></tr>
<tr><td>Employee No.</td><td></td><td></td></tr>
<tr><td>Department</td><td></td><td></td></tr>
<tr><td>Name</td><td></td><td></td></tr>
<tr><td>Date</td><td></td><td></td></tr>
<tr><td>OT Paid?</td><td></td><td></td></tr>
<tr><td colspan="3"></td></tr>
<tr><td colspan="3">Overtime</td></tr>
<tr><td>Date</td><td>Description</td><td>No. of hours</td></tr>
<tr><td></td><td></td><td></td></tr>
<tr><td></td><td></td><td></td></tr>
<tr><td></td><td></td><td></td></tr>
<tr><td></td><td></td><td></td></tr>
<tr><td></td><td></td><td></td></tr>
<tr><td></td><td></td><td></td></tr>
<tr><td></td><td>Total</td><td></td></tr>
</table>

Figure 22.1: The Time sheet form

<table>
<tr><td colspan="3">

Staff Details

V / P
</td></tr>
<tr><td>Employee No:</td><td></td><td></td></tr>
<tr><td>Department:</td><td></td><td></td></tr>
<tr><td>Surname:</td><td></td><td></td></tr>
<tr><td>Forename:</td><td></td><td></td></tr>
<tr><td>Start Date:</td><td></td><td></td></tr>
<tr><td>Annual Salary:</td><td></td><td></td></tr>
<tr><td>Paid Overtime?:</td><td></td><td></td></tr>
<tr><td colspan="3"></td></tr>
<tr><td>Signatures:</td><td>Employee:</td><td></td></tr>
<tr><td></td><td>Line Manager:</td><td></td></tr>
<tr><td>Date:</td><td></td><td></td></tr>
<tr><td colspan="3"></td></tr>
</table>

Figure 22.2: The Staff Details form

The data from the Time Sheet forms will be entered into the spreadsheet each month in order to calculate the amount of overtime pay earned by each employee. When an employee joins the company, or details on an existing employee need to be changed, a Staff Details form is completed and the Finance Department enters this data into the spreadsheet.

Spreadsheet structure

The various functions of the Overtime Collection System will be accessed from a front-end menu which will have the following structure.

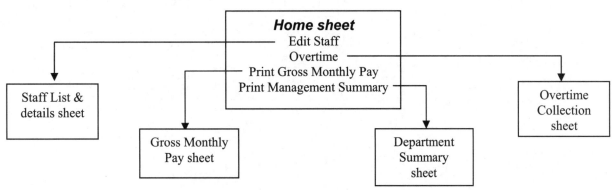

Figure 22.3: The menu structure

Worksheet structure

The layouts for the individual worksheets are shown on the following pages.

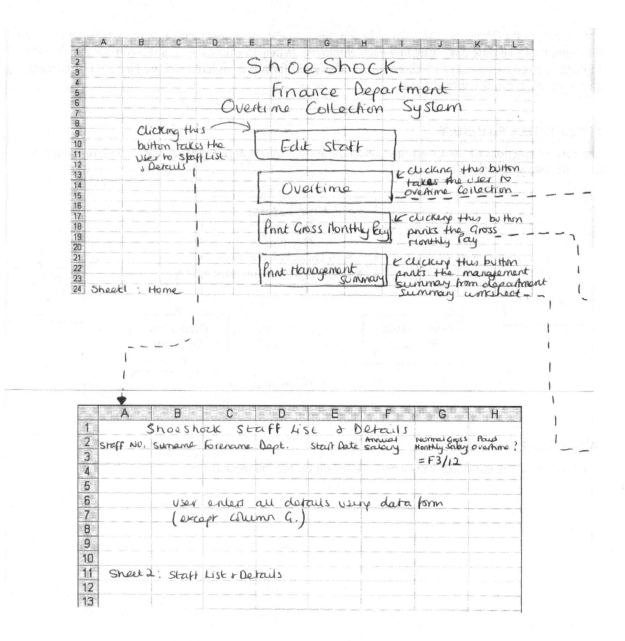

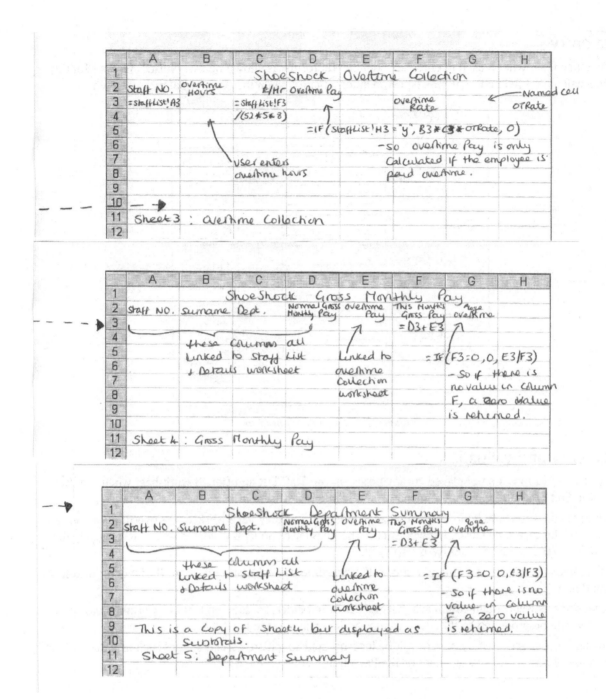

Figure 22.4: Contents of the worksheets

Data entry

A data entry form will be used to enter staff details. Its format is shown below. Normal Gross Monthly Pay is a calculated field and will be displayed automatically when the Annual Salary is entered.

Figure 22.5: The data input form

Data entry and validation

The data entry form will be displayed automatically on the **Staff List and Details** worksheet when the user selects the **Edit Staff** option from the menu on the **Home** worksheet.

Each month, the Overtime hours worked by each employee (if they have worked any overtime) are entered directly into the **Overtime Collection** worksheet. The number of hours is validated and, if it is outside the range 0.5 to 20.0, an error message is displayed.

Not all employees receive overtime pay and so the overtime pay calculation uses an 'IF' function to test for this condition.

Some worksheets will contain comments that will act as reminders to data input staff. Certain areas of worksheets will be protected so that users cannot accidentally change fixed data.

Command buttons activated by macros will be incorporated to initiate certain actions such as data input and the printing of reports for management or the Payroll Bureau.

Calculations and functions

The following calculations are performed in order to produce the required output.

Calculation	Formula required
Normal Gross Monthly Salary	Annual Salary/12
£ per Hr	Annual Salary/(52*5*8)
This Month's Gross Pay	Normal Gross Monthly Salary + Overtime Pay

The following IF functions are used.

Overtime Collection worksheet:

Overtime Pay = (If Paid Overtime? = "y" **Then** Overtime Hours * £ per Hr* Overtime Rate **Else** 0)

Gross Monthly Pay worksheet:

%ge Overtime = (If This Month's Gross Pay =0 **Then** "0" **Else** Overtime Pay/This Month's Gross Pay)

Using a template

The new system will be installed from the template ShoeShocktemplate.xlt. This contains headings and formulae but no data.

Output

The following printed information must be output from the new system for the Payroll Bureau.

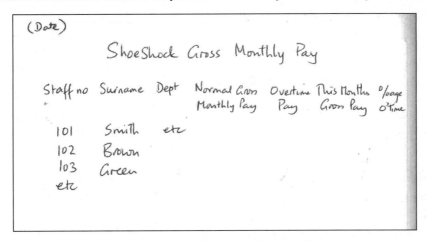

Figure 22.6: Layout for Payroll Bureau Report

The **Management Summary Report** will have the following format:

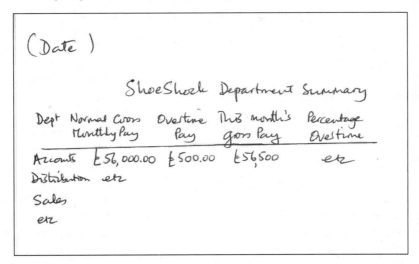

Figure 22.7: Layout for the Management Summary Report

Test Plan

The system testing must cover the following areas:

- ❑ Checking that validation rules and error messages work correctly on all worksheets by inputting valid, invalid and extreme data.
- ❑ Checking that conditional formatting works correctly.
- ❑ Checking that worksheet/workbook security is working by testing passwords and protected cells.
- ❑ Using the Auditing toolbar to test that every formula is correct.
- ❑ Testing command buttons and assigned macros under different circumstances.
- ❑ End-user testing to establish whether the system meets the requirements of the end-users.

The following tests will be carried out.

Test No.	Type of test	Data to be used	Expected result
1	Test protected cells in worksheets.	Any text	Error message.
2	Test Auto_Open macro	N/A	Should open at Home.
3	Test the formula to calculate Normal Gross Monthly Salary.	Random number	Result entered into column G of Staff List & Details worksheet.
4	Test the formula to calculate Overtime Pay.	Random number	Result entered into column D of Overtime Collection worksheet.
5	Test the formula to calculate This Month's Gross Pay.	Random number	Result entered into column F of Gross Monthly Pay worksheet.
6	Test the formula to calculate the %ge Overtime.	Random number	Result entered into column G of Gross Monthly Pay worksheet.
7	Enter the details of a new member of staff using the Edit Staff command button.	New staff details	The details are entered on all worksheet lists.
8	Edit the details of a member of staff using the Edit Staff Command button.	Change the annual salary of a staff member	The details are changed on all worksheet lists.
9	Delete the details of a member of staff using the Edit Staff command button.	Any of the existing employees	The details are deleted on all worksheet lists.
10	Move to the Overtime collection worksheet using the Overtime button.	N/A	The user is moved to the Overtime Collection sheet and an input message is displayed.
11	Data validation on overtime entries.	-2	Error message
		0	Error message
		0.5	Value accepted
		10	Value accepted
		20	Value accepted
		52	Error message
12	Print out a report using the Print Gross Monthly Pay button.	N/A	Gross Monthly Pay worksheet is printed.
13	Print out a report using the Print Management Summary button.	N/A	Department Summary is printed.
14	Print out a Management Summary after a new member of staff has been added.	New staff details	The subtotals and the summary data should be updated.

15	Reopen the workbook to test the Auto_Open macro.	N/A	The workbook should reopen at the Home worksheet.
16	Clear out the overtime payments from previous month	N/A	O/T payments deleted
17	Attempt to delete formula from Overtime sheet	N/A	Cannot delete formula in protected sheet
18	Print out Management summary for the new month	N/A	Results reflect different amounts of overtime worked.

Development Plan

The planned schedule for development is shown below:

Week beginning	Task	Comments
19-02-01	Detailed design specification	
26-02-01	Worksheets created	
05-03-01	macros written	
12-03-01	menu worksheet created	
17-03-01	Testing and modifications	Complete test plan
24-03-01	Testing and modifications	Use 'real' data from Finance Department
31-03-01	Documentation	Technical manual and User manual
14-04-01	Installation and user training	Delivery to end-user with two days on-site support

Chapter 23 – Documentation

Objectives

✓ To keep records of spreadsheet drafting, testing and refinement
✓ To show how problems were resolved
✓ To write technical documentation
✓ To show the results of testing

23.1. Checking the assessment criteria

Developing your spreadsheet is probably going to be the most enjoyable part of the project, but don't forget, **it is only a small part of the assessment criteria**. Look again at the Assessment criteria in Appendix D. Even to get a Grade E, you must produce Design documentation, clear technical documentation, clear user documentation and evidence of testing. To get a Grade C you had better get all this in on time. If you will settle for nothing less than a Grade A, then you must keep comprehensive records of how you developed your spreadsheet, the problems you encountered and how you solved them.

23.2. Keeping a log

From the day you first start work on your project, you should keep a hand-written log of what you do each session and what problems you encounter. This will not only help you to remember where you have got to next time you work on it, but it also forms an essential part of the documentation required for a Grade A. Your spreadsheet is inevitably going to end up somewhat different from how you originally planned it. Some things won't work and you will have to try an alternative. Better ideas will come to you as you work on the project. **Write them all down!** Here is a short extract from a developer's log.

Date	Work done/Problems/Solutions
26 Feb	Created and named the worksheets Home, Staff List & Details, and Overtime Collection. Entered 20 lines of test data in Staff List and Details. Links and formulae worked fine. When I added an extra line the formula did not appear automatically in the new line.
28 Feb	Solved my previous problem. Solution: Tools, Options, Edit, Extend list formats and formulas. I intend to use a data entry form to enter staff details and monthly overtime. Data, Form is supposed to do this but I got an error message that it couldn't identify the list. Solved the problem by removing the extra data for overtime rate, from beside the list. It doesn't seem to like extra data on the sheet.
...	
5th April	I was going to use a template containing staff names, pay rates etc which the user would load up each month and enter the overtime in. However I now realise that if the staff details change during the month, the template will still have the original data in

	it. So it would be better not to use the template, but to load up the previous month's spreadsheet and delete the overtime hours before entering the current month's data. I probably should put an extra button on the menu to 'Initialise new month'. This will run a macro to delete the Overtime hours.
7th April	The Management Summary Report does not work when a new member of staff has been added. I am going to modify the design to allow the user to select the correct range to be sorted. This also means adding an extra command button on the Department Summary worksheet.
...	

23.3. The contents of technical documentation

A Technical manual is for specialists who are competent Excel users. It records the design and development of the spreadsheet and would help your successors to install, modify or enhance the system once you have left the country with your lottery win! This manual could include:

- Details of the hardware, software and other resources required – for example, this should specify which version of Excel is required and the filename of the workbook and where it is stored.
- Instructions for opening and configuring the spreadsheet. This must include details of any passwords or protection that has been applied to the workbook. It should also include details of any hidden cells.
- Details of all calculations, formulae and functions used.
- Details of validation procedures that have been applied to certain areas of the spreadsheet.
- Details of all macros that have been incorporated into the system. A printout of the Visual Basic code can also be useful.
- Copies of the test strategy and test plan will help others to see any weaknesses that have been identified in the system and how they have been removed.
- Details of backup files.

You may not have a lot of actual program code in your application. However you can print out the Visual Basic code generated by your macros together with screenshots of worksheets and forms and explain how and why they are used. One of the aims of this documentation is to prove to the moderator that you have used advanced features of the package and that you can use technical language fluently, make good use of graphic images and use annotated screen prints to create effective documentation.

You should include evidence of thorough testing based on the test plan shown in your system specification. Screenshots can provide evidence of test output that shows the system works correctly.

To print the code generated by the macros select **Tools, Macro, Macros.** Select the macro you wish to print and press the **Edit** button. You can then copy and paste the code into your documentation.

On the following pages extracts from sample technical documentation are given.

23.4. Sample technical documentation

On the following pages is a sample of the type of technical documentation you should provide.

Technical Documentation

Software and hardware

The system was developed using Excel 2000 on a Pentium PC. The workbook is to be loaded initially from the template **Shoeshock.xlt** which is saved in the default **Templates** directory. Once the user has typed in the employees the first time, the workbook will be saved as **Shoeshockmonth.xls,** where *month* stands for the current month name.

Details of Processing

Formulae and Functions

The following formulae are used in the worksheets

Staff List & Details

In column G the Normal Gross Monthly Salary is calculated by dividing the Annual Salary in column F by 12.

	A	B	C	D	E	F	G	H
2	Staff No.	Surname	Forename	Dept.	Start Date	Annual salary	Normal Gross Monthly Salary	Paid Overtime?
3	101	Smith	Jack	Purchasing	31747	16500	=F3/12	y
4	102	Brown	Ian	Sales	36393	22000	=F4/12	n
5	103	Green	Jill	Distribution	36923	12000	=F5/12	y
6	104	Jones	Sally	Sales	34903	30000	=F6/12	n
7	105	Jones	Brian	Purchasing	33772	15500	=F7/12	y
8	106	James	Alan	Purchasing	35872	14000	=F8/12	y
9	107	Williams	Sarah	Accounts	36710	13000	=F9/12	y
10	108	Baker	James	Purchasing	35045	13000	=F10/12	y
11	109	Lamb	Charles	Sales	36264	22000	=F11/12	n
12	110	Gunn	Ben	Purchasing	32541	14000	=F12/12	y
13	111	Jackson	Jill	Management	34103	16000	=F13/12	n
14	112	Shaw	Bill	Management	31472	40000	=F14/12	n
15	113	Little	Sidney	Purchasing	35659	18000	=F15/12	y
16	114	Chaplin	Ian	Management	31472	35000	=F16/12	n
17	115	Philips	Marie	Sales	33785	22500	=F17/12	n
18	116	Collier	Robin	Distribution	35069	14000	=F18/12	y
19	117	Wilson	Harold	Accounts	36222	17000	=F19/12	y
20	118	Bottomley	Alice	Sales	34864	21000	=F20/12	n
21	120	Smythe	Gerald	Sales	35470	12500	=F21/12	n
22	121	Farrow	Helen	Purchasing	37033	17450	=F22/12	y
23	122	Beasley	James	Sales	37033	24750	=F23/12	n

Figure 23.1: Displaying formulae on the Staff List & Details worksheet

Overtime Collection

Column A is linked to column A on the **Staff List & Details** worksheet to insert the Staff No. In column C the £/Hr is calculated by taking the Annual Salary from the **Staff List & Details** worksheet and dividing it by 52 (number of weeks in the year) multiplied by 5 (number of working days in a week) multiplied by 8 (number of working hours in a day).

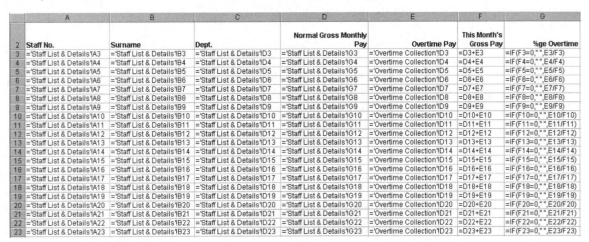

	A	B	C	D
2	Staff No.	Overtime Hours	£/Hr	Overtime Pay
3	='Staff List & Details'!A3		='Staff List & Details'!F3/(52*5*8)	=IF('Staff List & Details'!H3="y",B3*C3*OTRate,0)
4	='Staff List & Details'!A4		='Staff List & Details'!F4/(52*5*8)	=IF('Staff List & Details'!H4="y",B4*C4*OTRate,0)
5	='Staff List & Details'!A5		='Staff List & Details'!F5/(52*5*8)	=IF('Staff List & Details'!H5="y",B5*C5*OTRate,0)
6	='Staff List & Details'!A6		='Staff List & Details'!F6/(52*5*8)	=IF('Staff List & Details'!H6="y",B6*C6*OTRate,0)
7	='Staff List & Details'!A7		='Staff List & Details'!F7/(52*5*8)	=IF('Staff List & Details'!H7="y",B7*C7*OTRate,0)
8	='Staff List & Details'!A8		='Staff List & Details'!F8/(52*5*8)	=IF('Staff List & Details'!H8="y",B8*C8*OTRate,0)
9	='Staff List & Details'!A9		='Staff List & Details'!F9/(52*5*8)	=IF('Staff List & Details'!H9="y",B9*C9*OTRate,0)
10	='Staff List & Details'!A10		='Staff List & Details'!F10/(52*5*8)	=IF('Staff List & Details'!H10="y",B10*C10*OTRate,0)
11	='Staff List & Details'!A11		='Staff List & Details'!F11/(52*5*8)	=IF('Staff List & Details'!H11="y",B11*C11*OTRate,0)
12	='Staff List & Details'!A12		='Staff List & Details'!F12/(52*5*8)	=IF('Staff List & Details'!H12="y",B12*C12*OTRate,0)
13	='Staff List & Details'!A13		='Staff List & Details'!F13/(52*5*8)	=IF('Staff List & Details'!H13="y",B13*C13*OTRate,0)
14	='Staff List & Details'!A14		='Staff List & Details'!F14/(52*5*8)	=IF('Staff List & Details'!H14="y",B14*C14*OTRate,0)
15	='Staff List & Details'!A15		='Staff List & Details'!F15/(52*5*8)	=IF('Staff List & Details'!H15="y",B15*C15*OTRate,0)
16	='Staff List & Details'!A16		='Staff List & Details'!F16/(52*5*8)	=IF('Staff List & Details'!H16="y",B16*C16*OTRate,0)
17	='Staff List & Details'!A17		='Staff List & Details'!F17/(52*5*8)	=IF('Staff List & Details'!H17="y",B17*C17*OTRate,0)
18	='Staff List & Details'!A18		='Staff List & Details'!F18/(52*5*8)	=IF('Staff List & Details'!H18="y",B18*C18*OTRate,0)
19	='Staff List & Details'!A19		='Staff List & Details'!F19/(52*5*8)	=IF('Staff List & Details'!H19="y",B19*C19*OTRate,0)
20	='Staff List & Details'!A20		='Staff List & Details'!F20/(52*5*8)	=IF('Staff List & Details'!H20="y",B20*C20*OTRate,0)
21	='Staff List & Details'!A21		='Staff List & Details'!F21/(52*5*8)	=IF('Staff List & Details'!H21="y",B21*C21*OTRate,0)
22	='Staff List & Details'!A22		='Staff List & Details'!F22/(52*5*8)	=IF('Staff List & Details'!H22="y",B22*C22*OTRate,0)

Figure 23.2: Displaying formulae on the Overtime Collection worksheet

Monthly Gross Pay

Column A is linked to column A in the **Staff List & Details** worksheet to insert the Staff No. The surname, department and Normal Gross Monthly Pay are linked in the same way. The Overtime Pay in column E is linked to the **Overtime Collection** worksheet. This Month's Gross Pay in column F is calculated by adding Normal Gross Monthly Pay to Overtime Pay. Percentage Overtime is Overtime Pay divided by This Month's Gross Pay – it is blank if there is no This Month's Gross Pay in column F.

	A	B	C	D Normal Gross Monthly Pay	E Overtime Pay	F This Month's Gross Pay	G %ge Overtime
2	Staff No.	Surname	Dept.				
3	='Staff List & Details'!A3	='Staff List & Details'!B3	='Staff List & Details'!D3	='Staff List & Details'!G3	='Overtime Collection'!D3	=D3+E3	=IF(F3=0,"",E3/F3)
4	='Staff List & Details'!A4	='Staff List & Details'!B4	='Staff List & Details'!D4	='Staff List & Details'!G4	='Overtime Collection'!D4	=D4+E4	=IF(F4=0,"",E4/F4)
5	='Staff List & Details'!A5	='Staff List & Details'!B5	='Staff List & Details'!D5	='Staff List & Details'!G5	='Overtime Collection'!D5	=D5+E5	=IF(F5=0,"",E5/F5)
6	='Staff List & Details'!A6	='Staff List & Details'!B6	='Staff List & Details'!D6	='Staff List & Details'!G6	='Overtime Collection'!D6	=D6+E6	=IF(F6=0,"",E6/F6)
7	='Staff List & Details'!A7	='Staff List & Details'!B7	='Staff List & Details'!D7	='Staff List & Details'!G7	='Overtime Collection'!D7	=D7+E7	=IF(F7=0,"",E7/F7)
8	='Staff List & Details'!A8	='Staff List & Details'!B8	='Staff List & Details'!D8	='Staff List & Details'!G8	='Overtime Collection'!D8	=D8+E8	=IF(F8=0,"",E8/F8)
9	='Staff List & Details'!A9	='Staff List & Details'!B9	='Staff List & Details'!D9	='Staff List & Details'!G9	='Overtime Collection'!D9	=D9+E9	=IF(F9=0,"",E9/F9)
10	='Staff List & Details'!A10	='Staff List & Details'!B10	='Staff List & Details'!D10	='Staff List & Details'!G10	='Overtime Collection'!D10	=D10+E10	=IF(F10=0,"",E10/F10)
11	='Staff List & Details'!A11	='Staff List & Details'!B11	='Staff List & Details'!D11	='Staff List & Details'!G11	='Overtime Collection'!D11	=D11+E11	=IF(F11=0,"",E11/F11)
12	='Staff List & Details'!A12	='Staff List & Details'!B12	='Staff List & Details'!D12	='Staff List & Details'!G12	='Overtime Collection'!D12	=D12+E12	=IF(F12=0,"",E12/F12)
13	='Staff List & Details'!A13	='Staff List & Details'!B13	='Staff List & Details'!D13	='Staff List & Details'!G13	='Overtime Collection'!D13	=D13+E13	=IF(F13=0,"",E13/F13)
14	='Staff List & Details'!A14	='Staff List & Details'!B14	='Staff List & Details'!D14	='Staff List & Details'!G14	='Overtime Collection'!D14	=D14+E14	=IF(F14=0,"",E14/F14)
15	='Staff List & Details'!A15	='Staff List & Details'!B15	='Staff List & Details'!D15	='Staff List & Details'!G15	='Overtime Collection'!D15	=D15+E15	=IF(F15=0,"",E15/F15)
16	='Staff List & Details'!A16	='Staff List & Details'!B16	='Staff List & Details'!D16	='Staff List & Details'!G16	='Overtime Collection'!D16	=D16+E16	=IF(F16=0,"",E16/F16)
17	='Staff List & Details'!A17	='Staff List & Details'!B17	='Staff List & Details'!D17	='Staff List & Details'!G17	='Overtime Collection'!D17	=D17+E17	=IF(F17=0,"",E17/F17)
18	='Staff List & Details'!A18	='Staff List & Details'!B18	='Staff List & Details'!D18	='Staff List & Details'!G18	='Overtime Collection'!D18	=D18+E18	=IF(F18=0,"",E18/F18)
19	='Staff List & Details'!A19	='Staff List & Details'!B19	='Staff List & Details'!D19	='Staff List & Details'!G19	='Overtime Collection'!D19	=D19+E19	=IF(F19=0,"",E19/F19)
20	='Staff List & Details'!A20	='Staff List & Details'!B20	='Staff List & Details'!D20	='Staff List & Details'!G20	='Overtime Collection'!D20	=D20+E20	=IF(F20=0,"",E20/F20)
21	='Staff List & Details'!A21	='Staff List & Details'!B21	='Staff List & Details'!D21	='Staff List & Details'!G21	='Overtime Collection'!D21	=D21+E21	=IF(F21=0,"",E21/F21)
22	='Staff List & Details'!A22	='Staff List & Details'!B22	='Staff List & Details'!D22	='Staff List & Details'!G22	='Overtime Collection'!D22	=D22+E22	=IF(F22=0,"",E22/F22)
23	='Staff List & Details'!A23	='Staff List & Details'!B23	='Staff List & Details'!D23	='Staff List & Details'!G23	='Overtime Collection'!D23	=D23+E23	=IF(F23=0,"",E23/F23)

Figure 23.3: Displaying the formulae on the Gross Monthly Pay worksheet

Macros

The following macros are used:

The EditStaffList macro is assigned to the Edit Staff command button situated on the Home worksheet. It moves the user to the Staff List & Details worksheet and displays a data form. It leaves the user back in the Home worksheet.

```
Sub EditStaffList()
'
' EditStaffList Macro
' Macro recorded 14/06/2001 by richards
'

'
     Sheets("Staff List & Details").Select
     Range("A3").Select
     ActiveSheet.ShowDataForm
     Sheets("Overtime Collection").Select
     Range("A28").Select
     Sheets("Home").Select
End Sub
```

Figure 23.4: The EditStaffList macro

The Overtime macro takes the user to the Overtime Collection worksheet so that the user can enter overtime hours.

```
Sub Overtime()
'
' Overtime Macro
' Macro recorded 14/06/2001 by richards
'

'
     Sheets("Overtime Collection").Select
     Range("B3").Select


End Sub
```

Figure 23.5: The Overtime macro

The PrintReport macro is assigned to the Print command button on the Home worksheet. This prints the Gross Monthly Pay worksheet that is sent to the Payroll Bureau.

```
Sub PrintReport()
'
' PrintReport Macro
' Macro recorded 14/06/2001 by richards
'

'
     Sheets("Gross Monthly Pay").Select
     ActiveWindow.SelectedSheets.PrintOut Copies:=1, Collate:=True
End Sub
```

Figure 23.6: The PrintReport macro

(You should describe all the other macros and command buttons in a similar fashion.)

Testing

The test plan shown in the Design Specification was used. Results of testing are shown below.

Test 1 – Test protected cells in worksheets

Result – An error message is displayed

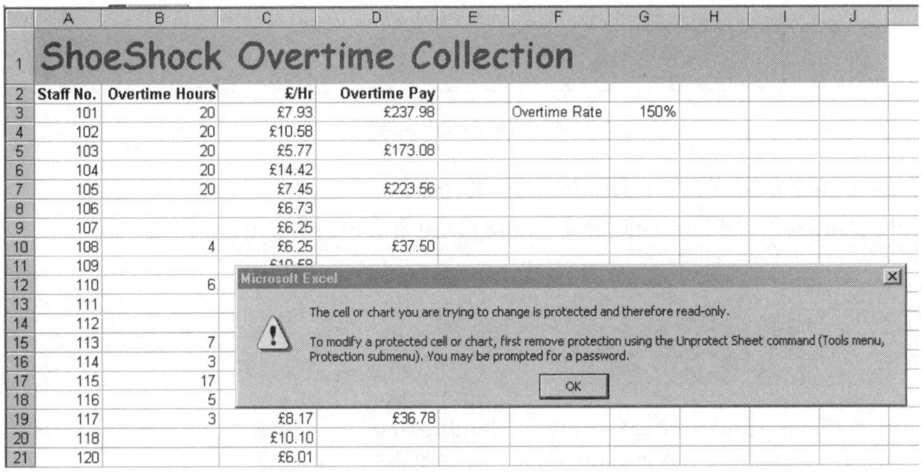

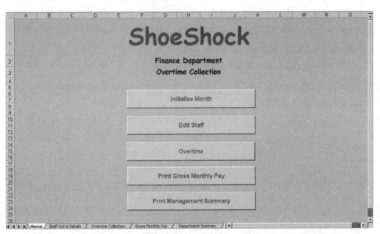

Figure 23.7: Test 1

Test 2 – Test the Auto_Open macro.

Result – Opens at the menu on the Home worksheet.

Figure 23.8: Test 2

Test 3 – Test the formula to calculate Normal Gross Monthly Salary.

Result – Correct result entered into column G of the Staff List & Details worksheet.

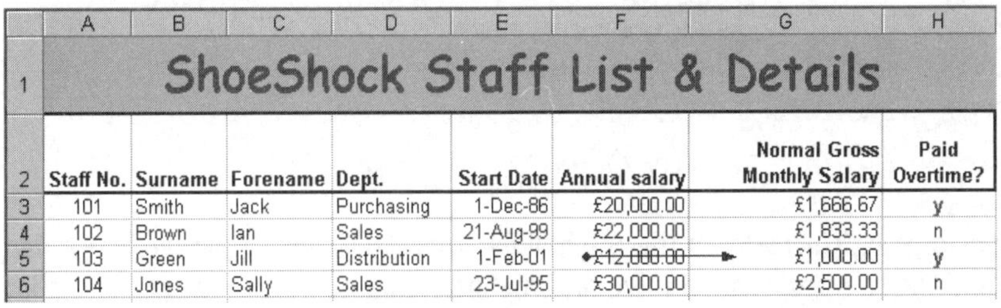

ShoeShock Staff List & Details

Staff No.	Surname	Forename	Dept.	Start Date	Annual salary	Normal Gross Monthly Salary	Paid Overtime?
101	Smith	Jack	Purchasing	1-Dec-86	£20,000.00	£1,666.67	y
102	Brown	Ian	Sales	21-Aug-99	£22,000.00	£1,833.33	n
103	Green	Jill	Distribution	1-Feb-01	£12,000.00	£1,000.00	y
104	Jones	Sally	Sales	23-Jul-95	£30,000.00	£2,500.00	n

Figure 23.9: Test 3

Test 4 – Test the formula to calculate Overtime Pay.

Result – Correct result entered into column D of the Overtime Collection worksheet. If a y does not appear in the Paid Overtime column on the Staff List & Details worksheet then no value is displayed.

Staff No.	Overtime Hours	£/Hr	Overtime Pay		
101		£7.93	£237.98	Overtime Rate	150%
102	20	£10.58			
103	20	£5.77	£173.08		
104	20	£14.42			
105	20	£7.45	£223.56		
106		£6.73			

Figure 23.10: Test 4

Test 5 – Test the formula to calculate This Month's Gross Pay.

Result – Correct result entered into column F of the Gross Monthly Pay worksheet.

	A	B	C	D	E	F	G
1	ShoeShock Gross Monthly Pay						
2	Staff No.	Surname	Dept.	Normal Gross Monthly Pay	Overtime Pay	This Month's Gross Pay	%ge Overtime
3	101	Smith	Purchasing	£1,666.67	£57.69	£1,724.36	3.35%
4	102	Brown	Sales	£1,833.33		£1,833.33	
5	103	Green	Distribution	£1,000.00	£25.96	£1,025.96	2.53%
6	104	Jones	Sales	£2,500.00		£2,500.00	
7	105	Jones	Purchasing	£1,291.67		£1,291.67	
8	106	James	Purchasing	£1,166.67	£10.10	£1,176.76	0.86%
9	107	Williams	Accounts	£1,083.33		£1,083.33	

Figure 23.11: Test 5

Test 6 – Test the formula to calculate the %ge overtime.

Result – Correct result entered into column G of the Gross Monthly Pay worksheet i.e. 10.10 is 0.86% of 1,176.76 (rounded to 2 decimal places).

.

.

.

Test 14 – Print out Management summary after a new member of staff has been added.

1 2 3		A	B	C	D	E	F	G	H
	1	ShoeShock Department Summary						
	2	Staff No.	Surname	Dept.	Normal Gross Monthly Pay	Overtime Pay	This Month's Gross Pay	%ge Overtime
	6			Accounts Total	£3,875.00	£84.74	£3,959.74	5.88%
	9			Distribution Total	£2,166.67	£36.06	£2,202.72	3.39%
	13			Mgmnt Total	£7,583.33		£7,583.33	
	22			Purchasing Total	£10,995.83	£294.23	£11,290.06	20.63%
	30			Sales Total	£13,062.50		£13,062.50	
	31			Grand Total	£37,683.33	£415.02	£38,098.36	29.90%
	32	125	Vincent	Accounts	£833.33		£833.33	
	33							
	34							

Figure 23.12: Test 14

This test did not perform satisfactorily in the original version. The new employee is not included in the summary. This was a difficult problem to solve and meant a change in the design. The command button on the menu now goes to the Department Summary Sheet, deletes all the existing subtotals and copies cells A3 to G50 from the Gross Monthly Pay worksheet. A message is displayed asking the user to select the range to be sorted prior to the summary report being printed, and then to press a command button which will do the sorting and subtotalling.

(You should show the results of all your tests and explain how you fixed any problems.)

Conclusion

It is extremely difficult in Excel to have everything done from command buttons without using Visual Basic code. When a new employee is added, the summary report cannot adjust automatically without a new range being selected. The application will require some knowledge and intelligence on the part of the user.

The system does have some limitations, for example it can only handle 50 members of staff. However, as there are only currently 18 members of staff this should be adequate.

It is possible to enter duplicate staff numbers into the system. This could be solved quite simply by using a formula that adds one to the previous staff number. The new staff number would appear automatically on the data input form.

Chapter 24 – User Documentation

Objectives

✓ To write a user manual

24.1. Introduction

The User Manual is for a non-technical user and should explain clearly all the functions of the system. It should help them to use your custom spreadsheet, not explain to them how to use Excel. You must write user instructions that are simple to understand, including:

- ❑ an introduction giving an overview of the application;
- ❑ how to start the program and how to gain access using a password;
- ❑ examples of the route through the spreadsheet;
- ❑ instructions about data entry and validation rules that have been applied;
- ❑ advice on how to respond to error messages if they type in something incorrectly;
- ❑ examples of data output screens and printed copy;
- ❑ advice on backing up;
- ❑ who to contact to get help if they get into trouble;
- ❑ a title page and Table of Contents.

24.2. Word processing your user manual

In Unit 1 you learned how to use outlining to generate an automatic Table of Contents. You will also need to use headers and footers to specify what the document is, the page number etc.

24.3. Sample user manual

Sample extracts from a user manual for the Shoe Shock Overtime Collection system are given on the next few pages. The title page and Table of Contents are omitted but you should include them in your documentation.

ShoeShock Overtime Collection System
User Manual

Introduction

ShoeShock does not run a payroll system in-house but employs a Payroll Bureau to provide this service for them. The company's Finance Department supplies details of each employee's gross pay and the Bureau calculates deductions for Income Tax and National Insurance, arranges bank transfers and produces payslips for the employees.

The new Overtime Collection System will automate the currently manual system that updates staff details, enters their monthly overtime hours and calculates their gross monthly pay.

The data to be input will be taken from the Time Sheets submitted by each employee (for overtime claims) and Change to Staff Detail forms submitted by employees or management (for changes to personal details or pay rises).

Initial system set up

If this is the first time the system has been used you will have to enter the following details for all members of staff (supplied by Personnel):

Staff No., Surname, Forename, Department, Start Date, Annual Salary, and "y" or "n" to indicate if they are paid overtime.

Enter these details as follows:

- Load MS Excel and select **File, New.**
- Click on the **ShoeShocktemplate.xlt** icon and click **OK.**

The following opening screen will be displayed:

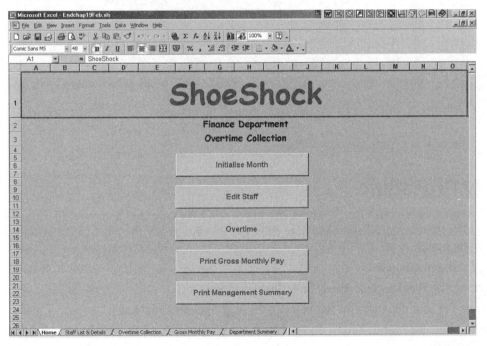

Figure 24.1: The opening screen

- Click the **Staff List & Details** tab at the bottom of the screen.
- You will be moved to the **Staff List & Details** worksheet.
- Enter the details of the employees, pressing **Tab** between fields.
- Save the workbook as *ShoeShockmonth.xls*, where *month* is the current month e.g. June.

Editing Staff Details

From time to time the Finance Department will receive Staff Details forms which show any changes to staff details including details of staff joining or leaving the company.

To edit staff details:

- Open the file **ShoeShockmonth.xls** (e.g. **ShoeShockJune.xls**).
- Click the **Edit Staff** button and use the data form that appears on the **Staff List & Details** worksheet to make the changes. Use either the scroll bar or the **Find Next** and **Find Prev** buttons to find the record you wish to edit.

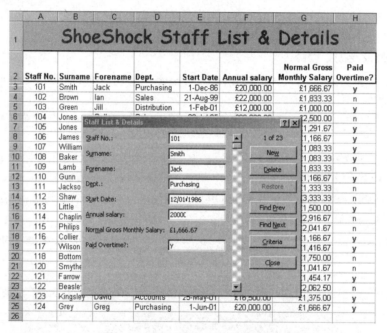

Figure 24.2: Editing Staff Details

- When the edits are complete click **Close**.

Monthly Procedure

By the beginning of each month the Finance Department will have collected a number of Time Sheet forms detailing staff overtime claims. These should be collected together ready for input to the system during the first week of the month.

To initialise for the new month

- Open the file **ShoeShockmonth.xls** (e.g. **ShoeShockJune.xls**).
- Save the file with the name for the new month (e.g. **ShoeShockJuly.xls**).
- Click the **Initialise Month** button on the **Home** worksheet menu. This will clear out last month's overtime hours.

Entering overtime payments

- Click the **Overtime** button on the **Home** worksheet to take you to the **Overtime Collection** worksheet.
- In column B enter the overtime hours for each member of staff.

	A	B	C	D	E	F	G	H
1		ShoeShock Overtime Collection						
2	Staff No.	Overtime Hours	£/Hr	Overtime Pay				
3	101		£9.62			Overtime Rate	150%	
4	102		£10.58					
5	103		£5.77					
6	104		£14.42					
7	105		£7.45					
8	106		£6.73					
9	107		£6.25					
10	108		£6.25					
11	109		£10.58					
12	110		£6.73					
13	111		£7.69					
14	112		£19.23					
15	113		£8.65					
16	114		£16.83					
17	115		£11.78					
18	116		£6.73					
19	117		£8.17					
20	118		£10.10					
21	120		£6.01					
22	121		£8.39					
23	122		£11.90					
24	123		£7.93					
25	124		£9.62					
26								

Figure 24.3: Entering overtime payments

Printing the Gross Monthly Payments report

- Return to the **Home** worksheet by clicking on the **Home** tab at the bottom of the screen.
- Click the **Print Gross Monthly Pay** button to print the report to be sent to the Payroll Bureau.
- Return to the **Home** worksheet by clicking on the **Home** tab at the bottom of the screen.

The report will be printed as follows:

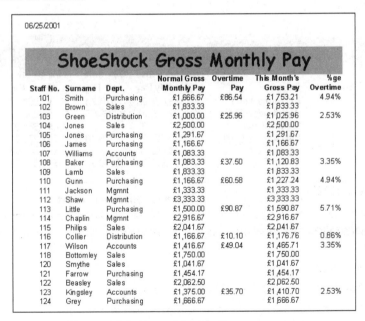

06/25/2001

ShoeShock Gross Monthly Pay

Staff No.	Surname	Dept.	Normal Gross Monthly Pay	Overtime Pay	This Month's Gross Pay	%ge Overtime
101	Smith	Purchasing	£1,666.67	£86.54	£1,753.21	4.94%
102	Brown	Sales	£1,833.33		£1,833.33	
103	Green	Distribution	£1,000.00	£25.96	£1,025.96	2.53%
104	Jones	Sales	£2,500.00		£2,500.00	
105	Jones	Purchasing	£1,291.67		£1,291.67	
106	James	Purchasing	£1,166.67		£1,166.67	
107	Williams	Accounts	£1,083.33		£1,083.33	
108	Baker	Purchasing	£1,083.33	£37.50	£1,120.83	3.35%
109	Lamb	Sales	£1,833.33		£1,833.33	
110	Gunn	Purchasing	£1,166.67	£60.58	£1,227.24	4.94%
111	Jackson	Mgmnt	£1,333.33		£1,333.33	
112	Shaw	Mgmnt	£3,333.33		£3,333.33	
113	Little	Purchasing	£1,500.00	£90.87	£1,590.87	5.71%
114	Chaplin	Mgmnt	£2,916.67		£2,916.67	
115	Philips	Sales	£2,041.67		£2,041.67	
116	Collier	Distribution	£1,166.67	£10.10	£1,176.76	0.86%
117	Wilson	Accounts	£1,416.67	£49.04	£1,465.71	3.35%
118	Bottomley	Sales	£1,750.00		£1,750.00	
120	Smythe	Sales	£1,041.67		£1,041.67	
121	Farrow	Purchasing	£1,454.17		£1,454.17	
122	Beasley	Sales	£2,062.50		£2,062.50	
123	Kingsley	Accounts	£1,375.00	£35.70	£1,410.70	2.53%
124	Grey	Purchasing	£1,666.67		£1,666.67	

Figure 24.4: Gross Monthly Payments report

Printing the Management Summary report

- Click the **Print Management Summary** button. This will take you to the **Department Summary** worksheet, where you will see a message on a blue background asking you to select the range to be summarised for the report. You should select the heading row and all the data (e.g. A2 to G25 in the screenshot below).

	A	B	C	D	E	F	G	H	I	J	K	L
1		ShoeShock Department Summary							Please select the range to be sorted, starting in A2, and then click the button below to print the summary			
2	Staff No.	Surname	Dept.	Normal Gross Monthly Pay	Overtime Pay	This Month's Gross Pay	%ge Overtime					
3	101	Smith	Purchasing	£1,666.67	£86.54	£1,753.21	4.94%					
4	102	Brown	Sales	£1,833.33		£1,833.33						
5	103	Green	Distribution	£1,000.00	£25.96	£1,025.96	2.53%					
6	104	Jones	Sales	£2,500.00		£2,500.00						
7	105	Jones	Purchasing	£1,291.67		£1,291.67						
8	106	James	Purchasing	£1,166.67		£1,166.67						
9	107	Williams	Accounts	£1,083.33		£1,083.33						
10	108	Baker	Purchasing	£1,083.33	£37.50	£1,120.83	3.35%					
11	109	Lamb	Sales	£1,833.33		£1,833.33			Click here to Print Summary			
12	110	Gunn	Purchasing	£1,166.67	£60.58	£1,227.24	4.94%					
13	111	Jackson	Mgmnt	£1,333.33		£1,333.33						
14	112	Shaw	Mgmnt	£3,333.33		£3,333.33						
15	113	Little	Purchasing	£1,500.00	£90.87	£1,590.87	5.71%					
16	114	Chaplin	Mgmnt	£2,916.67		£2,916.67						
17	115	Philips	Sales	£2,041.67		£2,041.67						
18	116	Collier	Distribution	£1,166.67	£10.10	£1,176.76	0.86%					
19	117	Wilson	Accounts	£1,416.67	£49.04	£1,465.71	3.35%					
20	118	Bottomley	Sales	£1,750.00		£1,750.00						
21	120	Smythe	Sales	£1,041.67		£1,041.67						
22	121	Farrow	Purchasing	£1,454.17		£1,454.17						
23	122	Beasley	Sales	£2,062.50		£2,062.50						
24	123	Kingsley	Accounts	£1,375.00	£35.70	£1,410.70	2.53%					
25	124	Grey	Purchasing	£1,666.67		£1,666.67						
26												

Figure 24.5: Preparing to print the Management Summary report

- Now press the large **Print Summary** button. The report will be displayed on screen as follows and if all is satisfactory, you can press **Print** to obtain a hard copy.

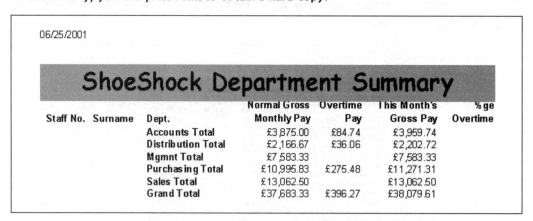

06/25/2001

ShoeShock Department Summary

Staff No.	Surname	Dept.	Normal Gross Monthly Pay	Overtime Pay	This Month's Gross Pay	%ge Overtime
		Accounts Total	£3,875.00	£84.74	£3,959.74	
		Distribution Total	£2,166.67	£36.06	£2,202.72	
		Mgmnt Total	£7,583.33		£7,583.33	
		Purchasing Total	£10,995.83	£275.48	£11,271.31	
		Sales Total	£13,062.50		£13,062.50	
		Grand Total	£37,683.33	£396.27	£38,079.61	

Figure 24.6: The Management Summary report

- Save the file as *ShoeShockmonth.xls*.

Appendix A
Standard Ways of Working

Introduction

Every organisation has rules about the way it operates. These may not be formal rules and regulations that are written down – they may be just conventions and ways of working that all members of staff adhere to. Standard ways of working are important when working with ICT systems because they can help to protect three of the organisation's most important assets: information, equipment and employees.

Managing your work

Planning

Whether you are at school, college or in the workplace, you will often be faced with a number of tasks that need to be completed. If you can plan your work effectively you will be more likely to complete those tasks successfully. Spending some time drawing up a plan to organise your work will pay off in the long run and is something you should become used to doing as a matter of course. The plan will depend on you clearly identifying the task to be completed and discussing the details with whoever has set it. You need to establish the priority of the task, how long it is likely to take you and what deadline has been imposed. If you feel that the deadline is unrealistic it is always worth trying to renegotiate it, but you will have to be able to put up a good case! It is often useful to identify 'milestones' leading up to a deadline so that you can check your progress and that you are on target for completing in time.

Working with files

Almost all of the work that is created using a computer is stored in a *file* (a 'unit of storage'). These files are stored in folders on a storage device – often the hard drive on your computer. Every file is given a name and it is important that you use sensible filenames that remind you of the contents. Once you are in the workplace the files that are created and stored belong to the organisation. This means that they need to be accessible to other people within the organisation so a well-organised file structure is vital.

My Documents is a desktop folder that provides you with a convenient place to store documents, graphics, or other files you want to access quickly. On your desktop it is represented by a folder with a sheet of paper in it. Often users will create their own subfolders within My Documents creating a simple path to where their files are stored.

Fault Logging

Many problems can arise when working with ICT systems. Often the 'faults' are not problems with the system but occur because users do not fully understand how to operate the software, or what messages mean. This is why initial user training and good user documentation are vital to the success of a new ICT system.

However the resolution of many genuine faults can be speeded up if clear and precise information is passed on to the technical people supporting the system. When reporting a fault the following information should be provided:

- The way the fault manifests itself. If there is an error message, it should be relayed exactly as it appears on the screen.
- The exact sequence of events that gave rise to the fault.
- Details of the equipment and its precise location.

A fault log should always be kept near to a PC and all details of the problem entered neatly. These records can help to identify equipment that has a recurring fault and provide information on how the fault has been fixed in the past.

Keeping information secure

Computer systems must have adequate controls to ensure that only authorised personnel have access to data. There are a number of ways in which this can be achieved:

Passwords

Most networks require a user to log on with their password before they can gain access to the computer system. Additional passwords may be required to gain access to certain programs and data. For example in an organisation everyone may be able to access word processing programs and files, but only people working in the Finance department may be able to access the accounting system. It is clearly important that these passwords are not divulged to other people and it is recommended that passwords are frequently changed. In fact many systems are set up to automatically prompt you after a set number of days to change your password.

Communications controls

These controls ensure that only authorised people can connect to a computer from an external link. Some organisations have dial-back systems: when someone attempts to log on to the remote computer, they are positively identified and the computer disconnects them and immediately dials them back to ensure they are an authorised user.

Virus checks

Viruses are generally developed with a definite intention to cause damage to computer files or, at the very least, cause inconvenience and annoyance to computer users. The first virus appeared at the University of Delaware in 1987, and since then the number of viruses has escalated to tens of thousands. The virus usually occupies the first few instructions of a particular program on an 'infected' disk and relies on a user choosing to execute that program. When an infected program is executed, the virus is the first series of instructions to be performed. In most cases the virus's first action is to copy itself from the diskette onto the PC and 'hide' within obscure files, the operating system code or within unused disk blocks which are then marked as being 'bad' and unavailable for reuse. The virus can then proceed to perform any of a number tasks ranging from the irritating to the catastrophic such as reformatting the hard disk.

Some viruses lie dormant, waiting to be triggered by a particular event or date – the 'Friday 13th' virus being a well-known one. The virus then infects other diskettes, perhaps by modifying operating system programs responsible for copying programs. From there, the next PC to use the diskette will be infected.

Virus checkers need to be installed on all computer systems so that they automatically check for any infected data when the computer is started up. Manual checkers can also be used to check for viruses on floppy disks.

Backup systems

Routine backups of the computer system should be made so that in the case of serious emergency, the system can be recreated to the last full backup. Backups can be made to a variety of media – magnetic tape, CD-ROM, Zip drive etc. They are made on a daily, weekly or monthly basis depending on the importance of the data to be backed up. The backup media must be clearly labelled and should be stored in a fire-proof safe, or better still on a different site, so that should a disaster or emergency occur, the backup media will be safe.

Copyright

Computer software is copyright material – that means it is protected in the UK by the Copyright, Designs and Patents Act 1988. It is owned by the software producer and it is illegal to make unauthorised copies.

When you buy software it is often supplied in a sealed package (e.g. CD ROM case) on which the terms and conditions of sale are printed. This is called the software licence and when the user opens the package they are agreeing to abide by the licence terms.

Software licences usually permit the user to use one copy on any single computer. It is considered to be in use if it is loaded into either the computer's temporary memory (RAM) or onto the hard disk drive. With network licences the software is often loaded onto the file server and the licence specifies how many users on the network can access it at any one time.

It is illegal to make copies of the software, except for backup purposes, so you are breaking the law if you copy some software from a friend to use on your own computer.

Data that is held on computer is often subject to copyright. For example not everyone has the ability or opportunity to draw or to take photographs and you often want to include copies of someone else's work in your documents. These images may well be copyright and belong to the original artist or photographer. If this is the case it may be possible to contact the publisher for permission to use the material, but this can be a lengthy process. To be outside the copyright law, the artist/photographer/writer has to have been dead for 70 years. If this is the case and you would like to use, for example, some old photographs, you may do so freely, but it is often best to acknowledge the source somewhere in your document.

Computer Misuse Act 1990

In the early 1980s in the UK, hacking was not illegal. Some universities stipulated that hacking, especially where damage was done to data files, was a disciplinary offence, but there was no legislative framework within which a criminal prosecution could be brought. This situation was rectified by the Computer Misuse Act of 1990 which defined three specific criminal offences to deal with the problems of hacking, viruses and other nuisances. The offences are:

- ❑ unauthorised access to computer programs or data;
- ❑ unauthorised access with a further criminal intent;
- ❑ unauthorised modification of computer material (i.e. programs or data).

To date there have been relatively few prosecutions under this law – probably because most organisations are reluctant to admit that their system security procedures have been breached, which might lead to a loss of confidence on the part of their clients.

Principles of Data Protection

The Data Protection Act 1998 came into force on 1 March 2000. It sets rules for processing personal information and applies to paper records as well as those held on computers. It strengthens and extends the rules about data protection laid down in the Data Protection Act 1984, which it has now replaced.

The rules

Anyone processing personal data must comply with the eight enforceable principles of good practice. They say that data must be:

- ❑ fairly and lawfully processed;
- ❑ processed for limited purposes;
- ❑ adequate, relevant and not excessive;
- ❑ accurate;
- ❑ not kept longer than necessary;
- ❑ processed in accordance with the data subject's rights;
- ❑ secure;
- ❑ not transferred to countries without adequate protection.

Personal data covers both facts and opinions about a living person. It also includes information regarding the intentions of the data controller towards the individual, although in some limited circumstances exemptions will apply. For more information on Data Protection visit the following web site: www.dataprotection.gov.uk.

Working safely

Computers and health

Computers can be held responsible for a whole raft of health problems, from eyestrain to wrist injuries, back problems to foetal abnormalities, stomach ulcers to mental collapse. Articles appear regularly in the newspapers relating stories of employees who are suing their employers for computer-related illnesses.

Not so long ago it was thought that the widespread use of these fantastic machines, that could perform calculations and process data with lightning speed and complete accuracy, would free up humans to work maybe only two or three hours a day, while the computer did the lion's share. In fact, people seem to be working harder than ever, trying to keep up with the output of their computers. Human beings are the weak link in the chain, needing food, rest, a social life; prone to headaches, stress, tired limbs and mistakes.

Figure 1: Stress at work

Stress

Stress is often a major factor in work-related illness. Simply thinking about computers is enough to cause stress in some people. It is stressful to be asked to perform tasks which are new to you and which you are not sure you can cope with. It is stressful to know that you have more work to do than you can finish in the time available. It is stressful, even, to have too little to do and to be bored all day.

The introduction of computers into the workplace can have detrimental effects on the well-being of information workers at many different levels in an organisation. For example:

- Some companies may use computers to monitor their workers' productivity, which often increases their stress levels. Symptoms include headaches, stomach ulcers and sleeplessness.

- Many people are afraid of computers and fear that they will not be able to learn the new skills required, or that their position of seniority will be undermined by younger 'whizz kids' with a high level of competence in ICT.

- It can be almost impossible for some people to get away from work. Pagers, mobile phones, laptop computers and modems mean that even after leaving the office, there is no need to stop work – indeed, should you even think of stopping work? As a busy executive, can you afford to waste 45 minutes on the train to Ipswich reading the newspaper or just gazing out of the window, when you could be tap-tap-tapping on your laptop, or infuriating your fellow passengers by holding long and boring conversations on your mobile phone?

- 'Information overload' means that managers are often bombarded with far more information than they can assimilate, producing 'information anxiety'. Try typing the words 'Information Overload' into one of the World Wide Web's search engines and within seconds, it will have searched millions of information sources all over the world and come up with thousands of references all presorted so that those most likely to be of interest are at the top.

- A survey of 500 heads of ICT departments revealed that over three-quarters of respondents had suffered from failing personal relationships, loss of appetite, addiction to work and potential alcohol abuse. The continuing developments within ICT ensure that it is always in the minds of business executives and also that it is blamed for most corporate problems. The very speed of development, for which ICT is now famous, and the need to keep pace with this is also a major contributing factor to ICT stress-related illness.

Repetitive Strain Injury (RSI)

RSI is the collective name for a variety of disorders affecting the neck, shoulders and upper limbs. It can result in numbness or tingling in the arms and hands, aching and stiffness in the arms, neck and shoulders, and an inability to lift or grip objects. Some sufferers cannot pour a cup of tea or type a single sentence without excruciating pain.

The Health and Safety Executive say that more than 100,000 workers suffer from RSI.

Eyestrain

Computer users are prone to eyestrain from spending long hours in front of a screen. Many computer users prefer a dim light to achieve better screen contrast, but this makes it difficult to read documents on the desk. A small spotlight focussed on the desktop can be helpful. There is no evidence that computer use causes permanent damage to the eyes, but glare, improper lighting, improperly corrected vision (through not wearing the correct prescription glasses), poor work practices and poorly designed workstations all contribute to temporary eyestrain.

Extremely low frequency (ELF) radiation

In normal daily life we are constantly exposed to ELF radiation not only from electricity mains and computer monitors but also naturally occurring sources such as sunshine, fire and the earth's own magnetic field. Research into the effects of ELF radiation is increasing and seems to indicate that it may be connected to some health problems. Several studies have tried to establish whether there is a link between monitor use and problems in pregnancy such as early miscarriages. The results are not clear-cut, because although some studies seem to show a correlation between an increased rate of miscarriages and long hours spent at a VDU in the first trimester of pregnancy, other factors such as stress and poor ergonomic conditions could have played a part.

Computers, health and the law

Occupational health and safety legislation in Britain is researched, guided and structured by the Health and Safety Executive (HSE), a government body. An EEC Directive on work with display screen equipment was completed in the early 1990s, with member states required to adapt it to become part of their own legislation. As a consequence, the Health and Safety at Work Act of 1974 incorporated legislation pertaining to the use of VDUs, and the relevant section is now referred to as The Health and Safety (Display Screen Equipment) Regulations 1992.

This legislation is intended to protect the health of employees within the working environment, and employers, employees and manufacturers all have some responsibility in conforming to the law.

Employers are required to

- Perform an analysis of workstations in order to evaluate the safety and health conditions to which they give rise.

- Provide training to employees in the use of workstation components.

- ❏ Ensure employees take regular breaks or changes in activity.
- ❏ Provide regular eye tests for workstation users and pay for glasses.

Employees have a responsibility to

- ❏ Use workstations and equipment correctly, in accordance with training provided by employers.
- ❏ Bring problems to the attention of their employer immediately and co-operate in the correction of these problems.

Manufacturers are required to ensure that their products comply with the Directive. For example, screens must tilt and swivel, keyboards must be separate and moveable. Notebook PCs are not suitable for entering large amounts of data.

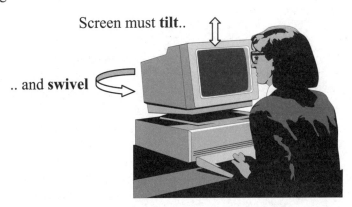

Screen must **tilt**..

.. and **swivel**

Figure 2: Workstations must be ergonomically designed

The ergonomic environment

Ergonomics refers to the design and functionality of the environment, and encompasses the entire range of environmental factors. Employers must give consideration to:

- ❏ Lighting. The office should be well lit. Computers should neither face windows nor back onto a window so that the users have to sit with the sun in their eyes. Adjustable blinds should be provided.
- ❏ Furniture. Chairs should be of adjustable height, with a backrest which tilts to support the user at work and at rest, and should swivel on a five-point base. It should be at the correct height relative to a keyboard on the desk.
- ❏ Work space. The combination of chair, desk, computer, accessories (such as document holders, mouse and mouse mats, paper trays and so on), lighting, heating and ventilation all contribute to the worker's overall well-being.
- ❏ Noise. Noisy printers, for example, should be given covers to reduce the noise or positioned in a different room.
- ❏ Hardware. The screen must tilt and swivel and be flicker-free, the keyboard must be separately attached.
- ❏ Software. Software is often overlooked in the quest for ergonomic perfection. The EEC Directive made a clear statement about the characteristics of acceptable software, requiring employers to analyse the tasks which their employers performed and to provide software which makes the tasks easier. It is also expected to be easy to use and adaptable to the user's experience.

Appendix B
Victory Publishers Ltd

Victory Publishing Ltd

Introduction

Victory Publishing Ltd is an educational publishing company publishing a wide range of textbooks for schools and colleges throughout the UK. The company was founded some 20 years ago and has been built up by the Managing Director into a company with some 40 employees and an annual turnover of £30 million. They publish approximately 400 different titles.

The company is located in a Business Park in Ipswich. The premises comprise a suite of offices and a warehouse where the books are stored and dispatched. Most of the offices are fairly large and shared by several members of a department, with the Heads of each department having their own offices. The building is cabled up for a computer network and everyone (except the packers in the warehouse, who do not have desks) has their own computer on their desk. There is comprehensive provision for phone and fax, and an ISDN line for Internet access. E-mails can be sent and received from any computer both internally and externally.

The company is divided into several departments, namely Editorial, Foreign Rights, Production, Sales, Marketing, Distribution, Finance and Administration. The rather 'flat' organisation within the company means that there is a maximum of three levels below the Managing Director, a Head of each department, sometimes two or more managers in a large department and the rest of the staff in the department.

The Departments

Editorial Department

The Chief Editor is in charge of this department and his job is to decide what titles the company will produce, commission new authors, decide on print runs and ensure that the quality and profitability of their range is maintained. Under him there is one commissioning editor and two copy editors who proofread and edit manuscripts, which are then sent to Production to be typeset.

Foreign Rights

Many of Victory's titles are published in several other countries, in the local language. It is the task of the Foreign Rights department to make new overseas contacts, negotiate foreign rights and occasionally also to buy rights themselves to books published in another country, usually the USA.

Production

The production department does the typesetting of the books and also some of the graphic work such as cover design. Sometimes this work is contracted out to a firm of graphic designers. They also prepare the disks to be sent to the printers. The books are not printed by Victory Publishing, but by specialist book printers in different parts of the country. Sometimes books are printed in Spain, Italy or Hong Kong. They are also in charge of Stock Control and ensuring that they do not run out of a particular title, or conversely, get left with thousands of unsaleable books.

Sales Department

There are basically three different types of customer; wholesale, retail and direct (schools and colleges). The sales staff is divided into three teams, each with its own manager. One team is assigned to School and College sales and goes round to various institutions and exhibitions displaying books and talking to teachers to assess their needs. This information is relayed back to the Marketing Department.

The second team consists of sales people who visit bookshops and wholesalers. Sometimes they travel abroad, especially to Southern Ireland, where they have a strong presence.

The third team is back in the office taking and entering orders, answering customer queries and liasing with the Marketing and Distribution Departments. For example when a special promotion is implemented, such as an advertisement or flyer with an order form for a particular book, they will set up a special response code for orders resulting from the flyer so that the Marketing team can gauge how successful the promotion has been.

Marketing Department

The Marketing Department is in charge of designing and sending out catalogues and questionnaires, organising special promotions, gathering and analysing responses to questionnaires and promotions, organising stands at exhibitions and placing advertisements in magazines or on web sites belonging to other organisations.

Distribution

When orders are received they are entered into the Sales Order Processing system and invoices printed out, usually once a day at about 12 noon. The dispatch notes are sent to the warehouse with a Picking List showing how many of each book is required to fulfil all the orders. The books are picked off the shelves and placed in a packing area where the orders are assembled and packed ready for collection by courier at around 4pm. The invoices are printed in the warehouse and attached to the outside of each parcel.

The Distribution Department is also in charge of receiving stock into the warehouse and recording where each title is located. The stock file is updated to show the revised quantity in stock.

Finance

The Finance Department is split into two teams each with its own manager, namely Sales Ledger and Purchase Ledger. Sales Ledger staff are responsible for receiving and recording customer payments and chasing up late payers. Purchase Ledger staff are responsible for paying suppliers. The Head of Department is a chartered accountant who keeps the monthly and annual accounts and is responsible for ensuring that the company is in sound financial health. The payroll is not handled within the company but is contracted out to a Payroll Bureau. Each month details of salaries, sick pay, pension payments, tax codes etc are assembled and e-mailed to the Bureau, who calculate the payslips and e-mail the results back to the payroll clerk in the Finance Department, who transfers the net salaries into the employees' bank accounts.

Administration

The Administration Department has a Head of Department and 4 other members of staff, two of whom are computer personnel responsible for keeping all the company's hardware and software systems running smoothly. They also install and test new software and customise it to individual or company requirements. The other staff in this department are responsible for the general running of the company, from the maintenance of the premises to the hiring, care and training of employees.

Appendix C
ShoeShock Ltd

ShoeShock UK Ltd

Introduction

ShoeShock UK Ltd is a wholly owned subsidiary of SportsShu International Inc. They market, sell and distribute a range of footwear throughout the UK, including hiking boots, multi-sport high-quality trainers, after sport shoes ('jungle mocs') and sandals. All of the footwear is designed by a Design Committee comprising 4 people who meet in the Head Office in the USA, and who with the aid of colourists and designers come up with a range of shoes which then has to be approved. Once approved, the range is shown to distributors such as ShoeShock UK and their equivalent companies in Europe, Canada and the US, and each distributor will choose the products he wishes to stock and market, typically 50%-75% of the whole range.

All the footwear is made in Asia, mainly in China, Vietnam and Thailand, and then imported into the UK by ShoeShock.

The company is run by David Reed, the Managing Director, who for the past 17 years has run a successful business in Peterborough manufacturing and selling camera cases, bags and rucksacks, from a building owned by his company, CamCase. Eleven years ago he took the opportunity to expand his business interests by taking on the distribution of the SportsShu footwear range, and both companies now operate side-by-side from the same building.

The building is a two-storey block with offices on the top floor. The downstairs is divided into office space, cutting rooms and warehouse space for CamCase.

This case study is concerned only with ShoeShock UK Ltd, which currently has a turnover of over £20,000,000.

The Company structure

The company has a total of 18 employees, structured into different departments. The main departments are Sales/Marketing, Import/Distribution, and Finance/Credit/IT. The structure is shown in graphical form in Figure 1.

Organisation Chart for ShoeShock UK

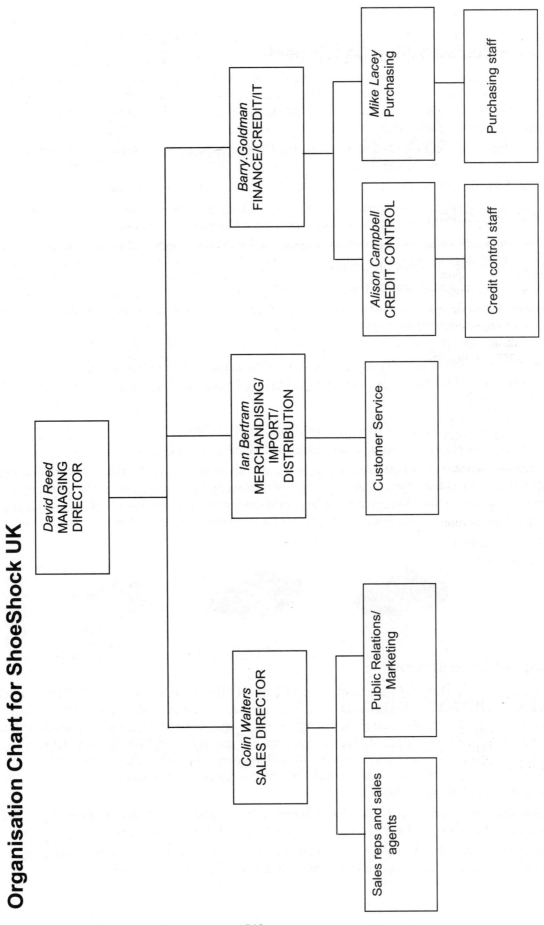

David Reed
MANAGING
DIRECTOR

Colin Walters
SALES DIRECTOR

Ian Bertram
MERCHANDISING/
IMPORT/
DISTRIBUTION

Barry.Goldman
FINANCE/CREDIT/IT

Sales reps and sales agents

Public Relations/ Marketing

Customer Service

Alison Campbell
CREDIT CONTROL

Mike Lacey
Purchasing

Credit control staff

Purchasing staff

The Sales/Marketing Department

Charles Walters, the Sales Director, is on the Design Committee and was the brains behind the extraordinarily successful new range of 'after-sport' footwear which resulted in a 30% company growth in a single year. He also has responsibility for Marketing and uses a variety of methods to market each season's footwear including:

- Trade shows in the USA, Europe and the UK where the company takes a stand and prospective customers come to see the range;
- Four showrooms in various cities in the UK which trade customers can visit
- Sales representatives/agents visit UK stores, taking samples with them. There is also a network of showrooms throughout the country where the wider range can be displayed.
- Point of Sale advertising such as posters, special display stands and shelves in stores.
- Advertising in Trade magazines
- A film was made last year which was shown in cinemas.

Market Research is also carried out through an agency which interviews people in the street. Five percent of the company's turnover is spent on marketing.

ShoeShock distributes to the mid- to upper-end of the market. Their customers include

- Outdoor shops such as Field and Trek, Cotswold Camping, Millets/Blacks
- Sports outlets such as J D Sports
- Style accounts such as Raw, Aspecto, Sole Trader, Office
- High Street and Department stores such as Debenhams and Clarks.

There are approximately 600 customer accounts representing about 1,200 different stores – for example Millets is one account which orders centrally for their many stores nationwide. The company has to be selective who they sell to because some large customers who purchase say £1 million worth of goods annually would not purchase if the same product were available in more down-market stores.

Import/Distribution

Ian Bertram is in charge of the import and distribution of the goods. Once the Trade shows have taken place, an initial order is placed based on the orders already taken and the reaction of major customers. The order is sent to the Head Office in the US, which then places orders for the finished goods with factories in China, Vietnam and Thailand. The company has 120 employees in Asia who look for new manufacturers, negotiate prices, check quality and try to ensure that the rights of the workers are respected. For example, they will not deal with any factory that employs underage workers or which has unacceptable working conditions.

Typically, ShoeShock stocks about 300 different styles of shoe, each of them in an average 2.5 different colours and about 10 different sizes – giving about 7,500 different stock units.

Once the order is placed with Head Office, it is forwarded to a Chinese or Vietnamese factory who give an estimated date of delivery, which is entered into ShoeShock's stock control system.

It is Ian's job to decide, based on orders received and potential orders expected, how many of each stock unit to order. He is also in charge of ordering goods on a weekly basis. Each week he goes through the stock report which highlights what needs to be ordered, and based on a combination of facts, figures and experience, places his orders. This process is dependent on the use of a spreadsheet model which Ian developed himself. It calculates, for each of the 750 different styles and colour of shoe, the breakdown of sales of each size. For example, if 500 pairs of *Black Polar Extremes* have been sold and need to be reordered, the spreadsheet will use detailed sales data collected over a period of weeks to calculate that say 35 pairs of size 5 should be ordered, 67 pairs of size 6 and so on to make up the 500 pairs.

The company uses a third party 'Pick and Pack' warehouse called P&P (located in Bradford) to hold and dispatch the goods. When the orders arrive in the UK they are cleared through Customs and then sent directly to P&P, who keep their own separate stock control system. A Goods Received note is sent from P&P to ShoeShock, where stock quantities are input to the ShoeShock system and the balances updated.

Ian also has to make sure that the goods are dispatched to the customers. When an order is received, a Pick Note is prepared on the computer system. Each day a batch of Pick Notes is dispatched to P&P, who use them to pick the goods off their warehouse shelves, pack and dispatch them to the customers with a delivery note. Data on what has been dispatched is then transmitted back to ShoeShock who invoice the customer and update the stock control information.

Finance/Credit/IT

Barry Goldman is in charge of Finance. He looks after the financial side of the business, purchasing office supplies, payment of regular overheads such as rates, electricity, phone bills, etc and prepares the company accounts.

Reporting to him is Alison Campbell who is in charge of credit control. This involves establishing each customer's credit limit, ensuring that customers do not exceed their credit limit without special dispensation, and chasing up customers who are late with their payments, which she does by telephone.

The Payroll is outsourced to an independent consultant working from home who maintains the payroll files for the organisation, prepares the weekly and monthly payslips, Inland Revenue returns and any required forms such as P45 for employees who leave and P46 for end-of-year tax returns.

The IT function is also outsourced to a company who are under contract to maintain both the hardware and software. The basic accounting and stock control system was originally purchased about 17 years ago by David Reed, the MD, for CamCase from a company called AXEL. Since then the system has grown with the needs of both CamCase and ShoeShock, with new functions and reports being added and updated as required. The staff at AXEL are online to ShoeShock and, if there are any problems, they can view any particular screen from their offices in Lincoln and generally fix it fairly quickly.

There is no Personnel Department as such. David Reed hires new employees when the need arises and very occasionally terminates an employee for non-performance or serious breaches. Most employees stay with the firm for many years and a handful have been with the company since its inception.

Information flow within the organisation

Information has to be communicated both internally and externally, for example:

- ❑ between departments at ShoeShock's offices in Peterborough
- ❑ between ShoeShock and P&P, the Pick and Pack warehouse
- ❑ between ShoeShock and AXEL, the software suppliers
- ❑ between ShoeShock and the salesmen and agents who go round the stores
- ❑ between ShoeShock and the WWW Head Office in New York
- ❑ between ShoeShock and the Customs and Excise Department when goods received from Asia arrive in the UK and need to be cleared through Customs
- ❑ between ShoeShock and their customers.

Appendix D
Assessment Evidence for Units 1-3

Unit 1: Presenting Information

ASSESSMENT EVIDENCE

You need to produce:

- six original documents created by you for different purposes to show a range of writing and presentational styles. The documents may be in printed form or shown on-screen. They must include one designed to gather information from individuals and one major document of at least three A4 pages

- a report describing, comparing and evaluating two different standard documents used by each of three different organisations (total of six documents).

To achieve a grade E your work must show:	*To achieve a grade C your work must show:*	*To achieve a grade A your work must show:*
E1 new information that is clear, easy to understand, uses a suitable style and is at a level that suits the intended readers	C1 by presenting original draft copies with proof-reading corrections and annotations, how you achieved a coherent and consistent style, made good use of standard formats, placed information in appropriate positions and ensured correct and meaningful content	A1 a good understanding of writing style, presentation techniques, standards for special documents and attention to detail by organising a variety of types of information into a single coherent, imaginative, easy-to-read presentation of several pages
E2 text styles, page layout, paragraph formatting and, where appropriate, common standards for layout that suit the purpose of each document		
E3 combinations of text, graphics, tables, borders and shading used effectively	C2 detailed descriptions of the content, layout and purpose of the six collected documents, accurately evaluating good and bad points about the writing and presentation styles of similar items, commenting on their suitability for purpose and suggesting how they could be improved	A2 effective skills in the appropriate use of software facilities to automate aspects of your document production, such as bullets and numbering, paragraph and heading styles, standardised layout, contents lists and indexes
E4 location, use and adaptation of existing information to suit a presentation, and a list of your information sources in an appropriate form		
E5 a clear and accurate description of each of the six collected documents, which identifies the common elements of similar documents	C3 that you can work independently to produce your work to agreed deadlines.	A3 appropriate use of lines, borders, shading, tables, graphics and writing style to create a form that is easy to understand and easy to use to enter data and retrieve the information collected
E6 careful checking of the accuracy of the layout and content of your six original documents and your report, and that you have proof-read them to ensure that few obvious errors remain.		A4 effective skills in the use of graphics to improve a presentation by making appropriate use of pictures, drawings, clip art, lines and borders, graphs or charts.

Unit 2: ICT Serving Organisations

ASSESSMENT EVIDENCE

You need to produce a case study analysing a suitable organisation.

To achieve a grade E your work must show:	To achieve a grade C your work must show:	To achieve a grade A your work must show:
E1 clear descriptions, with the aid of diagrams, of the main function(s) of the organisation, its associated customers (or clients) and suppliers, the function of each department, the structure of the organisation and the relationships between the main departments and outsiders	C1 a well-structured case study, fluent use of technical language, appropriate conclusions and suitable references to the information sources used	A1 detailed explanations, with the aid of diagrams and definitions of the data, of how information moves from a customer or client through the organisation to result in the delivery of a product or service
E2 descriptions of the ICT provision for each of the organisation's departments (or functions) and identify possible extensions or improvements to the use of ICT that would benefit the organisation	C2 detailed explanations of how information used in the organisation is processed, including details of the data-capture techniques, any processing or calculations involved and the specification and style of data output	A2 use of examples to recommend improvements to the organisation's internal ICT systems (this may cover items such as integration of existing systems, specialised equipment or software, database development, LAN or WAN – wide area network – systems)
E3 using diagrams, clearly how information essential to successful operation moves within the organisation and to and from outsiders	C3 that you can work independently to produce your work to agreed deadlines.	A3 detailed description of how the organisation might benefit from more extensive use of new communication technologies, such as the Internet, mobile communications, E-mail, e-commerce or EDI
E4 detailed descriptions of the purpose and operation of an important ICT application used within the organisation, including examples of input and output data and the job functions and personnel involved		A4 a description of how the organisation might use a management information system to monitor or control activities and decision making.
E5 that your case study is presented clearly as a coherent report and is checked for meaning and accuracy.		

Unit 3: Spreadsheet Design

ASSESSMENT EVIDENCE

You need to produce:

- a spreadsheet solution to meet specified user requirements, involving the use of at least six of the more complex spreadsheet facilities

- user and technical documentation, including a test report.

To achieve a grade E your work must show:	To achieve a grade C your work must show:	To achieve a grade A your work must show:
E1 a clear design specification that meets user requirements, including appropriate selection of more complex facilities, details of sources of data, outline screen data entry forms, calculations required, user aids to operation and how output is presented	C1 a good understanding of spreadsheet design and attention to detail by creating an imaginative customised spreadsheet that makes good use of design and layout facilities	A1 a good understanding of the purpose and value of more complex facilities by using them effectively in your spreadsheet design
E2 suitable data entry facilities, including input messages and macros that reduce keystrokes and improve user efficiency	C2 detailed test specifications together with examples of a full range of acceptable and unacceptable input, associated expected output and any associated error messages	A2 customised data input using facilities such as forms, dialogue boxes and list boxes that are clear, well laid out, suitably labelled and that validate data input
E3 suitable printed or screen output that makes appropriate use of cell formats, charts or graphs, page or screen layout and graphic images	C3 that you can work independently to produce your work to agreed deadlines.	A3 comprehensive records of spreadsheet drafting, testing and refinement that show how the spreadsheet was developed and how any problems were resolved
E4 clear technical documentation identifying formulae and functions used, and screen and printed report layouts		A4 high-quality, clear user documentation making good use of graphic images in detailed instructions for use with examples of menus and data input screens, types of output available and possible error messages.
E5 clear user documentation with copies of menus and screens and examples of input and output		
E6 testing of your spreadsheet against the design specification and careful checking of the accuracy of the data used and the output generated.		

Index

You may photocopy these blank worksheets to use in your Design documentation. Cut them out and arrange them on an A3 sheet, and design your sheets using different coloured pens for cell names and formulae, highlighter pens to show protected or unprotected cells, arrows to indicate links between sheets, etc.

	A	B	C	D	E	F	G	H	I	J	K	L
1												
2												
3												
4												
5												
6												
7												
8												
9												
10												
11												
12												
13												
14												
15												
16												
17												
18												
19												
20												
21												
22												
23												
24												

	A	B	C	D	E	F	G	H	I	J	K	L
1												
2												
3												
4												
5												
6												
7												
8												
9												
10												
11												
12												
13												
14												
15												
16												
17												
18												
19												
20												
21												
22												
23												
24												